FOOTBALL
SKILLS & DRILLS

SECOND EDITION

TOM BASS

HUMAN KINETICS

Library of Congress Cataloging-in-Publication Data

Bass, Tom.
 Football skills & drills / Tom Bass. -- 2nd ed.
   p. cm.
 ISBN 978-0-7360-9076-6 (soft cover) -- ISBN 0-7360-9076-2 (soft cover)
 1. Football--Training. 2. Football--Coaching. I. Title. II. Title:
Football skills and drills.
 GV953.5B364 2012
 796.332--dc23
                                2011052795

ISBN-10: 0-7360-9076-2 (print)
ISBN-13: 978-0-7360-9076-6 (print)

Copyright © 2012, 2004 by Tom Bass

Acquisitions Editor: Justin Klug; **Developmental Editor:** Carla Zych; **Assistant Editor:** Claire Marty; **Copyeditor:** Bob Replinger; **Graphic Designer:** Keri Evans; **Graphic Artist:** Julie L. Denzer; **Cover Designer:** Keith Blomberg; **Photographer (cover):** Chris Graythen/Getty Images; **Photographer (interior):** Neil Bernstein; **Visual Production Assistant:** Joyce Brumfield; **Photo Production Manager:** Jason Allen; **Art Manager:** Kelly Hendren; **Associate Art Manager:** Alan L. Wilborn; **Illustrations:** © Human Kinetics; **Printer:** Versa Press

We thank Rantoul High School in Rantoul, Illinois, for assistance in providing the location for the photo shoot for this book.

Human Kinetics books are available at special discounts for bulk purchase. Special editions or book excerpts can also be created to specification. For details, contact the Special Sales Manager at Human Kinetics.

Printed in the United States of America   10 9 8 7 6 5 4 3 2 1

The paper in this book is certified under a sustainable forestry program.

Human Kinetics
Website: www.HumanKinetics.com

United States: Human Kinetics
P.O. Box 5076
Champaign, IL 61825-5076
800-747-4457
e-mail: humank@hkusa.com

Canada: Human Kinetics
475 Devonshire Road Unit 100
Windsor, ON N8Y 2L5
800-465-7301 (in Canada only)
e-mail: info@hkcanada.com

Europe: Human Kinetics
107 Bradford Road
Stanningley
Leeds LS28 6AT, United Kingdom
+44 (0) 113 255 5665
e-mail: hk@hkeurope.com

Australia: Human Kinetics
57A Price Avenue
Lower Mitcham, South Australia 5062
08 8372 0999
e-mail: info@hkaustralia.com

New Zealand: Human Kinetics
P.O. Box 80
Torrens Park, South Australia 5062
0800 222 062
e-mail: info@hknewzealand.com   E5075

This book is dedicated to Michele, my wife and partner, who constantly provides positive encouragement and insight for all my writings. I cannot thank her enough.

CONTENTS

CONTENTS

ACKNOWLEDGMENTS

A word of praise and admiration goes out to the thousands of junior high and high school football coaches who every year give their time, energy, and knowledge to help to shape teenage football players into young adults. I hope this book provides them with information that can enhance their present programs.

A number of very dedicated and organized people have contributed to the preparation and completion of this new edition of the book. A special thanks goes to each of them, starting with Carla Zych, my developmental editor, who provided great insight, understanding, and motivation. It was great working with her on this project. I would also like to thank Claire Marty, assistant editor, and Neil Bernstein, photographer, who worked hard to make the book come alive. A very special thanks also goes to Coach Shane Carter, head football coach of the Rantoul High School Eagles, and all of his players, who contributed their time and energy to make the book the best it can be.

A special thanks to my daughter, Shana, who was always there when Dad needed to discuss the usage and spelling of a word or the wording of a phrase or concept. Her suggestions and ideas were greatly appreciated.

Finally, thanks to my good friend and fellow football coach, the late Harry Johnston, for providing a sounding board for the endless discussion of all things football and life.

INTRODUCTION

Young athletes learning to play football within the rules, to the best of their ability, and with great sportsmanship face a tremendous challenge. Football is a demanding game both physically and mentally. It is a game in which desire, determination, and willingness to work hard and to play as a member of a team are very important. Most of all, it is a fun sport.

Although football is the ultimate team sport, on each play every player is involved in an individual battle. Winning or losing this battle determines the success or failure of each play. The challenge is to win as many of these individual battles as possible. Even so, no single player is ever bigger than the team. No individual player can succeed without the aid and contributions of his teammates.

Teamwork starts with the attitude teammates have toward each other. Having fun by kidding around is one of the ways players deal with the pressures of the game, but caring for teammates and giving them encouragement is much more important than spending time joking around.

Teamwork also means treating everyone on the squad with respect, a sign of true sportsmanship. A starting player who knows he will play in every game may find it easier to put in the hours at practice. Each week, this player sees the reward of his hard work and will feel that practice is worth the time and effort. But what about the player who practices just as hard but rarely gets in the game? When I played, these teammates were the ones I came to admire the most. They were the players who ran the opponent's plays and defenses during practice. Their role was to make it possible for the team to succeed. They practice hard and got banged up and bruised, but never complained even though they knew they probably would never get a chance to play in the game. Their contribution and reward was to see the starters improve and their team have a chance to win. This group of players represents teamwork at its best.

Coaches need to remember that players need to know that you care about them as individuals before they will start caring about the team. It is important for coaches to take the time to encourage the players who rarely get to play in the game. These are the players who make it possible for the team to be prepared.

A word of encouragement and appreciation from the coach can mean a lot to someone who rarely gets to play. It is very important to let these players know how much their teamwork helps the team to win. Teach by giving praise for effort as well as performance.

Learning to come together with other players and to work as a team toward a common goal is one of the most important lessons players will take away from the game.

PRACTICING TO IMPROVE

The battles on the field are decided by how players play the game. Understanding and performing the necessary skills and techniques is essential to winning each battle on the field. Mastering these small techniques will greatly increase the level of performance.

In addition, the more a coach and player learn about what their opponent is trying to do, the easier it becomes to defeat his actions. Watching video from a previous game or even seeing an opponent play live, if possible, can help players and coaches gain this knowledge. The more a team sees an opponent and can chart and diagram their offensive and defensive scheme, the better the team can anticipate what the opponent will do and plan successfully to stop them.

Every day in practice coaches will be challenged to help players improve. Coaches should emphasize that the players must do their part by listening carefully and then trying to correctly do what is asked. Players must concentrate and work hard if they want to get better and help the team to be successful.

During practice, players should watch the more experienced players, listen when the coach corrects what the more experienced players are doing, and remember how it should be done. When they get their chance, less experienced players can recall the instruction given to other players and try to do the skill the correct way. Every minute of practice time needs to be used for learning, even by players who are not involved in the drill.

All players must work on staying strong and in good condition throughout the year. Each player should be physically prepared to play as hard in the fourth quarter as in the first. Players can give themselves this edge by making certain they do extra work when it is needed.

DRILLING FOR SUCCESS

The techniques in this book are explained and illustrated so that the player can work on his own as well as with a coach. Players in every position should practice getting into their stances and working on their starts away from the field.

Some techniques require another person to observe and assist in their practice. This other person can be a teammate who plays the same position. In this way, players can help each other raise the level of their performances and become better players.

When first learning a technique, players should work on their footwork against air. Once they perfect the movement, they can execute the technique at half speed versus a bag and then with a player from the same position. Finally, they can practice the technique against an opponent from the opposite side of the ball at full speed. Early in the season, when conditioning is one of the major goals, players should practice without pads. This is an excellent time for players to learn and practice footwork drills that do not involve contact as well as to learn assignments.

Competition and contact are two major distractions in learning good technique. Coaches should teach each technique without these two elements at first and then slowly introduce them into the drill.

This book includes technique instruction and drills to help any player improve at any position. Detailed illustrations and photo sequences enhance the text and improve understanding and retention. The first chapter covers five fundamental skills needed by every player—tackling, catching the ball, running with the ball, recovering a fumble, and generating power by rolling the hips. The following chapters discuss each position in detail, with complete skill instruction, technique photos, and diagrams where appropriate. The book concludes with vital information on the unique positions in special-teams play.

My goal is to help you become the very best football coach or player. My priority is to provide the best skills and drills that I have learned throughout my 30 years of coaching. Good luck as you work your way toward becoming a success both on and off the field.

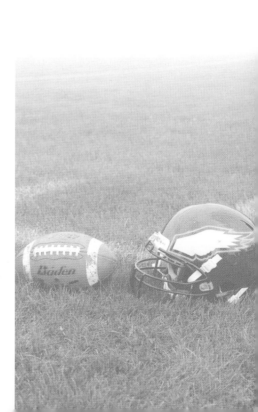

KEY TO DIAGRAMS

QB	Quarterback
HB	Halfback
FB	Fullback
TB	Tailback
CN	Center
RB	Running back
TE	Tight end
WR	Wide receiver
LT/RT	Left, right tackle
LG/RG	Left, right guard
OG	Offensive guard
OT	Offensive tackle
OL	Offensive lineman
NT	Nose tackle
K	Kicker
P	Punter
LDE/RDE	Left, right defensive end
LDT/RDT	Left, right defensive tackle
DE	Defensive end
DB	Defensive back
LB	Linebacker
ILB	Inside linebacker
OLB	Outside linebacker
SS	Strong safety
FS	Free safety
CB	Cornerback
BC	Ballcarrier
TK	Tackler
C	Coach
⟶	Running path
—————⟨	Blocking path
- - - - - - - -	Ball path

ALL PLAYERS

Every football player needs to learn and master a number of skills. These skills are not specific to any position but are instead basic skills that every player may be called on to use at some point during any game. These skills include tackling, catching the ball, running with the ball, recovering a fumble, and generating power by rolling the hips. During the course of the game or season, a punter might have to make a tackle, a defensive back might make an interception, a linebacker might be able to pick up a fumble and advance the ball to the opponent's goal line, and a special-teams player might need to block on a kick return. The list of opportunities for players to use skills not typically required in their particular positions goes on and on, so these fundamentals are in this first chapter. Individual skills for position play are covered in other chapters, but this is a great place for any player to start.

TACKLING

Tackling is to defense what blocking is to offense—a vital technique for every defensive player. At the same time, many games are won because an offensive player, punter, or placekicker makes a tackle and stops the opposing team from scoring. Just as vital to good tackling on defense is good tackling by all special-teams coverage players. Special teams are made up of offensive and defensive players who come together to function as one unit. All players must therefore be able to tackle.

Often the placekicker or punter is the last man in position to stop a long return from going all the way. Therefore, kickers need to spend time learning how to get in front of the ballcarrier, make contact, and slow the runner down until help arrives. The play may come down to knocking the ballcarrier out of bounds at the sideline. The punter and placekicker have to be ready to make the tackle or shove the ballcarrier out of bounds if the opportunity arises.

Offensive players who are not part of the special teams will need to tackle after an interception or fumble recovery. On a turnover, the offensive player must quickly go from blocking to tackling. Offensive linemen, who seldom have to make a tackle, may find that they are in perfect position when a defensive player with the ball tries to cut back across the field. They will be able to make the tackle if they are prepared.

In the case of an interception, the first two players to realize that an interception has occurred are the intended receiver and the quarterback. These players should be the first to react to the interception, and they can minimize the interception return if they have tackling ability. The receiver is in position to chase down the defensive ballcarrier quickly because he is usually the closest to the defensive man. The quarterback is the first to see the interception, allowing him to move where he can meet the defensive ball-carrier and make the tackle or knock the ballcarrier out of bounds.

Defensive players are prepared to tackle on every play. All players on special teams must anticipate having to tackle, and offensive players must know that at any moment they may have to switch to defense and prepare to make a tackle. No one on the team can think that he has the luxury of going through the game without having to tackle. Every player on the team must know how to tackle in a safe and sure manner.

Tackling Desire

Good, hard tackling is the heart of any great football team. At times a player will make a sure open-field tackle. On these tackles, technique is key. At other times, a player might only be able to reach out with one hand and try to grab the ballcarrier's jersey while warding off a blocker. Although many tackles are made with less than perfect technique, players must know and understand how to make a good tackle. Good tackling technique, if the situation allows it, increases the chance of successfully tackling the ballcarrier.

The first trait that a tackler needs is desire. The player has to want to get there. On every offensive play, defensive players must go 100 percent to get a piece of the man with the ball. Every coverage player on special teams has to have the desire to sprint downfield and get in on the tackle. On every interception, three or four offensive players need to go all out to tackle the defensive ballcarrier. Every week of the season great defensive players and special-teams players shed blockers and run all over the field to track down a speedy ballcarrier. These players do not give up until the ballcarrier is down or out of bounds. Desire drives these men to run quickly and make the play.

A player puts himself in position to make a tackle by anticipating the movements of the ballcarrier and aggressively putting himself between the ballcarrier and the goal line. He must recognize and defeat potential blockers before reaching the ballcarrier. Defensive and special-teams players are aware of potential blockers, but offensive players must also be taught to look out for blockers so that they can protect themselves as they move toward the ballcarrier. After the tackler has defeated and shed any blockers, he must focus his attention on the ballcarrier and adjust his body position to make the tackle using the proper technique.

Tackling Technique

When first learning to tackle, players should start at half speed or less. Only after they have mastered the proper techniques should the speed of any tackling drill increase. Every player is somewhat afraid the first time that he lines up to tackle someone. As he learns the techniques and gains more confidence, this fear will decrease.

Good tackling technique is designed to produce a picture-perfect tackle. Obviously, this rarely happens during a game. The player's major objective when making a tackle is to stop the ballcarrier; how he gets it done doesn't really matter. He can stop the ballcarrier by getting to the ballcarrier, grabbing him in any way possible, and keeping him from moving forward until teammates can arrive to help or sending him out of bounds.

The keys to good tackling are getting in the correct position (figure 1.1a, page 4) and generating an explosion at the point of impact. The number one tackling technique is bending the knees. Many beginning tacklers make the mistake of bending at the waist instead of bending at the knees. Bending at the waist causes the back to bow, brings the head and eyes down, and increases the chance of injury.

After bending the knees, the tackler lowers his body in preparation for impact. He keeps his back straight and his head up at all times, focusing his eyes directly on the ballcarrier's chest. Every player needs to keep his head up and eyes open during the tackle. The tackler should never lower his helmet because doing so could result in neck injuries. Players should be reminded repeatedly to make contact with their shoulder pads, never with any part of their helmets.

At the point of impact, the tackler takes off on the foot nearest the ballcarrier. If the ballcarrier cuts to his left (the tackler's right), the tackler should take off from his left foot (figure 1.1b, page 4). When the tackler uses this foot as his explosion foot, his body will be in the correct position: head in front of the ballcarrier and eyes focused on the center of the ballcarrier's chest. Exploding off the proper foot and taking short, choppy steps to maximize leg drive help the tackler make clean contact with the ballcarrier.

When the tackler feels his pads hit the ballcarrier's body, he drives his shoulder pads up and through the side of the ballcarrier and slams both arms into him (figure 1.1c, page 4). The tackler's forearms make the first contact. His front arm makes contact with the ballcarrier's belly and his back arm makes contact with the ballcarrier's lower back. The tackler automatically raises his hands to the front and back of the ballcarrier's jersey and grabs the jersey securely in both hands. The tackler continues his leg drive up and through the ballcarrier and finishes by taking the ballcarrier to the ground.

Figure 1.1 Tackling technique: Player (a) sets up in proper position, (b) drives off the foot nearest the ballcarrier, and (c) makes contact with the arms.

One of the most difficult situations for a tackler occurs when the ballcarrier is running up the sideline and the tackler is the last player in position to make the stop. The difficulty is not the actual tackle but the tremendous amount of open field that the tackler must protect. In this situation, the tackler must understand that making the tackle should be the only thing on his mind. If necessary, he may have to allow the ballcarrier to advance 1 or 2 yards up the field to ensure that he does not miss the ballcarrier completely.

When preparing to make a sideline tackle, the tackler needs to keep the ballcarrier between himself and the sideline by approaching the ballcarrier at a 45-degree angle. The tackler balances his stance by bringing his feet even and keeping his knees bent as he continues to run in place. He keeps his back straight, his head up, and his eyes focused on the ballcarrier. He must stay calm, be patient, and prepare for the ballcarrier to go up the sideline or back into the center of the field. In either case, the tackler takes a quick, open step in the direction that the ballcarrier is going. The tackler picks a spot 2 or 3 yards in front of the ballcarrier and proceeds to that spot, using it as his tackling point. After he reaches the spot, he explodes off the foot closer to the ballcarrier, driving up and through the ballcarrier. If the tackler takes a crossover step instead of an open step, he will not be able to correct his position if the ballcarrier cuts back in the other direction.

Players should expect the ballcarrier to make head and shoulder fakes to avoid tackles. The tackler must hold his ground and not lunge at the ballcarrier. He should allow the ballcarrier to fake in one direction or the other, because the ballcarrier must slow down to fake, giving the tackler's teammates time to get there and help make the tackle.

To be good tacklers, players must remember these key points:

- Good tackling is crucial to a good football team.
- Tackling starts with desire.
- Proper technique leads to successful tackles.
- Not every tackle will be perfect; the important thing is to stop the ballcarrier.
- The ballcarrier is not down until the whistle blows.
- Players must never use any part of the head when making a tackle.

Making an open-field tackle against a good ballcarrier is a considerable challenge. The tackler must anticipate the ballcarrier's moves and be ready to react if the ballcarrier tries to cut or run over him. But the challenge increases the satisfaction of getting the job done. The tackler who sets and drives the ballcarrier back with a solid tackle receives a real thrill. Executing a good, solid tackle is one of the fun parts of playing football.

Tackling Drills

Defensive players should perform one tackling drill each day that they are in pads; kickers and offensive players should tackle at least once a week. Driving the ballcarrier to the ground during tackling practice is unnecessary and not advised. Players should save that part of tackling for the game.

ANGLE TACKLING

Purpose: To provide all players the opportunity to improve tackling skill and confidence.

Procedure:

1. **Ballcarriers and tacklers line up 15 yards apart, facing one another (figure 1.2). Defensive linemen work against defensive linemen, linebackers versus linebackers, defensive backs versus defensive backs, and so on. The placekicker and punter should work with smaller defensive backs.**

2. **On the coach's command of "Hut," the first ballcarrier and tackler advance toward each other at half speed for 5 yards. Only one ballcarrier and tackler go at a time.**

3. **At 5 yards, the ballcarrier cuts to his right or left at a 45-degree angle and the tackler mirrors his move. The coach signals the ballcarrier which way to cut. The ballcarrier should have the ball in the arm on the side of his cut.**

4. **When the tackler makes contact, the ballcarrier gives with the tackle. After the tackle, the tackler goes to the end of the ballcarrier line and the ballcarrier moves to the end of the tackling line. The next two players then take their turn.**

Coaching points: As the tackler approaches the ballcarrier, he needs to shorten his stride, widen his base, flex his knees, lower his center of gravity, and be ready to explode into the ballcarrier. In this position, the tackler can react to any cut that the ballcarrier might make. When tackling, players should think of driving up and through, not just into, the ballcarrier.

Variation: After players are tackling properly, all pairs can go at once instead of one pair at a time. After players have run through the drill a number of times, the ballcarrier can decide which way to cut.

Figure 1.2 Setup for the angle tackle drill.

STRAIGHT-AHEAD TACKLING

Purpose: To provide all players the opportunity to improve tackling skill and confidence.

Procedure:

1. Ballcarriers and tacklers line up 10 yards apart (figure 1.3).
2. On the coach's command of "Hut," the ballcarrier and tackler move toward each other at half speed.
3. The tackler assumes the proper position to make the tackle. The coach tells the tackler which shoulder to use when making the tackle. The tackler steps directly into the ballcarrier using the foot on the same side as the shoulder that the coach has told him to use. His head slips to the side of the ballcarrier. The tackler should try to drive his face mask into the ball as his head slides to the side.
4. The ballcarrier jumps in the air as contact is about to be made.

Coaching points: The tackler uses the same techniques used in the angle tackling drill except that both arms and hands encircle the ballcarrier and make contact with the back of his jersey.

Figure 1.3 Setup for straight-ahead tackling drill.

SIDELINE TACKLING

Purpose: To give all players practice making sideline tackles. This drill is a good one for punters and kickoff men.

Procedure:

1. The ballcarrier and the tackler begin 7 yards apart. The tackler is even with the coach 7 yards from the sideline. The ballcarrier is 4 yards from the boundary (figure 1.4). Both players face the coach.

2. The coach begins the drill by tossing the ball to the ballcarrier. When he catches the ball, the ballcarrier turns and faces up the field.

3. As the ball is in the air, the tackler moves two steps forward and angles his body to the sideline, keeping his feet evenly spaced.

4. The ballcarrier moves upfield and cuts to the inside or goes straight ahead without faking.

5. The tackler moves on the ballcarrier and tries to tackle him. If he cannot tackle the ballcarrier, he should at least try to push the ballcarrier out of bounds.

6. After the tackler successfully stops the ballcarrier, the two players switch roles and perform the drill again.

Coaching points: The tackler should react correctly to the ballcarrier's motion, whether he moves to the inside, up the field, or begins to cross. Players should work this drill on both sidelines until the coach is confident that they can make this crucial tackle in a game.

Variation: After players are comfortable with the drill, the ballcarrier can make one or two fakes.

Left foot takeoff
Left shoulder tackle

Figure 1.4 Setup for sideline tackling drill.

CATCHING THE BALL

Like tackling, catching the ball is a basic skill that every player on the team needs to learn. In catching, the focus naturally shifts to wide receivers, tight ends, and running backs because they make the majority of catches in a game. But other players on both sides of the ball may have the opportunity to make a catch that helps the team win a game. Defensive players may have a chance to make an interception. An offensive lineman may catch a batted ball or a pass when lined up as a tight end in a short-yardage or goal-line situation. Nothing is more exciting or fun for the entire team than seeing an offensive or defensive lineman make a catch, secure the ball, and then try to move like a running back.

Some teams design plays in which the running back takes the ball from the quarterback, starts a wide run in one direction, and then throws the ball back to the quarterback, who has gone the opposite way after handing off the ball. A team may line up to kick a

Figure 1.5 When the receiver's hands are in the correct position, he can see both the ball and his hands.

Figure 1.6 Palms-up catching technique.

field goal but have the holder quickly get to his feet on taking the snap, roll out one way, and then throw the ball back across the field to the placekicker, who has faked a block and gone down the sideline. Often the kicker will be wide open, and his ability to catch the ball can lead to a touchdown. A team has an advantage if every player knows the right way to catch the ball.

Players must learn to focus all their attention on the flight of the ball as it moves toward them and block out any distractions from opposing players. To make a reception, players must concentrate on seeing the ball all the way into their hands. Many good receivers talk about seeing the point of the ball as it comes through the air and being able to block out the players around them. Every pass is theirs, and they demonstrate tremendous desire and pride in catching every ball thrown in their direction.

Catching a pass is a skill that players can improve with technique instruction. In the heat of a game, players do not have time to think through each step when making a catch. Therefore, players must spend time on and off the practice field working on receiving.

One of the most important skills is the positioning of a player's hands (figure 1.5). The way that he sets his hands for a catch depends on the flight and location of the ball. When players drop passes, the usual cause is that they positioned their hands wrong or did not extend their arms far enough to see both the ball and their hands at the same time. When the receiver focuses on the flight of the ball but keeps his hands near his body where he cannot see them, he has to coordinate his hand position with the flight of the ball in an instant, at the moment of the catch.

Correct hand position allows the receiver to see both the ball and his hands, giving him more time to adjust before the ball arrives.

To catch a ball at the level of the numbers on his jersey or lower, the receiver uses the palms-up technique (figure 1.6). He places the little fingers of his hands together, turning the palms up. He opens both hands and spreads his fingers and thumbs to form a secure, oval catching area for the ball.

The same palms-up catching technique is used to make an over-the-head or over-the-shoulder reception. When a receiver is running up the field and must make a reception over his head or shoulder, he should reach high and back with his hands so that he can see his hands and the ball together (figure 1.7).

When the receiver must catch a ball coming directly at him at shoulder height or higher, he should use the thumbs-together hand position (figure 1.8). For this type of pass, the receiver puts his thumbs together and has his palms facing out and slightly down. The fingers of both hands are open and spread, forming a cradle for the catch. The receiver catches this pass while facing the ball, not looking over his shoulder.

To keep from dropping the ball, the receiver cocks both wrists (figure 1.9). Even with the thumbs and fingers in the correct position, many receivers have trouble making a reception when the ball is shoulder high or above because their palms are turned down to the ground. Rather than catch the ball when it reaches their hands, they deflect it to the ground. To prevent this type of error, the receiver must cock his wrists and keep the hands back so that his palms are turned up, not down.

When making a reception to either the right or left, regardless of how high the ball is, the receiver should position his hands so that the palm of the hand on the side of the ball acts like a baseball mitt and comes in contact with the point of the ball, stopping its flight (figure 1.10).

This approach is especially helpful when a receiver is in the difficult position of having to catch a low pass that is wide to either side or out in front of him. He can use the palm of the hand farthest from the ball to stop the flight of the ball and use the other hand to surround and help secure it.

During a game, a single receiver may have only a few opportunities to catch the ball, but he must be prepared so that when an opportunity does come, he is able to make the catch. When the ball comes his way, the receiver must have his hands in the proper position, focus completely on the ball, and see the ball and his hands as he makes the catch.

Immediately after making the catch, the receiver must secure the ball. After the ball reaches his hands, he immediately brings it into his body with both hands. The hand on the side of the reception covers the front tip of the ball as he pulls it snug against his ribs. The uncovered tip of the ball is secure in his armpit.

The receiver also needs to be aware of defenders and expect to be hit. All players, especially receivers, must be taught that any time they touch a ball, whether they catch it or drop it, they probably will get hit. They need to concentrate on the flight of the ball, make the reception, and instantly secure the ball close against their ribs.

Catching is a skill that everyone needs to know. Wide receivers, tight ends, and running backs must be prepared to make a reception on any pass play called in the huddle. Defensive players must be ready to make an interception any time the opposing quarterback goes back to throw. All other players should learn to catch the ball in case the opportunity comes up in a game and they are in position to make the catch.

Figure 1.7   **Hands in position for an over-the-head catch.**

Figure 1.8   **Thumbs-together hand position.**

Figure 1.9   **Palms-up, wrists-cocked position.**

Figure 1.10   **Mitt technique for stopping a ball coming to the side.**

PALMS-UP CATCHING

Purpose: To reinforce proper catching technique when the ball is at the numbers or lower.

Procedure:

1. Players line up on a yard line 5 yards from the coach and face the coach.
2. The coach throws the ball to the first player in line.
3. The player makes the catch by placing the little fingers of both hands together, turning the palms up, opening both hands, and spreading the fingers and thumbs of both hands to form an oval catching area for the ball.
4. The coach throws the ball to the next player in line.

Coaching points: The receiver must extend his hands away from his body, and his little fingers must be touching. His palms should be up and not angled straight down toward the ground. He should be able to see his hands and the ball at the moment of the catch.

THUMBS-TOGETHER CATCHING

Purpose: To reinforce thumbs-together catching technique when the ball is shoulder high or higher.

Procedure:

1. Players line up on a yard line 5 yards away from the coach and face the coach.
2. The coach throws the ball to the first player in line.
3. The player makes the catch by putting his thumbs together with his palms turned out and slightly back, opening both hands and spreading his fingers to form a cradle for the catch.
4. The coach throws the ball to the next player in line.

Coaching points: The receiver must extend his hands away from his body, and his thumbs must be touching. His palms should be open to the ball and cocked slightly back away from the ground. He should be able to see his hands and the ball at the moment of the catch.

SIMULATED RECEIVING

Purpose: To reinforce proper catching technique.

Procedure:

1. When a player is learning hand position, starting without the ball is helpful. The coach faces the receiver and calls out the side (left or right) and location of the catch: knee, thigh, waist, chest, shoulder, or above the head.
2. The receiver stands in a comfortable position and then reaches out with his arms, simulating a pass reception at a particular location.
3. After players achieve the correct position, a ball is added to the drill.

Coaching points: The player's hands must be placed correctly for each reception, and his arms must be extended so that his hands are in view.

Variation: After working on passes of various heights to both the left and right, the receiver works on catching simulated passes at various heights directly in front.

RUNNING WITH THE BALL

Most of the time during a game, the offensive backs and receivers have the responsibility of carrying the ball. But all players on the team need to learn proper ball protection so that every player is prepared to carry the ball.

A player who does not usually carry the ball may make an interception or pick up a fumbled ball and find that he has a unique opportunity to advance the ball down the field and maybe even score (every defensive lineman's dream come true).

At these times, the player must understand that possession of the ball is his number one priority and that he must secure the ball so that it is not dislodged when contact occurs.

All players should be introduced to running with the ball, securing the ball tightly to their sides as they run, and protecting the ball with both hands if they see that contact is going to occur.

Securing the ball starts with the runner cradling the back tip of the ball in the crook of the elbow. The back tip of the ball needs to be securely wedged between the player's elbow and side. Coaches should emphasize that there must not be any separation or space at this juncture.

Next the forearm should be placed on the outside of the ball, forcing the ball into the ballcarrier's body. This contact point should be constant and must be maintained during the entire run.

The palm of the hand on the arm surrounding the ball should be over the front tip of the ball, with the fingers spread on two panels of the football (see figure 1.11). The hand exerts constant pressure, forcing the ball into the elbow joint.

Ballcarriers are now being taught to bring the front tip of the ball up to the top of the numbers on the front of the jersey, so that the ball is angled over the chest. The elbow joint forms a V rather than an L shape. Carrying the ball in this high, tight position makes it much more difficult for any potential tackler to cause a fumble by pulling the ball loose or knocking it forward out of the ballcarrier's arm.

Coaches should instruct bigger or less experienced ballcarriers and any ballcarrier who sees opposing players in position to attack him to secure the ball with both hands to prevent a fumble. In these situations the player should cover the front tip of the ball with his hand and use that arm to protect the bottom front quarter panel of the ball. The player should position the other arm across the top front panel of the ball; the forearm protects the ball, and the palm of the hand covers the back tip of the ball. Players should understand that although this method of carrying the ball may slow them down, it provides maximum ball protection (see figure 1.12).

Figure 1.11 Proper position for securing the ball while running.

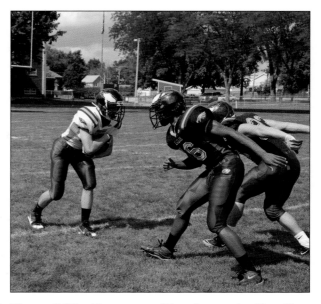

Figure 1.12 Proper position for protecting the ball when attackers are close.

RUNNING AND PROTECTING THE BALL

Purpose: To give players the experience of running with the ball while other players try to knock it loose.

Procedure:

1. The ballcarrier lines up on the yard line, 5 yards away from the first player in the tackling line. Tackling players are staggered in position every 3 yards.

2. The coach instructs the ballcarrier to carry the ball in one or both arms and to run in a straight line between the two rows of potential tacklers. The coach then hands the ball to the ballcarrier to start the drill.

3. The ballcarrier has 5 yards to get running momentum and secure the football properly.

4. Each player in line tries to knock the ball loose or reach out and strip the ball out of the ballcarrier's grasp.

5. After his run, the ballcarrier rotates to a position in the tackling line. The drill continues until every player has had the opportunity to carry the ball.

Coaching points: The ballcarrier must maintain forward momentum during the drill and exert constant pressure on the ball with all points of contact. The ballcarrier should keep his shoulders low and concentrate on protecting the ball as he drives by each potential tackler (as shown in figure 1.12). The drill can be run by position rather than as an entire team. Players can use handheld dummies for the drill. When using dummies the players strike and jolt the ballcarrier rather than grab at the ball.

FUMBLE RECOVERY: GAINING POSSESSION OF THE BALL

A play that often changes the momentum and outcome of a football game occurs when a team recovers a fumble, thereby gaining possession for their team. All players, whether on offense, defense, or special teams, need to be taught how to recover a fumble because the football may be jarred lose during any phase of the game.

Coaches should emphasize that although picking up and advancing the ball is a positive play, gaining and maintaining possession needs to be the number one priority, especially when the loose ball is in the midst of a large group of players.

In a crowded situation, the player needs to go to the ground, surround and secure the ball, and protect himself from contact by opposing players who may try to jar or rip the ball away.

To make the recovery, the player should go to the ground on his side, grasp the ball with both hands, bring it tightly to his belly, and surround it with both arms. From this position, the player should bring both knees to his chest, making sure to keep his legs and feet stacked and not separated. At the same time, the player should curl his head and shoulders forward, close his eyes and mouth to protect against the extended fingers of opposing players, and stay rolled into a ball until the whistle is blown to end the play (figure 1.13).

When the ball becomes free in the open field, the player must determine whether he should go the ground and maintain possession or pick up the ball and advance it toward the opponent's goal line, possibly to score a touchdown.

To pick up a free ball rolling on the ground, the player should come under control by shortening his stride, spreading his feet, bending his knees, and positioning the ball between his feet as he prepares to scoop it up (see figure 1.14).

The player needs to focus on the moving ball, extend both arms forward, and place the little fingers together so that the hands form a scoop to pick the ball up as the player moves forward.

After the player has the ball in his hands, he needs to bring it up and secure it in the protected position. Just as when recovering a ball on the ground, keeping possession of a recovered fumble must be the number one priority.

If the player was moving toward the opponent's goal line before he picked up the ball, he can continue his normal running motion. Otherwise, he must take short, choppy strides to come under control so that he can turn his momentum in the other direction.

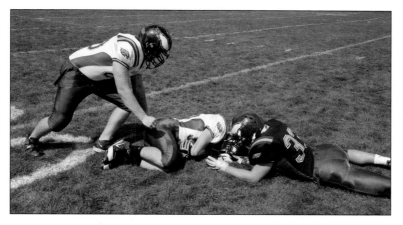

Figure 1.13 Technique for going to the ground to gain and maintain possession of the ball.

Figure 1.14 Technique for scooping up a loose ball.

GAINING POSSESSION ON THE GROUND

Purpose: To let players practice the proper technique for safely recovering a fumble by going to the ground to gain possession.

Procedure:

1. Players line up in one line 5 yards away from and facing the coach.
2. The coach then bounces the ball on the ground.
3. The first player in the line goes down to the ground on his side.
4. Reaching out with both hands, the player brings the ball into his belly, surrounds the ball with both arms, and, keeping one leg stacked on the other, brings both knees to his chest.
5. The player brings his shoulder and head in toward his chest while keeping his eyes and mouth closed.
6. The coach blows a whistle to end the drill, retrieves the ball from the player on the ground, and starts the drill with the next player in line.

Coaching points: The player must move close enough to the ball that he can easily reach it before going to the ground. The coach should emphasize to the player that other players will make contact and try to dislodge the ball, so the player must stay in position until the whistle blows.

RETRIEVING A FUMBLE IN THE OPEN FIELD

Purpose: To help players learn to pick up a loose ball, secure the ball, and keep running.

Procedure:

1. Players form one line alongside the coach and face the same direction. The coach designates the location of the opponent's end zone.
2. When the coach calls, "Ready," the first player assumes a football stance, and the coach throws the ball out on the ground.
3. The player sprints to the ball, spreads his feet, bends his knees, and positions the ball between his legs.
4. To pick up the ball, the player places the little fingers of both hands together with the palms up to form a scoop and slides his hands under the ball.
5. After scooping up the ball, the player secures it in a proper running position using one or two arms and runs for another 10 yards toward the opponent's end zone.
6. The player returns the ball to the coach, who starts the next player in line.

Coaching points: The coach should throw the ball on both sides of each player. The players need to focus on the ball, reach out to scoop it up, see both his hands and the ball when picking it up, and secure the ball immediately. The coach should change the drill by changing the location of the opponent's end zone so that players have to run in the opposite direction after recovering the ball.

ROLLING THE HIPS

Every beginning football player, regardless of position, should understand the importance of activating the hips to generate the power needed to sprint off the line, block, tackle, step to throw, and kick the ball.

When introducing this skill, coaches should focus on this one activity, rolling the hips, and not combine it with any other football technique.

The concept is to have the player start his body forward by thrusting his hips forward and propelling his body forward as far as he can in a diving motion. The player's hips must move in a forward direction and not toward the ground.

Coaches begin to teach players how to roll their hips by having them line up on a yard line across the field on their hands, knees, and toes so that they generate their movement by the forward thrust of their hips, not a push-off with their feet (as shown in figure 1.15).

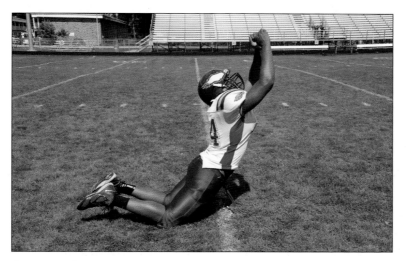

Figure 1.15 Hip roll.

ROLLING THE HIPS FOR FORWARD MOTION

Purpose: To let all players learn to use a strong hip thrust to start their forward movement.

Procedure:

1. The team lines up in equal lines a few yards apart across the field. The first player in each line stands just behind a yard line.

2. Have the first player in each line assume a stance on the ground on his toes, knees, and hands, with his fingers on the yard line.

3. On the coach's command, the players should thrust their hips forward, arch their backs, and move their arms forward and to the sky (as shown in figure 1.15). The goal is to see how far they can move forward by using only the hip thrust to propel their bodies before they land on the ground.

Coaching points: Players must keep their knees off the ground at the start of their movement and keep their heads up during the entire movement. They should land on their bellies, thighs, and hands. For added motivation, players can compete by position; the coach can record the longest forward thrust for every position, and the winners at each position can compete against the winners at all other positions.

QUARTERBACKS

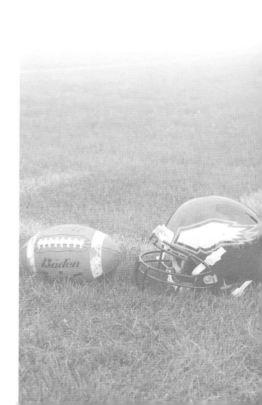

The quarterback leads the offense. This position carries a great deal of responsibility and can be loaded with pressure. Besides being a good leader, the quarterback must be an effective and quick decision maker and have the athletic ability to handle the physical demands of the position. Finally, the quarterback must be able to keep the team on course when it is playing well and rally the team when the going gets tough.

QUARTERBACK MIND-SET

The quarterback needs to know his offense and the defenses that he will face. A team's success depends on how well he studies the game and prepares mentally for each contest.

The quarterback should keep a written record of the plays that the team will use in the upcoming game and the down and distance when they will most likely be called. During the week, he should study the list—the game plan—away from the field. He must be confident that he knows how to call each play and what his responsibilities are on each play.

As a quarterback becomes more experienced, he should develop an understanding of the responsibilities of the other 10 players on the offense. He may not understand the techniques that each player uses, but he should be aware of their assignments on each play. To gain this understanding, the quarterback must study away from the field.

The thing that differentiates average, good, and great quarterbacks is not physical ability but mental toughness. Great quarterbacks stay focused on winning the game and never quit. Coaches and teammates want and need this mental toughness from their quarterback. Quarterbacks need to spend time on the mental aspect of the game in addition to physical skills.

The quarterback needs to understand the entire running and passing game. He must know when a receiver will come open and where and when to deliver the ball. The quarterback also needs to be able to read the defense and react appropriately. Reading defenses is a skill that takes years to perfect. The quarterback must first learn to recognize whether the defense is playing a man-to-man or a zone pass defense. The quarterback can then learn to identify the primary receiver and possibly the secondary receiver for each style of coverage.

The coach must teach the quarterback that he is the leader of the offense and that the other players on the offense look to him for direction. The quarterback must understand that it is his responsibility to understand the offense, to know his assignments as well as those of the other 10 offensive players, to take charge of the huddle by calling each play with authority and confidence, to be positive and offer encouragement to every player on the team, to listen to his coaches, and to think about the team first and his performance second.

The quarterback position is so complex that it is challenging for veterans, much less novices. To simplify things, the list can be shortened to three primary challenges: calling plays, knowing the formations, and throwing to the correct receiver. Individuals may experience more problems in one area than in the others. The quarterback and the coach must stay positive and continually work to improve the areas that the quarterback has trouble grasping.

The quarterback's coach must be adept at tutoring players who are best suited to be quarterbacks. The coach must teach the quarterback how to conduct himself in the huddle and in other aspects of the role not directly tied to executing plays. When the quarterback steps into the huddle, he should take over and convey a sense of confidence to the other 10 players. He must speak forcefully and make certain that he calls the play correctly, that the players understand the formation, and that every player hears the play, formation, and snap count. He then breaks the huddle and briskly gets the players up to the line and in the proper formation.

BASIC QUARTERBACK SKILLS

The quarterback must be able to both run and pass the ball. Although some skills, such as footwork, vary depending on the play, certain skills are basic to the position regardless of whether a pass play or a running play has been called. The quarterback needs to master these techniques—using the proper stance, controlling the snap, and securing the ball—to play the position proficiently.

To perform these skills, a quarterback must be in good physical condition. When the fourth quarter comes, the quarterback needs to step into that huddle ready to go. If he looks beat and out of shape, his teammates will feel the same way and their play will reflect it.

Stance

The quarterback has to move in a number of directions. He has to go forward, right, and left; retreat from the line to pass; and angle away from his starting position. His beginning stance must allow him to move easily in all these directions and perform the physical movements required to play the position.

Stance for a Traditional Snap. A quarterback has to be able to assume a proper stance without even thinking about it. To assume the proper stance (figure 2.1), the quarterback stands up straight and has his feet even and shoulder-width apart and his

Figure 2.1 Quarterback's stance for a traditional snap: *(a)* side view; *(b)* front view.

toes pointed straight ahead. He keeps his weight balanced on both feet, his back straight, and his head up. The quarterback needs good vision downfield so that he can see the defense, and his stance must provide him with a clear view of the field.

The quarterback begins to squat by bending his knees. He moves his shoulders forward until his head and shoulders are slightly in front of his hips. He extends his arms out in front and brings his hands together directly in front of and just below his crotch. He places the heel of his passing hand on top of the heel of his nonpassing hand and extends and separates his fingers and thumbs. He spreads his hands apart so that they are wide enough to receive the ball from the center.

All quarterbacks must practice getting into the stance until it becomes comfortable. When the quarterback practices without a center, he may not bend his knees enough or place his hands as low as he will need to when the center is there. The quarterback should always try to get his hands at the proper height and the correct bend in his knees, even when practicing without a center so that the position becomes natural for him. He will discover that the correct stance does not fatigue him as much when he is actually taking the ball from the center.

Figure 2.2 Quarterback's stance for a shotgun snap: (a) belt high snap; (b) chest high snap.

Shotgun Stance. More coaches are electing to position their quarterback off the line, usually 4 yards, in a shotgun position to receive the snap. When taking a snap in the shotgun position, the quarterback should assume the two-point balanced stance and extend both hands forward. The hands should be belt high with the palms up and little fingers touching if he expects the ball to arrive from the center at the belt line (figure 2.2a). If the snap is directed more to the chest area, the quarterback should have his thumbs together with the palms cocked slightly back to receive the snap (figure 2.2b). The quarterback should look the ball from the center into his hands and see the ball and both hands at the moment of the catch.

Snap

The quarterback must recognize the importance of the snap. Every successful offensive play begins with the quarterback receiving and controlling the ball from the center.

After the quarterback is in a comfortable stance that allows him to move the way that he needs to, he works with the center to guarantee a proper exchange of the ball. The quarterback must recognize that the center cannot change his height, so the quarterback needs to adjust the bend in his knees to ensure that his hands fit snugly in place (figure 2.3a). The quarterback's top hand should always be placed in the same location. He can guarantee this by placing his middle finger directly against the center seam of the center's shorts or pants. After the top hand is in place, the heels of both palms should be touching, his hands should be open, and his fingers should be open and spread apart. The quarterback presses up slightly to let the center know that he is ready for the snap. The quarterback must be ready to secure the ball with his bottom hand the instant that the center snaps it to him (figure 2.3b).

When practicing the snap, both the center and the quarterback should move one or two steps in the direction that the play calls for. This action makes practice more gamelike, helping the quarterback develop a feel for how the ball will be snapped during a game. On a running play, the center may step straight ahead, to his right, or to his left depending on the play called. The quarterback may move in the same direction as the center or in a different direction.

The quarterback needs to spend extra time with the center working on the snap for passing plays. When the center drops back in pass protection, he moves with the quarterback, not away. The center may lower his butt to move backward. This action is entirely different than that used in running plays, and the quarterback needs to be prepared for it. The quarterback must not only secure the ball but also move quickly away from the line of scrimmage to give the center enough room to make his block.

Even without the center, the quarterback can work on the snap. Another quarterback can get down on a knee in front of him and bring the ball up sideways from the ground into his hands. Although this setup is not the same as having a center, it is good practice for a quarterback who is working on gripping the ball and moving right or left or dropping back.

Many young quarterbacks are fine with the snap until they get into a game. At that moment, two things often occur:

Figure 2.3 Quarterback takes the snap: He *(a)* adjusts his body and puts his hands in place and *(b)* immediately secures the ball.

1. The center is anxious to block and snaps the ball slightly harder and not exactly in the proper position.

2. Anxious about the contact that happens in game conditions, the quarterback pulls out faster than he has practiced and fails to secure the ball properly.

The quarterback can overcome these problems by practicing taking the ball repeatedly, anticipating, and knowing where his center is going. For any offensive play to have a chance for success, the quarterback must be able to get the ball securely from the center.

The quarterback and center must work on the shotgun snap if it is to be a part of their team's offense. The quarterback has the responsibility for signaling the center when he is ready to take the snap by raising a leg or opening and closing his hands.

Focusing on the center and the ball is imperative when taking a shotgun snap, and the quarterback must resist the temptation to look down the field until he has caught and secured the ball in both hands. He should anticipate a good snap on each play but be prepared to bend down, jump in the air, or move right or left if the snap is not on target.

Ball Security

After the ball comes up from the center, the quarterback grips it with both hands and immediately brings it in to his belly. He keeps the ball secure near his body until he is ready to hand off or pass. His passing hand is over the laces, and his other hand is on the opposite side of the ball. He exerts the most pressure on the ball with the middle finger of his passing hand. From this position, the quarterback can either hand off the ball or set up to pass. If the ball does not come up correctly during the snap, he needs to make an adjustment to get the laces in the proper position if he is going to pass. He should keep the ball in both hands for as long as possible.

STANCE

Purpose: To reinforce proper quarterback stance so that it becomes automatic.

Procedure:

1. **Quarterbacks line up 2 yards apart facing the coach.**
2. **When the coach points to a player, the quarterback steps forward and assumes his stance.**
3. **The coach checks the player's stance to make sure that he is using the correct technique: Feet are even and shoulder-width apart, weight is balanced on both feet, the back is straight, head and shoulders are slightly in front of the hips, arms are extended, and fingers are spread.**
4. **After the quarterback is in his stance, the coach directs him to take a step up, right, left, and back.**
5. **The coach gives the players the snap count, and then each quarterback in turn moves into his stance and stays in that position for the entire cadence call.**
6. **After all quarterbacks are taking a proper stance, they can set up as a group to shorten practice time.**

Coaching points: The coach should observe each quarterback from the front and the side to make certain that his body is in proper alignment. The coach should also check each quarterback for balance and observe whether he is leaning too far forward or leaning back with the weight on his heels.

SNAP WITH MOVEMENT

Purpose: To solidify the connection between the center and quarterback during the snap.

Procedure:

1. **The center and quarterback assume their positions.**
2. **The coach calls a play and the blocking for the center. Plays can be called by giving a description (dive right or left with drive blocking, sweep right or left with reach blocking to the side of the play, a drop-back pass with pass blocking) or by using the team's terminology, which reinforces what the players will hear in the game. The idea is to have the center move with and move opposite the quarterback's movement, driving straight ahead and dropping back to pass protect.**
3. **The quarterback gives the cadence, and the center snaps the ball to the quarterback.**
4. **Both the quarterback and center take the initial steps of the play.**

Coaching points: When the quarterback and the center practice the snap together, both players should move one or two steps in the proper direction for the play that was called. This action helps the quarterback get the feel of how the ball will come to him during a game.

SHOTGUN SNAP WITH MOVEMENT

Purpose: To reinforce the proper quarterback stance and hand position when catching a shotgun snap.

Procedure:

1. The center and quarterback assume their positions.
2. The coach calls a play and the blocking for the center by giving a description or using team terminology to reinforce what the players will hear in the game. The idea is to have the center move as the ball is snapped.
3. The quarterback signals the center that he is ready and gives the cadence. The center snaps the ball to the quarterback.
4. The quarterback catches the snap and secures the ball. Both the quarterback and center take the initial steps of the play called.

Coaching points: When the quarterback and the center practice the shotgun snap together, both should move one or two steps in the proper direction for the play called. This action helps the quarterback get the feel for the various locations where the ball may come to him during a game. The quarterback should also practice fielding both low and high snaps and snaps to the right and left.

ADJUSTING THE BALL

Purpose: To give the quarterback experience adjusting to the ball from the snap.

Procedure:

1. The drill starts with the center snapping the ball to the quarterback or a player or coach handing the ball to the quarterback from the ground. The person snapping the ball should change the position of the laces so that the quarterback is forced to make the adjustment on the move.
2. The quarterback takes the snap and, holding the ball in both hands, adjusts it so that the laces are in the right location for him to grip the ball to pass (figure 2.4).
3. The quarterback starts his drop.

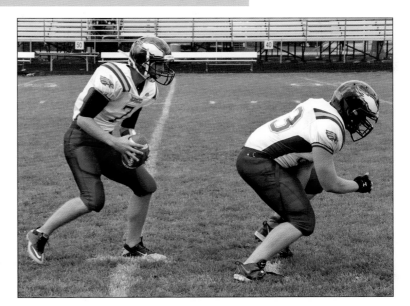

Figure 2.4 Quarterback takes the snap and adjusts the ball for a pass.

Coaching points: This drill takes only a few minutes each day, but it pays incredible dividends in a game. In the game, the center gives the quarterback the ball with the laces ready to be gripped. Game circumstances, however, may cause the center to alter the ball's positioning. The quarterback must be ready to adjust to the ball on the snap to prevent fumbles.

RUN PLAYS

Every quarterback needs to be able to execute both running and passing plays, even if his offense focuses more frequently on one or the other. For running plays, the quarterback needs to work on footwork, handoff technique, tossing or pitching the ball, and faking.

On all running plays the quarterback must make certain to deliver the ball to the ballcarrier. He must know the path that the running back is going to take and the exact spot where the exchange will take place. Until the handoff occurs, the quarterback must protect the ball by securing it in both hands and keeping it against his body.

When the quarterback is handing the ball to a running back, he approaches the handoff point with the ball in both hands. As he nears the running back, he extends the ball, taking away the hand closer to the ballcarrier. The quarterback is now in position to place the ball securely to the ballcarrier's midsection.

Each play requires specific footwork so that the quarterback and running back reach the handoff point at the proper time. The quarterback has to adjust to the size of each running back, just as he has to adjust to the size of each center on the team. Every dedicated pro quarterback practices his footwork on running plays. The challenge for the young quarterback is learning the footwork patterns for various running plays. A quarterback who neglects this skill is usually half a step short, which may cause him to overextend his arm and fumble the handoff.

Depending on the type of offense that the team uses, the quarterback can take four or five different paths to reach the handoff point. The footwork for each running play is different, so the quarterback needs to work on each path equally. On all plays, he must receive the ball from the center, secure it firmly in both hands, and bring it into his body at belt level.

The handoff is the quarterback's responsibility and should become automatic. The quarterback must turn his head quickly and focus on the exact spot where the handoff will take place. He must get the ball to the running back at the proper point on the field in a secure manner on all running plays.

The quarterback is also responsible for making certain that any pitch or option toss play is delivered correctly and to the proper location for the running back to make the catch and continue the play.

For a running play in which the running back comes straight down the line, the quarterback first takes a short directional cheat step with the foot on the same side as the handoff. He turns his hips in the direction of the cheat step and points them down the line, allowing his upper body and head to turn with his hips. The quarterback takes a longer second step with the other foot along the line of scrimmage. He must be in position to extend his arms, his hand, and the ball to the handoff point as the second foot makes contact with the ground (figure 2.5). To complete the handoff, he removes the hand nearest the ballcarrier's body and places the ball firmly to the ballcarrier's belly.

Figure 2.5 Quarterback hands off to a running back coming straight down the line.

This sequence of movements is also used when the quarterback is faking inside and then moving to the outside of the formation for an option play.

For a running play in which the quarterback needs to get the ball to a deep back who approaches the line at an angle (figure 2.6), the quarterback's footwork starts with a short step back with the foot on the same side as the handoff. The actual handoff takes place deep in the backfield, so this first step must be back. His second, longer step with the opposite foot carries him at an angle away from his original position. From here the rest of the handoff is the same.

A play in which the quarterback hands off to a running back who is coming across the formation on an off-tackle or sweep play requires a change in the quarterback's footwork. For his cheat step, he steps back with the foot opposite from the running back's direction. He takes his second, longer step back from the line, opening his body to put him in position to make the handoff to the back. When the quarterback executes this type of handoff, his body should be turned toward his goal line and away from the line of scrimmage (figure 2.7).

Figure 2.6 **Quarterback hands off to a deep back approaching at an angle.**

The footwork is the same when the quarterback executes a reverse pivot for a handoff or pitches the ball to the running back (figure 2.8). He takes a short step up with the foot on the side of the play. He pivots around on this foot with his second step. When he is in the pivot, he loses sight of the line of scrimmage for an instant. The action of the handoff is the same as on other running plays.

Figure 2.7 **Quarterback hands off to a running back coming across the formation.**

Figure 2.8 **Quarterback reverse pivots to hand off the ball to the running back.**

Figure 2.9 Quarterback pitches the ball to the running back.

Figure 2.10 Quarterback executes a one-hand fake.

When the quarterback pitches the ball (figure 2.9), he needs to adjust the location of the ball in his hands. As he pivots, the quarterback brings the ball to the hip on the same side as the play. On his second step, he quickly extends both arms and uses an underhand toss to send the ball to the running back.

The quarterback needs to understand exactly where the running back is going to line up before the start of the play—in an I-back location directly behind the quarterback or in a split-back position behind an offensive tackle. As he makes his pivot, the quarterback then knows how far he needs to pitch the ball so that the running back can make the catch at full speed.

For a smooth exchange, the quarterback should always put the ball to the center of the runner's belly. Most fumbles in the exchange occur when the ball only reaches the near hip of the runner or when the ball is too low and makes contact with the running back's thigh. Following a handoff, the quarterback must continue for at least three or four steps, setting up just as he would if the play were a play-action pass.

Faking the handoff is an important tool for the quarterback. Good fakes keep the defense off balance and make it easier to execute key plays at crucial moments in the game. One of the most important skills for the quarterback is attention to detail when giving or faking the ball to the ballcarrier.

The two main techniques for faking the handoff are the one-hand fake and the two-hand fake.

For the one-hand fake (figure 2.10), the quarterback needs to do the following:

1. Move the ball to the hand nearer the running back.

2. Secure the ball to his hip on that side.

3. Quickly put his empty hand to the ballcarrier's belly.

4. Remove his hand and continue his steps into his drop.

If the quarterback and the ballcarrier practice this motion enough, the running back may be able to deceive the defense into thinking that he is running with the ball after the fake handoff.

For the two-hand fake (figure 2.11), the quarterback keeps the ball firmly in both hands. As he reaches the handoff point, he uses both hands to extend the ball to the ballcarrier and then quickly pulls it back. Because the defensive players actually see the ball going to the ballcarrier's midsection, this way of faking is often the most effective. When the quarterback fakes with both hands, he also has greater control of the ball, lessening the chance for a fumble. The running back must not grip down on the ball.

The two-handed fake to a back is usually preferred when running an option play to the outside because it allows the quarterback to be in position to make a two-handed toss back to the trailing running back when necessary. When making the toss the quarterback must secure the ball in both hands and keep his thumbs together. The ball needs to be brought to his chest area and then pushed out with both arms toward the running back. Both hands need to open and rotate to the outside as the ball is released (figure 2.12). This action is often referred to as a basketball pass. When not making the toss, the quarterback should secure the ball in his outside arm and turn up the field.

Quarterbacks survive and become great because of the running game. To be successful, every quarterback must learn, understand, and practice the footwork, handoff techniques, and fake handoff techniques that are necessary for him to be effective. On running plays the quarterback's job after handing off to the running back is to carry out his fake. The quarterback of an option offense makes a much greater contribution to the running game.

Videotape of the quarterback's work on each handoff is useful. The coach and the quarterback can review the quarterback's footwork and body action on each handoff and make any necessary corrections.

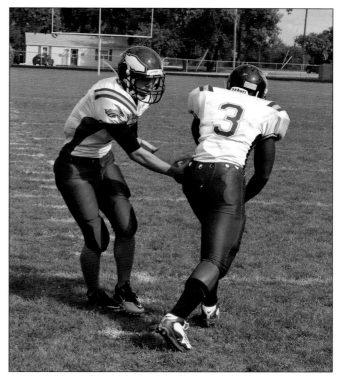

Figure 2.11 **Quarterback executes a two-hand fake.**

Figure 2.12 **Quarterback makes the toss to a back.**

COMING DOWN THE LINE

Purpose: To reinforce proper footwork during a running play from split position.

Procedure:

1. The quarterback and halfback line up in split position. The best approach is to have a center snap the ball to the quarterback, but if a center isn't available, the next quarterback in line can lift the ball to the quarterback who is executing the drill.
2. The quarterback calls the snap and executes the handoff to the halfback.
3. The halfback carries out the play by running at least 10 yards downfield with the ball. The quarterback carries out the fake and sets up to pass.

Coaching points: In this type of drill, the quarterback should call out the cadence and the players must start at the same time. The coach should check to see that the players come together at the proper point and that the ball is placed firmly to the ballcarrier's belly. The coach should make certain that the quarterback sets up properly after executing the handoff.

Variation: The same drill can be run with the quarterback executing a handoff or two-hand fake to the halfback and then continuing down the line for the option play.

READING FOR THE OPTION PLAY

Purpose: To drill the quarterback in making the decision to keep or toss on the option play based on the play of the end man on the line of scrimmage.

Procedure:

1. The quarterback and two running backs line up in split position. The best approach is to have a center snap the ball to the quarterback, but if a center isn't available, the next quarterback in line can lift the ball to the quarterback who is executing the drill.
2. The quarterback calls the snap and executes a two-handed fake handoff to the back running the dive on the side of the option call.
3. As the quarterback withdraws the ball after the fake, he should immediately locate an added player who serves as the outside defensive player.
4. On the coach's direction, the defender should either come toward the quarterback or start moving to the outside on the line of scrimmage.
5. If the defender moves to the quarterback, the quarterback should move to the defender and at the last moment toss the ball to the trailing running back.
6. If the defender moves away from quarterback, the quarterback should immediately secure the ball and turn up the field, becoming a running back and running at least 10 yards downfield with the ball.

Coaching points: The coach should observe that the quarterback makes a good fake with both hands on the ball and then brings the ball up to his chest ready to make the toss. The quarterback should be focusing on the end man on the line and reading the play of this defender correctly. The running back should be slightly in front of the quarterback when the toss is made. The coach should check that the quarterback makes the toss using both hands.

ANGLE FOOTWORK

Purpose: To reinforce proper footwork during a running play from the I-position.

Procedure:

1. The quarterback and tailback line up in the I-position. The best approach is to have a center snap the ball to the quarterback, but if a center isn't available, the next quarterback in line can lift the ball to the quarterback who is executing the drill.
2. The quarterback calls the snap and executes the handoff.
3. The tailback carries out the play by running at least 10 yards downfield with the ball. The quarterback carries out the fake and sets up to pass.

Coaching points: The coach should check to see that the quarterback's first step is away from the line, allowing him to move into the backfield. Because the tailback is coming from an I-position 7 yards from the line, the quarterback and the tailback may not come together smoothly at first. The coach should check to see that the tailback's path is correct and that he is not getting to the handoff spot too soon.

MAKING THE HANDOFF ON A SWEEP

Purpose: To reinforce proper handoff technique for a sweep play from split position.

Procedure:

1. The quarterback and halfback line up in split position. The best approach is to have a center snap the ball to the quarterback, but if a center isn't available, the next quarterback in line can lift the ball to the quarterback who is executing the drill.
2. The quarterback calls the snap and executes the handoff for a sweep.
3. The halfback carries out the play by running at least 10 yards downfield with the ball. After the handoff on a sweep, the quarterback fakes a bootleg action to the opposite side rather than drops back to set up to pass.

Coaching points: The quarterback must get his head around and quickly focus on the halfback. He should place the ball firmly to the ballcarrier's belly. After the handoff, the quarterback should move to the outside of the formation away from the halfback's path at a depth of 7 yards from the line. After learning the technique, the quarterback should also look to see whether anyone is watching his fake as he moves to the outside, as he would do in a game.

TURNING ON A REVERSE PIVOT

Purpose: To practice the execution of a handoff during a reverse pivot.

Procedure:

1. The quarterback and fullback line up in far position. The fullback is directly behind the quarterback 4 yards from the line. The best approach is to have a center snap the ball to the quarterback, but if a center isn't available, the next quarterback in line can lift the ball to the quarterback who is executing the drill.
2. The quarterback calls the snap and executes a reverse pivot to make the handoff to the fullback.

(continued)

Turning on a Reverse Pivot *(continued)*

3. The fullback carries out the play by running at least 10 yards downfield with the ball. The quarterback carries out the fake and sets up to pass.

Coaching points: The quarterback should take a short step up with the foot closer to his final direction to ensure that he secures the ball before making his pivot. The quarterback must turn his back to the line of scrimmage and turn his head and body with his second pivot step. He should be locating the fullback as he pivots around and keep the ball secure in both hands at the belt area until he is ready to make the handoff.

MAKING A PITCH FROM A REVERSE PIVOT

Purpose: To practice the execution of a pitch to a running back while using a reverse pivot.

Procedure:

1. The quarterback, fullback, and tailback line up in the I-position. The fullback is directly behind the quarterback 4 yards from the line, and the tailback is at 7 yards. The best approach is to have a center snap the ball to the quarterback, but if a center isn't available, the next quarterback in line can lift the ball to the quarterback who is executing the drill.

2. The quarterback calls for the snap and executes a reverse pivot to make the pitch to the tailback.

3. The tailback makes the catch and, with the fullback leading, runs at least 10 yards downfield with the ball. The quarterback carries out the fake and sets up to pass or runs a bootleg to the opposite side of the formation.

Coaching points: The quarterback should take a short step up with the foot closer to his final direction to ensure that he secures the ball before making his pivot. The quarterback must turn his back to the line of scrimmage and turn his head and body with his second pivot step to adjust the location of the ball in his hands. As he pivots, the quarterback brings the ball to the hip on the same side as the play. On his second step, he quickly extends both arms and uses an underhand toss to send the ball to the running back.

ONE-HAND FAKE

Purpose: To teach and reinforce proper one-hand faking technique.

Procedure:

1. The quarterback and running back line up in a predetermined play. No other players are necessary unless a center is available to start the play by making the snap.

2. The quarterback calls the snap and makes a one-hand fake.

3. The running back carries out the fake for 10 yards. The quarterback drops back to pass.

Coaching points: The quarterback should move exactly as he would if he were handing the ball to the running back. Any variation of steps or rising up will alert the defense that he is faking. The coach should check to see that the quarterback puts his empty hand to the running back's belly and that the running back leans forward and closes his arms as if he were receiving the ball.

TWO-HAND FAKE

Purpose: To teach and reinforce proper two-hand faking technique.

Procedure:

1. The quarterback and running back line up in a predetermined play. No other players are necessary unless a center is available to start the play by making the snap.
2. The quarterback calls the snap and makes a two-hand fake.
3. The running back carries out the fake for 10 yards. The quarterback drops back to pass.

Coaching points: The quarterback must securely grip the ball with both hands to guarantee that the running back does not jar it loose. The quarterback must quickly place the ball to the belly of the running back and then instantly bring it back to his own belt area. The running back can lean forward, but he must not close his arms around the ball.

PASS PLAYS

The passing game is a vital part of football. The quarterback must know the defense, call the right play, and consistently deliver the ball to the open receiver. A beginning quarterback should start with drop-back passing and then move on to play-action passes and passing on the move. Finally, the quarterback needs to spend a few minutes each week throwing the ball on the run while scrambling out of the pocket. He can improve all these passing skills with hard work and practice.

Throwing Technique

All quarterbacks want to pass the ball. A quarterback's success as a passer depends a great deal on the amount of time that he devotes to learning the proper mechanics for throwing the ball. One of the most important ways for the quarterback to grow is to master the throwing techniques.

If a quarterback is having trouble passing the ball accurately, the coach should take the time to review the basics of throwing. A quarterback should not be allowed to continue throwing bad passes. Before passing, the quarterback needs to master securing the ball in both hands, taking the drop that the play requires, and executing the footwork needed to prepare to pass. The quarterback also needs to know how to grip the ball and the movement that he should go through as he passes the ball.

Every good pass starts with the grip on the ball. Without a proper grip, the throw will lack the accuracy or velocity that the quarterback needs. The size of the quarterback's hands will cause some variation in the way that he is able to grasp the football. Regardless of the size of his passing hand, the quarterback grips the ball near the center (figure 2.13). He places the index or first finger of his throwing hand near the tip of the ball, off the laces and across the seam where the laces are located. He places the middle and third fingers across the laces. The fingertips of these two fingers are on the surface of the ball, not on the laces. The little finger just reaches the

Figure 2.13 Quarterback grips the ball for a throw.

Figure 2.14 Quarterback uses two hands to secure the ball until he is ready to pass.

laces of the ball. The coach should check the quarterback's grip during every practice.

The quarterback should feel the most pressure between the ball and his passing hand just behind the center point on the back of the ball. Depending on the size of his hand, the quarterback may need to adjust the base grip slightly, but he must keep the pressure in the same location.

Until the quarterback is ready to release the ball, he should keep his nonpassing hand on the ball, placing it lightly on the underside of the football to keep the ball more securely in his grasp (figure 2.14). Most quarterback fumbles occur during the exchange from the center or when the quarterback removes his nonpassing hand and starts running with the ball in only one hand. The quarterback does not have complete control of the center snap exchange, but he must have total control when he is going back to pass. He must keep both hands on the ball whenever possible.

The quarterback's passing motion begins with a step forward on the foot opposite his passing arm (figure 2.15a). The quarterback aims the toes of this lead foot directly where he wants the ball to go. The lead foot is important—the quarterback must step directly toward where he is going to pass the ball. The quarterback's body is now in position. With this step, the quarterback's entire body begins to point at the spot where he wants to deliver the ball. At this moment, his lead foot and hips are aimed at the target.

At the same time that the quarterback steps with his lead foot, he releases his nonpassing hand from the ball and brings

Figure 2.15 Quarterback's passing motion: The quarterback *(a)* steps forward with his lead foot, *(b)* brings his passing hand back, and *(c)* moves his hips and shoulders toward the target.

his passing hand back, bending the elbow on his passing arm (figure 2.15b). The ball is above his shoulder pads and slightly behind his helmet.

When the quarterback begins to deliver the pass, his hips and shoulders move toward the target, ahead of his passing arm and hand (figure 2.15c). An accurate passer who passes with touch and velocity always begins the passing movement with his entire body, not just his arm. The quarterback needs to understand that arm speed and ball velocity result from using his entire body to make the throw.

As the quarterback's body moves forward toward the passing area, his shoulder, passing arm, and hand also begin to move forward (figure 2.15d). His elbow is bent, and he holds the ball high. The quarterback finally allows his passing arm to come forward as he delivers the pass.

As the passing arm comes forward, the quarterback's lower arm passes over and in front of his elbow. The hand and the ball extend forward, and the ball comes out of his hand in a tight spiral. When the quarterback releases the ball, he points his hand and fully extended passing arm directly at the passing target. After the release, the passing hand rotates to the inside and the palm of the passing hand finishes the passing motion turned down to face the ground (figure 2.15e).

Quarterbacks need to practice throwing to make it one smooth motion. At the moment of release, every part of the quarterback's body should point directly at the passing target. His body should be in a direct line to the passing area. The lead foot, hips, shoulders, head, eyes, and passing hand should all point in the same direction. The coach may want to have a quarterback who is just learning the passing motion practice setting up and going through the entire sequence without the ball until the player becomes comfortable and the coach thinks that the player is doing it correctly every time.

The quarterback needs to step to throw to all areas of the field, not just to the middle or to the side of his passing hand.

Figure 2.15 *(continued)* Quarterback's passing motion: The quarterback *(d)* moves his passing arm forward and *(e)* releases the ball and finishes by rotating his hand.

Drop-Back Passing

When the quarterback perfects the running game and play-action pass, the drop-back pass attack will be that much better. For the passing game to be successful, the timing of the quarterback's throws must be as exact as possible. Good timing during a passing play depends on two people, the receiver and the quarterback. The receiver contributes to the timing of the pass by running his routes at full speed and at the proper depth. The quarterback contributes to the timing by having disciplined drops for each pass and delivering the ball to the receiver at the correct time. The quarterback must know the proper drop and work on his footwork so that he has a consistent drop each time he moves away from the line of scrimmage.

Each drop has to become second nature for the quarterback. Every time that he sets up to pass, the quarterback must use the same steps and body movements. During the drop, the quarterback must control the ball before releasing the pass, have a smooth and consistent throwing motion, and release the ball the same way on every pass.

In learning to drop correctly, the quarterback should not throw the ball but should instead focus on footwork and timing. After he starts throwing, the throw becomes the focus, and in the beginning the quarterback needs to concentrate solely on his footwork.

A center is not necessary, but the quarterback should start each drop by taking a short step up with the foot opposite his passing arm. When the center joins in the practice, the quarterback will find that this slight step up guarantees that he gets a good exchange, stays with the center, and gets a good grasp of the ball.

The quarterback should use crossover steps as he drops away from the line (figure 2.16). Each drop has a specific number of steps that the quarterback takes before setting up and stepping to throw the ball.

To deliver the pass using a quick, efficient motion, the quarterback needs to be sure that the ball is in the correct position during the drop. Before the quarterback starts the drop, the coach should be sure that the quarterback has the correct grip on the ball, has the ball securely in both hands, knows to keep the ball at the middle of his chest during the entire drop, and understands that his arms should move forward and back in a normal motion.

The quarterback needs to adjust to the surface of the field. On a normal, dry playing field, the quarterback's final step can be somewhat longer and can be used to stop his movement away from the line. When playing on a wet or loose field, the quarterback must shorten his final step to keep his feet under him and prevent a slip as he sets to throw the ball.

Figure 2.16 **Quarterback's crossover step.**

Three-Step Drop. The quarterback should start by learning the three-step drop. This drop is used for all short pass patterns, which are pass patterns run 4 or 5 yards from the line of scrimmage, such as quick out, hitch, or slant. With all these passes, timing is essential. The quarterback must take the steps and deliver the ball without hesitation if the pass is to be completed.

The quarterback does not count the first, slight step forward that he uses in each drop. After the slight step, he steps away from the line of scrimmage with the foot on the same side as his passing hand. He follows this with a crossover step with the other foot and then another step with the foot on the same side as his passing hand. The quarterback's third step should stop his momentum and allow him to step in the direction that he is going to throw the ball.

Five- and Seven-Step Drops.

A quarterback needs a five- or seven-step drop for medium and deep pass routes, or pass patterns run beyond 5 yards. As a rule, the deeper the pattern that the receiver runs, the deeper the quarterback's drop should be.

The quarterback's goal on any pass play is to deliver the ball to the receiver on time and at the point in the receiver's pattern at which the receiver has the best opportunity to make the catch. The quarterback needs to have disciplined drops if his timing is to be correct.

For both the five- and seven-step drops (figure 2.17), the quarterback takes both the first step away from the line of scrimmage and the last step with the foot on the same side as his passing hand. He follows his first step with a crossover step. He continues the drop by alternating feet until he has taken the appropriate number of steps.

The quarterback should use a five-step drop on all medium pass routes: in, out, hook, cross, delay, quick post, and deep up. When he takes the final step in the drop, he should be nearly 7 yards from the line of scrimmage.

When a receiver is running an out pattern, the quarterback should expect him to make his break toward the sideline at 12 yards. When the quarterback takes the final step, he immediately starts the throwing motion by stepping with his front foot at a point 9 yards directly in front of the receiver's path. This amount of space is what the receiver normally covers while the ball is in the air.

The up pattern is a deep pass pattern but is thrown from a five-step drop. The quarterback must be prepared to throw the ball the minute that the receiver moves up the field and gets even with the defensive back, usually at 12 yards. The quarterback should throw the pass 10 yards in front of the receiver and 5 yards to his inside so that the receiver has a chance to run directly under the pass to make the catch.

The seven-step drop should be used for deep pass routes, such as post, corner, and comeback. The seventh step of the drop should take the quarterback 9 yards away from the line of scrimmage as he sets up.

Throwing a corner route requires the quarterback to take a full seven-step drop. He must be prepared to lead the receiver with the ball toward the corner of the field on the sideline. In a post pattern, after the receiver starts toward the center of the field at 10 yards, he quickly breaks to the outside to the corner of the field. The quarterback must anticipate this path change and be ready to step and throw the ball 12 yards in front of the receiver's path. Ideally he throws the ball in front of and to the outside shoulder of the receiver.

Figure 2.17 Drop-step patterns for a right-handed quarterback: After a five-step drop, he is about 7 yards from the line of scrimmage; after a seven-step drop, he is about 9 yards away.

On both of these drops, the quarterback sprints away from the line of scrimmage at a much greater speed than he does in the three-step drop. Because of this speed, the final step, the plant step, is crucial (figure 2.18). The quarterback extends the final step, unless he is on a wet or loose field, to stop his momentum away from the line of scrimmage. Then he gets in position to set up for his delivery. When on a wet or loose field, the quarterback shortens the plant step and keeps his feet under him to keep from slipping on the plant step or just as he tries to throw the ball.

After the quarterback stops his momentum away from the line of scrimmage, he brings his front foot back slightly so that he can plant both feet under his hips and get in position to begin the throw. The quarterback is in perfect position to step to any area of the playing field to deliver the pass. He holds the ball securely with both hands at chest height. He gathers his body and stands tall with both feet under his hips, and he then begins the passing motion.

Figure 2.18 Quarterback's plant step.

Screen Passing

The quarterback may be asked to throw two basic types of screen passes. The first is the quick, or bubble, screen thrown to an offensive player located in a position outside the offensive tackle. The second type of screen pass is a slow screen in which the intended receiver lines up in the backfield and, after setting up, releases to one side of the formation to catch the ball.

Bubble Screen. The quarterback takes the direct or shotgun snap from the center, secures the ball, and immediately throws the ball to the outside to a receiver. This quick-hitting play allows other offensive players to go downfield quickly and block any potential tacklers.

Slow Screen. For a slow screen to have success, the defensive players must believe that a drop-back pass play is taking place and rush the quarterback. After taking the snap, the quarterback needs to take a seven-step drop, set, and then drop a few more yards to invite the pass rush to come up the field. At the same time, one of the backs should set up, brush block any assigned rusher, and then release to the outside, staying on the offensive side of the line of scrimmage. As the back moves to the outside, he should turn to the outside to receive the screen pass and then turn up the field following his offensive linemen, who have moved to the outside to block for his run.

Play-Action Passing

As the quarterback begins to master the mechanics of drop-back passing, he can start working on the footwork and mechanics of passing the ball after faking a run. Play-action passing requires even more work, but it is an important part of a team's attack.

Everyone has seen a great quarterback move to a running back and appear to hand off the ball. All the fans and a majority of the defense are certain that the play is a run. Then at the last second the quarterback quickly removes the ball, sets up at 7 yards, and delivers a perfect pass to an open receiver. Play-action passing, or throwing a pass after faking a run, can be a tremendous weapon for an offensive team.

A successful play-action pass is the result of a combination of actions by the quarterback and the ballcarrier. Success requires coordination between the quarterback and the running back. When the quarterback hands off the ball, he must sell the pass to the defense. How well he carries out his fake pass not only sets up the play-action pass in subsequent plays but also may cause the defense to hesitate, which helps the running back.

Success all starts with selling the fake. Although a number of factors are ultimately important, it begins with the quarterback's execution of actual running plays. When he hands the ball to the running back, he must carry out his assigned fake. His body movement should be the same whether the play is a run or a pass. The coordination between the quarterback and the running back should look the same in this first phase of the play-action pass.

The running back's effectiveness in faking the handoff, hitting the hole, and driving on a play-action pass can greatly affect the success of the play. But the running back's fake is not enough. If the quarterback is going to have the time he needs to complete the pass, his fake of the handoff must be just as convincing as the running back's fake.

Successful play-action passing is based on offensive deception that results in defensive indecision. Everyone on the offensive team must try to convince the defense that the play is a running play because the goal of the offense is to make the defenders play the run. Convincing the defense that the play is a run slows down the pass rush, keeps the linebackers near the line of scrimmage, and ideally causes at least one defensive back to leave his coverage and come up to tackle the running back, leaving the receivers open.

The quarterback uses the same footwork for play-action passes that he uses for running plays. When faking a toss to the running back from an I-formation, the quarterback takes a short step up with the foot on the side of his final directional fake. The quarterback turns his back to the line of scrimmage and gets his head and body around with his second pivot step. From this position, he extends both hands and fakes tossing the ball to the running back, who goes through the motions of making a catch. After the quarterback brings the ball back to his belly, he begins his crossover drop for three additional steps, taking him 7 yards from the line of scrimmage. This type of play-action pass can be used with any of the medium patterns run by a receiver.

At the point where the quarterback would normally put the ball to the running back's belly for the run, he fakes the handoff (figure 2.19). The coach needs to tell the quarterback whether to use a one- or two-hand fake. After the quarterback completes the fake, he sets up at the proper depth using a three- or five-step drop. He gathers his feet under him to be in position to throw just as he would on a drop-back pass.

Figure 2.19 Quarterback fakes a handoff to the fullback and completes a play-action pass to the tight end.

Most play-action passes are thrown from inside the pocket, giving the quarterback time to set his feet properly and go through the normal throwing motion. The quarterback should practice making the fake, setting up, and stepping to pass to all areas of the field. He must be sure to maintain the proper mechanics of the throw.

The time that a quarterback spends practicing play-action passes can greatly enhance his ability. This practice should be an important part of the workout program.

Passing on the Move

After learning play-action passing, the quarterback should progress to movement passing, in which he will learn to move out of the pocket to one side or the other and deliver the ball while he is on the move.

Most of the quarterback's passes are either drop-back or play-action passes. Both have predetermined steps and a certain spot at which the quarterback sets up, and both provide the quarterback time to step and throw at his target. When throwing on the move, however, all that changes. The quarterback does not have the benefit of setting up and going through his normal throwing motion, so throwing on the move requires him to think in a different way.

The offense may have different types of passes that require the quarterback to move out of the pocket and throw on the run. These are designed plays, not instances in which he is forced out of the pocket by defensive pressure. For example, in a sprint-out or rollout pass (figure 2.20), the quarterback follows the movement of one or more of the offensive backs to one side of the formation. Other movement passes include waggle or bootleg plays (see figure 2.21), in which the backs go in one direction and the quarterback, after faking the run, comes out with the ball on the other side of the formation.

If the quarterback knows how to throw while on the run, he can throw any type of movement pass. The first thing that the quarterback must do is get his hips turned down the field, pointing directly at the target. He begins to move his body in the direction of the pass by stepping with the foot opposite his throwing arm. He must take this lead step directly toward his target.

When the quarterback is moving to the same side as his passing arm, getting turned is much easier than it is when moving in the other direction to throw the ball. When the quarterback moves to the side opposite his throwing arm, he needs to go a little deeper to give himself room to get turned upfield before delivering the ball.

When the quarterback's hips and opposite foot lead the throw, the passing arm is free to come through in a normal throwing motion. The quarterback needs to carry the ball high. He moves forward during the entire throwing motion and keeps his momentum moving at the target. He delivers the ball as his body continues to move over the lead foot, and he finishes with a continuing step, using the foot on the side of his passing arm.

Quarterbacks who get into trouble when throwing on the move don't turn their hips and bodies toward the target; instead their hips point at the sideline. They end up trying to throw across their bodies or stopping and trying to deliver the ball to the receiver with only their arms.

Figure 2.20 Quarterback makes a rollout pass to the left.

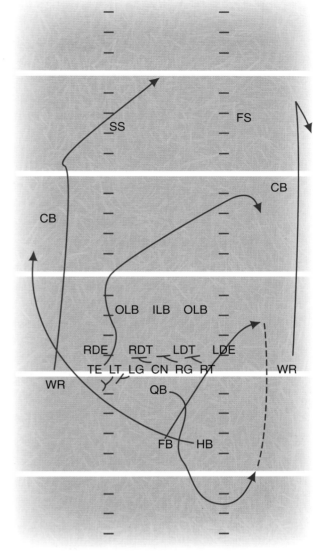

Figure 2.21 Quarterback fakes the run and sends a bootleg pass to the right.

CENTER AND QUARTERBACK PASS PLAY

Purpose: To reinforce to the quarterback the importance of moving back on passing plays so that the center has room to block in pass protection.

Procedure:

1. The center and quarterback set up.

2. The center and quarterback execute the snap and then execute their moves for a drop-back pass.

3. The center moves with the quarterback, and the quarterback backs away far enough to allow the center to move into pass protection. The center retreats off the line 2 yards, and the quarterback takes his normal five-step drop, reaching 7 yards in depth. During this drill the quarterback should not throw the ball.

(continued)

Center and Quarterback Pass Play *(continued)*

Coaching points: At the exchange point between the center and the quarterback, the ball must be brought up properly to the quarterback's hands. The quarterback should take a short cheat step up with the foot farther from his passing hand so that he can securely grasp the ball. The center should not step back too far as he makes the snap so that he does not step on the quarterback's foot.

THREE-STEP DROP

Purpose: To reinforce the proper technique for the three-step drop.

Procedure: The coach lines up on the defensive side of the ball, facing the quarterback and the center. If no center is available, another quarterback can lift the ball to the quarterback to start the drill when the snap count is called out.

1. The coach tells the quarterback the pattern and the snap count.
2. The quarterback takes his stance, calls out the cadence, takes the snap, and executes the three-step drop.
3. As the quarterback drops back, the coach points in the direction of the pass. The quarterback steps in that direction and goes through the throwing motion without releasing the ball.

Coaching points: Although no receiver participates in the drill, the coach needs to make certain that the quarterback practices stepping to all areas of the field—right, center, and left—after setting up with the three-step drop.

THROWING THE BUBBLE SCREEN

Purpose: To allow the quarterback to time the throw for the bubble screen.

Procedure:

1. The coach lines up on the defensive side of the ball, facing the quarterback and the center. If no center is available, another quarterback can lift the ball to the quarterback to start the drill when the snap count is called out.
2. Two wide receivers line up wide on either side of the ball.
3. The coach tells the quarterback the side of the bubble screen, the receiver, and the snap count.
4. The quarterback takes his stance, calls out the cadence, takes the snap, secures the ball, and immediately throws the ball to the designated wide receiver.
5. The quarterback must step in that direction and go through his normal throwing motion.

Coaching points: All four receivers should get the ball. The quarterback should practice stepping to both sides of the formation when making the pass and should have the experience of throwing to a receiver who is moving directly at him.

FIVE- AND SEVEN-STEP DROPS

Purpose: To reinforce the proper technique for the five- and seven-step drops.

Procedure:

1. The coach lines up on the defensive side of the ball, facing the quarterback and the center. If no center is available, another quarterback can lift the ball to the quarterback to start the drill when the snap count is called out.

2. Two wide receivers line up wide on either side of the ball.

3. The coach tells the quarterback the pattern, the receiver, and the snap count.

4. The quarterback takes his stance, calls out the cadence, takes the snap, secures the ball, and takes a five- or seven-step drop. As he drops, he looks at the coach to get the direction of the pass.

5. The quarterback must step in that direction and go through his normal throwing motion, but he does not need to make the throw.

Coaching points: The coach should repeat the drill so that the quarterback can practice stepping to all areas of the field (right, center, and left) after he has taken the five- or seven-step drop and set up properly.

SLOW SCREEN ACTION

Purpose: To give the quarterback practice in throwing a slow screen to a running back.

Procedure:

1. With one player acting as the center, another as the running back, and a third as a defensive rusher, the quarterback takes the snap and starts his drop.

2. At seven steps the quarterback should hesitate and then drop a few more steps.

3. The running back should set in place for three counts and then release to the outside to receive the ball.

4. The quarterback should throw the ball to the running back as soon as he turns back to receive the pass.

Coaching points: The defender should rush the quarterback at three-quarter speed. After making the snap, the center can set for three counts and then move to the outside in front of the running back to lead him up the field. The quarterback may need to loft the ball over the head of the rusher to the running back.

ARM STRENGTH

Purpose: To increase arm strength and to emphasize that using the entire body to make the throw produces arm speed and ball velocity.

Procedure:

1. Two quarterbacks stand 10 yards apart (figure 2.22).

2. Each quarterback takes a turn stepping and throwing three passes to the other quarterback.

3. After three passes, one quarterback moves back an additional 5 yards, creating a 15-yard separation. The quarterbacks throw three more passes to one another.

4. The quarterbacks continue the drill, increasing the distance by 5 yards after three passes each, until one of the quarterbacks starts to change his natural body motion to make the pass or releases the ball at an excessively high trajectory. When one of these actions occurs, the quarterbacks return to the previous distance and throw five passes each at that distance. If possible, quarterbacks with similar arm strength should be matched up.

① First set of passes – 10 yards
② Second set of passes – 15 yards
③ Third set of passes – 20 yards

Figure 2.22 Setup for the arm strength drill.

Coaching points: The coach should never allow a quarterback to keep practicing a labored throw. When one of the quarterbacks shows a breakdown in technique, all the quarterbacks should return to the previous distance where they threw with ease. Quarterbacks should keep a daily record of the distance and the number of passes thrown correctly.

MULTIPLE QUARTERBACKS, MULTIPLE RECEIVERS

Purpose: To increase the number of passing attempts for each quarterback during practice.

Procedure:

1. This drill requires three quarterbacks and three receivers. Two quarterbacks line up on the hash marks, and one quarterback lines up in the center of the field. A tight end gets in position in the center of the field, and two wide receivers line up, one near each sideline (figure 2.23).

2. The coach calls out a pass route to the three receivers. The outside receivers run the same route; the tight end runs a companion route.

3. The quarterback in the center of the field calls the cadence for the snap count. On the snap, all three quarterbacks execute the proper drop for the pattern called. The receivers run the correct routes.

4. The quarterbacks on the hash marks pass to the wide receiver on their sides. The quarterback in the center of the field passes to the tight end.

5. After throwing the passes, the quarterbacks rotate from left to right so that each has the opportunity to throw a variety of passes in all directions to a number of receivers.

Coaching points: The drill starts with short passes that use a three-step drop and progresses to medium and deep routes that use a five- or seven-step drop. Quarterbacks should try to throw as many passes as possible during practice time. Correction and instruction should be kept to a minimum during the drill, especially for the receivers. This drill is designed primarily to increase passing opportunities for the quarterbacks.

Figure 2.23 Setup for the multiple quarterbacks, multiple receivers drill.

TURNING AND STEPPING TO THE TARGET

Purpose: To give the quarterback experience passing while on the move.

Procedure:

1. The quarterback lines up behind the center. The coach tells the quarterback the direction that he should move after taking the snap. Another quarterback, acting as a receiver, is positioned downfield at 12 yards, near the sideline and facing the quarterback.
2. After receiving the snap, the quarterback moves to the right or left, taking a path that puts him at least 7 yards off the line of scrimmage.
3. As the quarterback moves to the outside, he brings the ball up to chest level and prepares to make the throw.
4. The quarterback positions his body so that he steps directly at the receiver as he starts the throwing motion and releases the ball. As the drill is repeated, the receiver moves to various positions on the field so that the quarterback must adjust his path to prepare to throw.

Coaching points: The quarterback should move to the right and left and execute the pass on the move. His front foot, hips, chest, and shoulders should point at and move directly toward the target so that his passing arm can come forward in a normal passing motion.

FAKING THE PITCH AND RUNNING A BOOTLEG

Purpose: To give the quarterback experience faking the pitch play, running a bootleg to the opposite side of the formation, and throwing the pass while on the move.

Procedure:

1. The quarterback lines up behind the center. The coach tells the quarterback the direction of the fake pitch and the direction that he should move after making the fake. Another quarterback, acting as a receiver, is positioned downfield at 12 yards, near the sideline and facing the quarterback.
2. After receiving the snap, the quarterback pivots to the right or left and fakes a pitch to the tailback.
3. After faking the pitch, the quarterback turns and moves to the opposite side of the formation.
4. The quarterback should take a path at least 7 yards off the line of scrimmage and toward the sideline.
5. As the quarterback moves to the outside, he brings the ball up to chest level and prepares to make the throw.
6. The quarterback must turn and position his body so that he can easily step directly at the receiver as he starts the throwing motion and then releases the ball. As the drill continues, the receiver moves to various positions on the field so that the quarterback must adjust his path to prepare to throw.

Coaching points: When a right-handed quarterback is moving to his left to throw, he needs to run a path slightly farther back from the line of scrimmage so that he can turn his body correctly down the field to make the throw. The quarterback must keep moving forward as he makes his throw, and his front foot, hips, chest, and shoulders must point at and move directly toward the target so that his passing arm can come forward in a normal passing motion. The coach should remind the quarterback that he may or may not have a blocker in front of him when he throws a bootleg pass, so he needs to be aware of the outside rusher on defense.

ROLLOUT PASSING

Purpose: To give the quarterback experience faking a handoff, running a rollout to the same side of the formation as the movement of the running backs, and then throwing the pass while on the move.

Procedure:

1. The quarterback lines up behind the center. The coach tells the quarterback the direction of the fake sweep and the direction that the quarterback should move after making the fake. Another quarterback, acting as a receiver, is positioned downfield at 12 yards, near the sideline and facing the quarterback.

2. After receiving the snap, the quarterback opens up to the right or left and fakes a handoff on the sweep play to the halfback.

3. After faking the handoff, the quarterback turns and moves to the same side of the formation as the movement of the fullback and halfback.

4. The quarterback should take a path at least 7 yards off the line of scrimmage and toward the sideline.

5. As the quarterback moves to the outside, he brings the ball up to chest level and prepares to make the throw.

6. The quarterback must turn and position his body so that he can easily step directly at the receiver as he starts the throwing motion and releases the ball. As the drill continues, the receiver moves to various positions on the field so that the quarterback must adjust his path to prepare to throw.

Coaching points: When a right-handed quarterback is moving to his left to throw, he needs to run a path slightly farther back from the line of scrimmage so that he can turn his body correctly down the field to make the throw. The quarterback must keep moving forward as he makes his throw, and his front foot, hips, chest, and shoulders must point at and move directly toward the target so that his passing arm can come forward in a normal passing motion. The coach should remind the quarterback that he will usually have a blocker in front of him when he throws a rollout pass, so the outside rusher should not be of immediate concern.

SPRINT-OUT PASSING

Purpose: To give the quarterback the experience of taking the snap and immediately opening and running to the outside to throw the ball (figure 2.24).

Procedure:

1. The quarterback lines up behind the center. The coach tells the quarterback the direction of the sprint-out. Another quarterback, acting as a receiver, is positioned downfield at 12 yards, near the sideline and facing the quarterback. Another player can line up in a split-back position to the side of the sprint-out.

2. After receiving the snap, the quarterback opens up to the right or left and angles off the line of scrimmage toward the sideline, trailing the back who is leading to the same side.

3. The quarterback should take a path at least 7 yards off the line of scrimmage and move toward the sideline.

4. After he is in this position, the quarterback should use the same throwing technique that he used for a bootleg or rollout pass.

Figure 2.24 Sprint-out passing.

Coaching points: When a right-handed quarterback is moving to his left to throw, he needs to run a path slightly farther back from the line of scrimmage so that he can turn his body correctly down the field to make the throw. The quarterback must keep moving forward as he makes his throw, and his front foot, hips, chest, and shoulders must point at and move directly toward the target so that his passing arm can come forward in a normal passing motion. A sprint-out pass is usually a quicker movement pass than the others and is normally thrown to a receiver who is moving toward the sideline in the same direction as the quarterback. The coach should remind the quarterback that he will usually have a blocker in front of him when he throws a sprint-out pass, so the outside rusher should not be of immediate concern.

CHAPTER 3

OFFENSIVE LINEMEN

Offensive lineman is one of the least glamorous positions on the team, yet it is one of the most important. The position requires a player who possesses mental toughness in addition to physical skills and doesn't need a lot of public recognition.

The three qualities that set great offensive linemen apart are personal pride in what they do, a desire to dominate the players on defense, and the ability to motivate themselves.

To play the offensive line, a player needs to be able to do the following:

1. Get into a proper stance.
2. Get off on the snap.
3. Execute the drive, hook, and angle blocks.
4. Work with other players to execute double-team and combination blocks.
5. Block a linebacker.
6. Pull to lead the ballcarrier.
7. Set up for pass protection.

The most important skill for any offensive lineman is blocking. One play may require the offensive lineman to drive a defensive player off the line, and the next may require him to protect the quarterback as he drops back to pass.

STANCE

An offensive lineman has to block to his right, left, or straight ahead. On some plays, he has to move laterally behind the line of scrimmage. On pass plays, he retreats off the line to protect the quarterback. The beginning stance must be balanced, allowing him to perform all these movements.

The stance may vary depending on the team's style of offense. Most offensive linemen use a three-point stance. A four-point stance is more appropriate when a team uses blocking that is more straight ahead or is in a short-yardage or goal-line situation. The offensive linemen on a team that throws the ball a lot use a two-point stance.

In all three stances, some constants apply. In every stance an offensive lineman keeps his head up and his eyes focused straight ahead. He keeps his shoulders even and his back straight. He never leans to one side or the other. When an offensive lineman leans, he gives the defensive players the advantage of knowing where he is going before the play begins. He does not rock back on his heels.

A three-point stance gives the offensive lineman the ability to move in all directions. To get into a three-point stance (figure 3.1), the offensive lineman begins by standing straight up, placing his feet even and shoulder-width apart, and pointing his toes straight ahead. Keeping his head up and his back straight, he bends at the knees until he can rest his forearms on his inner thighs. Next, he takes a small step back with his outside foot. The toes of the back foot are even with the middle of the front foot. With his forearms resting on the inner thighs, he reaches out with the hand on the same side as his back foot and places

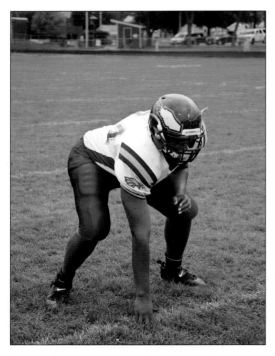

Figure 3.1 **Offensive lineman's three-point stance.**

the hand straight down and slightly in front of his shoulder. His shoulders are even, and his weight is evenly distributed on both feet, especially if the direction of his first step changes with each play. He has little or no weight on his down hand.

If he opens his hands with his fingers up instead of putting one hand on the ground, he is in a two-point stance (figure 3.2). The two-point stance is ideal for retreating off the line to protect a pass play.

The four-point stance (figure 3.3) is designed for drive blocking straight ahead or short-yardage plays. To get into a four-point stance, the offensive lineman starts with both forearms on his thighs. Next, he reaches forward with both arms, placing his hands on the ground slightly in front of his shoulders. His shoulders are even, his weight is on his hands, and the heels of both feet are off the ground. He now is in a good position to drive forward.

Figure 3.2　**Offensive lineman's two-point stance.**

Figure 3.3　**Offensive lineman's four-point stance.**

SNAP TIMING

Because the defensive players are so close, the offensive lineman needs to develop an explosive start off the line of scrimmage. Players must condition themselves to concentrate on the snap count. Offensive linemen need to stay square in their stances until the snap.

When exploding off the line, the offensive lineman should take short steps and move forward quickly (figure 3.4, page 50). This movement allows him to position himself into the defensive man. When blocking the defensive man, the offensive lineman must maintain a wide base, keep his back straight and his shoulders low and square, and move with his head up and eyes focused on the target.

One important goal when working on the start is to keep the momentum moving forward in one fluid motion. To develop this smooth, powerful motion, the player must

Figure 3.4 Offensive lineman exploding off the line.

have a wide base and take short, powerful steps. The offensive lineman must prepare for the defensive player to charge forward when the play begins because contact occurs much more quickly when the offensive lineman is working against a defensive man than it does when practicing with a blocking bag or sled. If the offensive lineman takes long steps, he will likely have a foot in the air when contact occurs, so getting the block will be much harder.

When a play is called in the huddle, the offensive lineman mentally reviews his assignment as he moves to the line of scrimmage. After he is at the line and in his stance, he concentrates on the quarterback's voice and prepares to react instantly when the snap count is called. Being late when moving on the snap usually allows a defender to win the battle, and moving early results in a penalty that moves the offense back 5 yards.

Crowd noise, defensive movement, and fatigue are three factors that can keep an offensive lineman from being mentally prepared to move on the snap. Blocking out crowd noise requires complete concentration on the quarterback's voice. Defensive movement may cause the lineman's blocking assignment to change before the snap, requiring the offensive lineman to adjust to a new assignment. Maintaining physical endurance throughout the season can help prevent fatigue.

GETTING OFF ON THE SNAP

Purpose: To develop an explosive start off the snap.

Procedure:

1. **This drill requires only the coach and the offensive linemen. The linemen go one at a time.**
2. **The offensive lineman lines up in his stance (two-, three-, or four-point).**
3. **When the coach gives the snap count, the lineman charges straight ahead for 5 yards.**
4. **After each player performs the drill correctly one at a time, they can go through the drill as a group.**

Coaching points: Offensive linemen should use short, quick steps off the line. They should move forward in one smooth motion.

BLOCKING

To be successful, an offense must have good blocking. Most of this blocking comes from the offensive linemen. Although every player has an important role, no offensive player— quarterback, running back, or receiver—will have a chance to do his job if the offensive line does not block the defense successfully.

Offensive linemen have to block while moving straight ahead (drive block), to their right or left (hook block and angle block), in combination with other linemen (double-team block and combination block), while moving laterally behind the line (pull and drive block), and when setting back off the line to protect the quarterback as he drops to throw (pass protection block).

Drive Block

On a drive block, the offensive lineman blocks the defensive lineman who has set up in front of him. The drive block is a fundamental technique that every offensive lineman must master. The goal of the drive block is to move the defender back off the line of scrimmage. Offensive linemen use drive blocks on most quick-hitting plays and on short-yardage and goal-line situations when defensive players are lined up in front of them.

To begin the drive block, the offensive lineman takes a short step up with his back foot the instant that he hears the snap (figure 3.5a). This quick step gets his momentum moving toward the defensive player. He maintains a wide base, keeps his feet spread apart, and takes short, rapid steps during the entire block. If his feet are too close together, the defender can easily push him aside.

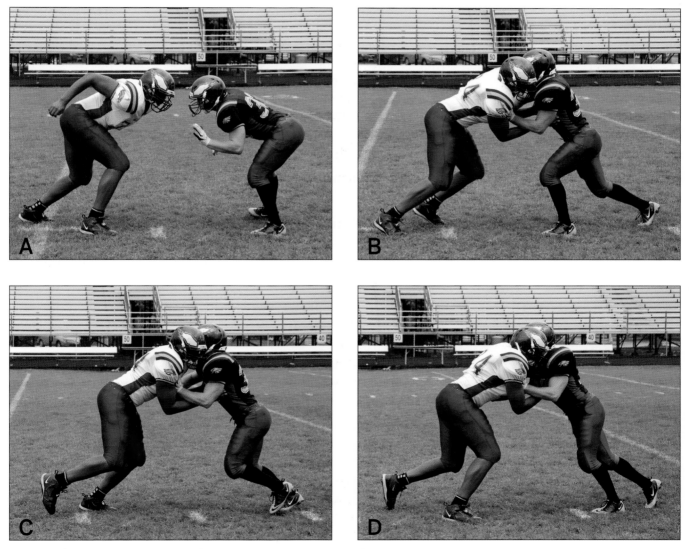

Figure 3.5 Offensive lineman executing a drive block: He *(a)* takes a short step on the snap, *(b)* makes contact on the second step, *(c)* plants his hands on the defender's chest, and *(d)* continues driving with his hips and legs.

As he moves forward, the offensive lineman keeps his shoulders square and his back straight. To avoid injury and keep the defender in his vision, he keeps his head up and his eyes looking directly at his target.

Most defenders line up directly across the line from the offensive linemen. The defensive lineman comes forward as the ball is snapped, and the offensive lineman should expect to make contact when his second step hits the ground (figure 3.5b). He continues driving with both feet the instant that he makes contact, keeping his momentum moving forward.

When the offensive lineman makes contact, he drives forward into the defensive lineman with his arms and hands (figure 3.5c). To get maximum leverage and force, he keeps his elbows close to his ribs. The inside position usually wins. The palms of both hands make contact with the middle of the defensive man's body in a strong, forceful manner.

Although the offensive lineman makes contact with his shoulder pad and hands, his legs do most of the work. At the instant that his hands make contact with the defender, he pushes his hips forward and upward, gathering his legs under him while keeping his feet driving with short, choppy steps (figure 3.5d). Blockers who are just learning to drive block tend to stop moving their feet at the moment of contact. To keep his feet driving and finish the block, the offensive lineman should pick a spot 2 or 3 feet past the defensive man as his goal.

Good offensive linemen take great pride in their ability to drive block. Players can practice the drive block by blocking into a big bag or blocking sled, but they need to realize that when they block a defensive player, the defensive player will be moving, not standing still.

At the start of the play, a linebacker lines up 3 to 4 yards off the line of scrimmage, directly opposite the offensive lineman. The offensive lineman needs to use a drive block, although contact occurs after the offensive lineman has taken a few steps (figure 3.6). The two major differences between this style of drive block and the drive block previously discussed are that the offensive lineman has to run to get to the defender, and the defender has a greater opportunity to move to his right or left as the offensive lineman comes forward to block him.

To block a linebacker successfully, the offensive lineman must get a quick start. He must know the snap count and take a fast step directly at the linebacker with his back foot. The blocker should keep a wide base and stay low as he moves across the line. The closer that he comes to the linebacker, the wider his base should be and the shorter his stride.

As the blocker prepares to make contact, he bends his knees and lowers his hips slightly in preparation for the block. His back is straight, and he keeps his head up and his eyes focused on the center of the linebacker's chest. The blocker initiates the block with the large muscles of the legs, coming up and through the defender in an explosive motion and keeping his legs moving.

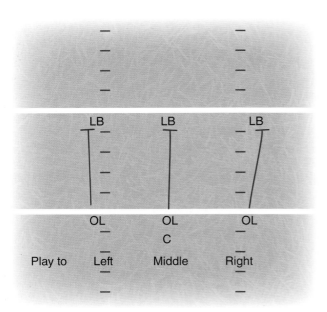

Figure 3.6 An offensive lineman must move quickly across the line to drive block a linebacker.

Hook Block

On a hook block, the offensive lineman blocks a defensive player who is lined up on his outside shoulder. The primary objective of a hook block is to stop the defender from penetrating the line of scrimmage because then the offensive lineman can stop the defender's pursuit and drive him back. Offensive linemen use this block most often on wide running plays to their side of the field.

On the snap, the offensive lineman takes a short position step with the foot on the same side as the defensive player. He takes this step laterally down the line of scrimmage. This step puts the offensive lineman's body in front of the defender and moves him into position for the block (figure 3.7a).

For his second step, the offensive lineman steps with his other foot directly at the defender. All the power for the block comes from this step. As the second step drives into the ground, the offensive lineman forces his far arm into the defender's chest. As he gets into position in front of the defender, the offensive lineman lifts the arm on the side of the block into the defender's chest (figure 3.7b). After he gets his body directly in front of the defender, he is able to drive the defensive player off the line of scrimmage (figure 3.7c). When the offensive lineman has stopped the defender's movement across the line, he continues to drive with his feet, using short, powerful steps as he would in a drive block.

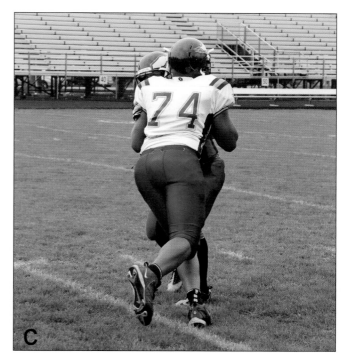

Figure 3.7 Offensive lineman executing a hook block: He *(a)* steps laterally to the defender, *(b)* steps into the block and puts his arm to the defender's chest, and *(c)* lifts his arm and drives into the defender.

Angle Block

In an angle block, the offensive lineman blocks a defender who is lined up in front of him to his right or left. When the play begins, the defensive lineman is focused on another offensive player, so his reaction to the angle block is secondary. The offensive lineman must execute the angle block with speed and quickness so that he drives into the defender before the defender can react.

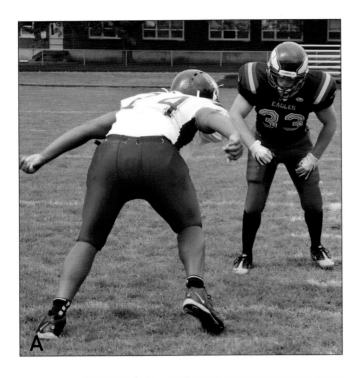

The offensive lineman needs speed and quickness to stop the defender's penetration across the line of scrimmage. When first learning the angle block, linemen often make the mistake of stepping to the spot where the defensive man lined up, not where he will be after the play begins and the defender moves forward. The defender will charge straight ahead, and the offensive lineman must anticipate this forward charge when moving to make the block.

To start the angle block, on the snap the offensive lineman takes a short step down the line of scrimmage with the foot nearer the defensive man whom he is to block (figure 3.8a). This step puts him in position to get his head in front of the defender. It also turns his hips and allows him to continue the block into the side of the defensive man's body. The offensive lineman does not narrow his base with this step, and he keeps a good bend in both knees.

The second step positions the offensive lineman's head, shoulders, and body squarely into the side of the defensive man (figure 3.8b). The offensive

Figure 3.8 Offensive lineman executing an angle block: He *(a)* steps laterally to the defender, *(b)* steps into the block and puts his shoulders and body into the defender's side, and *(c)* explodes into the defender with his shoulder pad and drives his palm into the defender's ribs.

lineman's back remains straight and his head and eyes stay up. He stays low and keeps his eyes on the defender. This second step generates most of the power for the block.

As his second step hits the ground, the offensive lineman explodes into the defender with the shoulder pad that is on the side of the second step. As his shoulder pad makes contact, he drives the palm of the hand on that side into the defender's ribs with as much power as he can (figure 3.8c).

From this initial explosion point, the offensive lineman maintains a wide base and continues to drive his legs in short, powerful steps. At the same time, he thrusts his hips forward and down, allowing him to drive up and through the defender. His goal is to drive the defender down the line of scrimmage away from the spot where the ballcarrier is going to run.

The offensive lineman should practice this block to both his right and left until he can execute it correctly in both directions. Because of the element of surprise and because the offensive lineman can attack the defender from the side, the angle block is one of the most devastating blocks that an offensive lineman can deliver.

Double-Team Block

The drive, hook, and angle blocks are performed by a single offensive lineman. In a double-team block, two offensive players work together to block one defensive player. The double team (figure 3.9) is the most powerful block an offense can direct at a defensive player. The combined size, weight, and power of two offensive players are directed at one defender. The defender should never win this battle. A good defensive player often reacts to the double team by merely dropping to the ground.

The double-team block is a combination of two blocks with slight adjustments. The offensive player directly in front of the defender uses a drive block, and the offensive player who blocks from the side of the defender uses a modified angle block.

Depending on the type of offense that the team uses, a double-team block may involve any offensive lineman and the tight end. In practice, the coach must work with every combination of offensive players who might execute this block together.

Figure 3.9 Double-team block by the center and offensive guard.

On the snap of the ball (figure 3.10a, page 56), the drive blocker takes a short position step with the foot on the same side as the angle blocker and explodes into the defender. The angle blocker takes a short position step with the foot on the same side as the drive blocker. After this short position step, the angle blocker explodes into the defender. After the two blockers take the position steps, they should be next to one another (figure 3.10b). From this position, the two bring their hips and shoulders together. Moving together side by side, they should be able to overpower the defender (figure 3.10c).

The drive blocker has the responsibility to prevent penetration by the defender. The angle blocker provides the added explosion to guarantee movement of the defensive player. The goal is to move the defender laterally down the line of scrimmage and back toward his goal line. When the offensive linemen accomplish this, they not only block the defender but also stop any other defender from pursuing the ballcarrier.

An offensive player may be either the drive blocker or the angle blocker on the double team, depending on the defender's position and the offense used. Even the tight end may be the drive blocker if a wingback is the angle blocker in a short-yardage or goal-line situation. All offensive linemen and tight ends need to practice both parts of the block.

Figure 3.10 Double-team block: The drive blocker and angle blocker *(a)* step to the defender, *(b)* are positioned side by side, and *(c)* with hips and shoulders together drive the defender down the line and back.

Combination Block

In combination blocking, two offensive linemen block two defensive players. The two players to be blocked are usually a defensive lineman and a defensive linebacker who are lined up next to each other. When executing the combination block, the offensive linemen should come off low on the snap. They need to keep their feet moving and take short, choppy steps. Offensive linemen should never cross their feet because doing so causes them to lose their base and power.

Offensive linemen use the combination block against stunting or slanting defenses. In a combination block, the offensive tackle and guard can work together or the guard and center can work together. In either case, the combination block starts with an attack on the defensive end on the line of scrimmage. The defensive end lines up directly in front of the tackle, and the inside linebacker is in front of the guard off the line of scrimmage (figure 3.11).

On the snap, both the guard and tackle step laterally with the outside foot. On his second step, the tackle strikes the defensive end in the chest with the palm of his inside hand, stopping the tackle's penetration across the line. With his first step, the guard checks the linebacker in front of him. If he sees the linebacker blitz, the guard must forget the combination block and direct all his power into blocking the linebacker. When the linebacker starts to move laterally, the guard strikes the defensive end with the palm of his outside hand on his second step. When both the tackle and guard have made contact with the defensive end, they can drive him off the line and determine whether he is playing to the inside or outside of the offensive tackle.

If the defensive end stunts or slants to the inside, the tackle should push the defensive end to the guard after making contact, release to the outside, move up the field, and prepare to block the inside linebacker as he comes behind the defensive end in pursuit (figure 3.12). On an inside stunt by the defensive end, the offensive guard should quickly come around in front of the defensive end, stop his penetration, and keep him from pursuit.

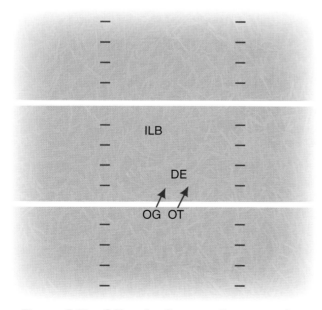

Figure 3.11 Offensive linemen line up and take a lateral step to set up the block.

Figure 3.12 The offensive guard and offensive tackle react to the defensive end's inside slant.

Figure 3.13 **The offensive guard and offensive tackle react to the defensive end's move to the outside.**

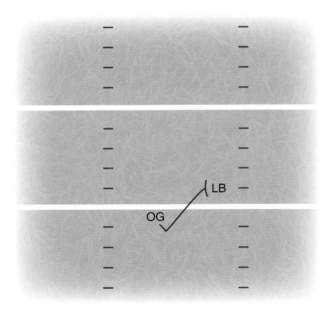

Figure 3.14 **The offensive guard pulls right and drive blocks the outside linebacker.**

If the defensive end moves to the outside, the guard can help the tackle start to move the defensive end off the line of scrimmage, but he must keep his vision on the linebacker (figure 3.13). If the linebacker starts to move to the inside, the guard must leave the combination block, release inside the defensive end, and use a running drive block on the linebacker.

To respond to various defensive fronts, players may execute a combination block to the outside or inside, or to the left or right. Players need to practice against every front with every combination of blockers.

Pull and Drive Block

Another running drive block that an offensive lineman needs to learn is the pull and drive block (figure 3.14). Instead of moving straight ahead to block a linebacker, he moves to his left or right down the line of scrimmage to block the defender.

The blocker has to establish a path behind his own offensive linemen. His path starts on the offensive line of scrimmage, but he runs toward the defensive side of the ball when blocking a defensive lineman or linebacker so that he can approach the defensive man from the inside and block him out of the hole. If he is pulling and leading the ballcarrier on a wide running play to the outside, he needs to give ground away from the line, take a path slightly back and away from the line of scrimmage, and then turn up the field to block a defensive back after he is outside the last block on the line of scrimmage. How far the blocker travels before making contact with the defender depends on his blocking assignment, the play being run, and the reaction of the defensive player.

The blocker should practice pulling. For this block, he must immediately change his direction from straight down the field to left or right on his first step. The first step, a short step with the foot in the direction that he will be going, establishes the path that he needs to follow to make the block. His path needs to go behind the offensive lineman next to him, so this first step brings him back from his original alignment and starts him in the direction of the block.

To change direction, the blocker takes a short angle step with the foot closer to his new path (figure 3.15). He swings the arm and shoulder that are on the same side as the foot back and around in a quick, hard motion. This motion also brings his upper body around and points his head and shoulders in the direction of the block. With his hand he pushes off the ground and back, and then he shoves off the opposite foot. During this motion, the blocker tries to stay as low as possible.

After his body is moving down the line, the blocker focuses on the defender whom he is assigned to block. Depending on the play, the blocker may be asked to block a defensive lineman, a linebacker, or a defensive back.

If he encounters the defender from the side, he should finish the block with the same action that he uses on an angle block. As he nears the defender, he explodes with the shoulder pad nearer the line of scrimmage into the exposed side of the defender's body. As his shoulder pad makes contact, he takes the palm of his hand on that side and drives it into the defender's ribs with as much power as he can. His head is in front of the defensive man. From this initial explosion point, the blocker maintains a wide base and continues to drive his legs in short, powerful steps. At the same time, he thrusts his hips forward and down, allowing him to drive up and through the defensive man.

The defender may see the blocker coming and turn to face him. When this occurs, the blocker is in

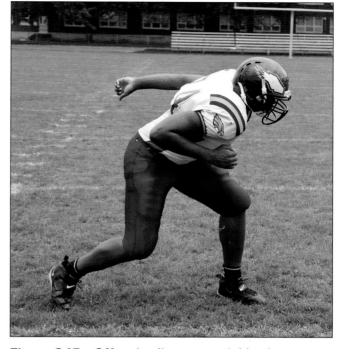

Figure 3.15 Offensive lineman quickly changes direction on the pull and drive block.

position to make a straight-ahead running drive block. As the blocker prepares to make contact, he bends his knees and lowers his hips slightly. His back is straight, and he keeps his head up and his eyes focused on the center of the defender's chest. The blocker initiates the block with the large muscles of the legs, coming up and through the defender in an explosive motion. The instant that his pads make contact, he punches into the numbers of the defender's jersey with both hands. The blocker finishes the block by driving his legs and moving the defender down the line of scrimmage away from the ballcarrier's path.

When the player is learning the proper path to run, a defender is unnecessary. After the blocker understands the path, a teammate can play defense while the player goes through each block at half speed. After he is comfortable with the pull, path, and block, he can increase the speed and go hard against a bag or pad. Finally, the defender reacts to the block, giving the blocker experience similar to what he will see during a game.

Blocking Drills

For each blocking drill, the offensive lineman should begin by working on the first step. Then he should work against a blocking bag. After working against the blocking bag, the offensive lineman can work against a defensive player at half speed. Finally, he can work against a defensive player at full speed. The defensive player should line up in the proper location for each block. The coach should give the blocker the snap count (first hut) and allow the blocker to get into his stance. Then the coach should start the cadence, and the snap count starts movement.

DRIVE BLOCK

Purpose: To reinforce proper technique for the drive block.

Procedure:

1. Two offensive linemen line up across from each other. One player holds a blocking bag.
2. On the snap, the blocker executes a drive block and drives the blocking dummy 4 yards off the line.
3. After the blocker learns the proper technique, he does the drill against a defensive player.

Coaching points: The offensive lineman should maintain a wide base and keep his feet moving, even after contact with the defender. He should keep his elbows close to his ribs as his hands make contact. He should keep his head up and his defender in sight.

BLOCKING A LINEBACKER

Purpose: To reinforce proper technique for a drive block on a linebacker who lines up off the line of scrimmage.

Procedure:

1. The linebacker lines up 3 to 4 yards off the line of scrimmage, directly opposite the offensive lineman. The linebacker can use a handheld blocking dummy at first.
2. The coach calls a running play and gives the blocker the snap count.
3. On the snap, the offensive lineman executes the drive block.
4. The coach should stand behind the blocker and indicate to the linebacker whether he should move straight ahead or to the right or left.

Coaching points: The coach should always call a running play so that the blocker knows in which direction the ball will be run. This heads-up gives the offensive player a good idea of how to anticipate and adjust to the movement of the defender.

HOOK BLOCK

Purpose: To reinforce proper technique for the hook block.

Procedure:

1. The defensive player holds a blocking dummy. He lines up just outside the blocker's right or left shoulder pad.
2. On the snap count, the blocker executes a hook block and attempts to drive the blocking dummy back 4 yards.
3. The defensive player alternates which side he lines up on. The blocker must learn to make the hook block in both directions.

Coaching points: The offensive lineman must use a short, lateral position step followed by a step directly at the defender. The offensive lineman gets into position in front of the defender and drives him back off the line of scrimmage.

ANGLE BLOCK

Purpose: To reinforce proper technique for the angle block.

Procedure:

1. The defensive player holds a blocking dummy. He lines up in an area that would be in front of the offensive lineman to the blocker's right or left. The player holding the blocking dummy positions himself so that he faces the direction of the block.

2. On the snap count, the blocker executes an angle block and attempts to drive the blocking dummy down the line of scrimmage and back off the line.

3. The defensive player alternates which side he lines up on. The blocker must learn to make the angle block in both directions.

Coaching points: The blocker should take a short step down the line with the foot nearer the defender. This first step allows him to get his head in front of the defender and stop him from crossing the line of scrimmage. The second step, taken with his other foot, is his explosion step and allows him to drive the shoulder pad on the same side as this step hard into the side of the defender. The blocker must continue to drive the defender with short, choppy steps.

DOUBLE-TEAM BLOCK

Purpose: To reinforce proper technique for the double-team block and give players experience from both sides of the double team.

Procedure:

1. In this drill, two offensive blockers work against one defender.

2. The defender lines up directly in front of one of the blockers.

3. On the snap count, the two blockers move in unison to block the single defender.

Coaching points: On the snap, the blocker directly in front of the defender should execute a drive block, and the offensive blocker to the side should start an angle block. Both blockers should use their shoulder pads and hips together to drive the defensive man back off the line for 4 yards.

COMBINATION BLOCK

Purpose: To reinforce proper technique for the combination block.

Procedure:

1. Two offensive blockers face a defensive lineman and a linebacker. The defensive lineman lines up directly in front of one of the blockers, and the linebacker lines up in front of the other.

2. After the blockers are in their stances, the coach directs the charge of the defensive lineman and the movement of the linebacker before calling out the snap count.

3. On the snap, the two blockers move in unison against the defensive lineman. Based on the movements of the defensive lineman and linebacker, the blockers separate so that one offensive blocker covers each defender.

(continued)

Combination Block *(continued)*

Coaching points: When players are first learning the combination block, the coach should indicate the direction that the defensive end and linebacker will move so that the offensive linemen can execute the block versus every charge. When executing the combination block, players should come off low, keep their feet moving, and take short, choppy steps. They should never cross their feet because doing so causes them to lose their base and power.

PULL AND DRIVE BLOCK

Purpose: To reinforce proper technique for the pull and drive block.

Procedure:

1. This drill requires two players. The defender can set up at various positions on the defensive line and in the secondary consistent with the play called by the coach.

2. On the snap, the blocker moves down the line and makes a running drive block on the defender.

Coaching points: The blocker must take a short angle step in the direction that he will be moving to make the block. He should swing back the arm and shoulder on the same side as his first step so that his body points in the direction of the block. At the same time, he needs to shove off his down hand and opposite foot. The blocker should stay low, shorten his stride, and widen his base as he nears the defender. At contact, his head should be in front of the defender, and he should drive his shoulder pad into the defender's side, driving him toward the sideline.

CENTER SNAP

This section focuses on a single position on the offensive line: the center. The center–quarterback exchange is vital to the success of every play.

Center is a demanding and important position on the offensive team. The center and the quarterback are the only two players who touch the ball on every offensive play, and the center's initial movement triggers the offensive play. The center must have great skill and be willing to bear tremendous responsibility. But all offensive linemen should learn to snap the ball so that a player is always ready to move over in case the center becomes injured. In this section, we focus on the skills required for the direct snap and the shotgun snap. The techniques for making short snaps for extra points and field goals and long snaps for punts are covered in chapter 10. Both types of snaps require special practice and are different from snapping to the quarterback.

Direct Snap to the Quarterback

The coach should face the offensive lineman who is learning to snap and check his stance and grip on the ball. The first step to learning the center snap is taking an even four-point stance (figure 3.16a). To start, the center gets into the stance and distributes his weight

Figure 3.16 Center prepares to snap: He *(a)* begins in a four-point stance, *(b)* lifts his snapping hand, and *(c)* grasps the ball.

equally on both feet and the fingers of both hands (no ball yet). The center lifts up the hand that he will use to snap the ball to the quarterback (figure 3.16*b*), and someone puts a ball on the spot where his hand was. The center reaches down and grasps the ball (figure 3.16*c*).

As the center grasps the ball, the laces of the ball are opposite the snapping hand. The palm of the hand is on the outside of the ball. The snapping hand is slightly in front of the ball. The center's fingers are securely under the ball, and his thumb rests over the top of the ball (figure 3.17).

When the center has a good grasp, he is ready to go through the actual snapping motion. The center needs to practice bringing the ball up to the quarterback until they both know that they can snap the ball without a fumble. Regardless of his blocking assignment, the center's first responsibility is to snap the ball securely to the quarterback at the proper time. As the center becomes more comfortable with the snap, he can move the ball more into the center of his body and lift his other hand off the ground. The next

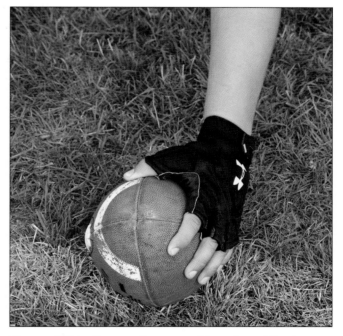

Figure 3.17 Proper finger and hand positioning for the snap.

technique that the center needs to practice is making the snap while moving as he does when making a block. The center needs to practice moving straight ahead, stepping to the right or left, and dropping straight back in pass protection.

Each center needs to spend time snapping to every quarterback on the team. No one can predict what will happen in a game. The more the center can prepare during practice, the better he will be able to handle whatever situation may come up during a game.

Shotgun Snap to the Quarterback

The shotgun snap is usually a blind snap in that after the center receives the signal that the quarterback is ready for the ball, the center raises his head, looks straight ahead, and prepares to block as he makes the snap.

For the shotgun snap, the center needs to assume a three-point stance and grip the ball as if he were throwing a pass. The ball needs to be rotated so that the laces are on the outside and lower part of the ball. The center should grip the ball by placing his first finger off the laces near the front tip, his second and third fingers over the laces, and his little finger on the laces near the center of the ball.

If possible, the center should keep his back level so that the shoulders and hips are at the same height. Lower hips often result in a low snap to the quarterback, and high hips can cause a high snap.

Younger players may need to use both hands when making the snap in a shotgun formation. The second hand grips the opposite side of the ball, and the thumb is on top and over the center of the ball for balance.

Before the snap, the center should look back between his legs and make certain that the quarterback is in position and ready. On the snap count, the center should pass the ball back between his legs in a smooth motion, allowing the snapping hand to rotate to the outside as he releases the ball (figure 3.18). The aiming point for the center should be from the belt to the chest of the quarterback.

Figure 3.18 Center delivering the shotgun snap: He looks back at the quarterback and delivers the ball in a fluid motion.

CENTER SNAP

Purpose: To fine-tune snapping technique without a ball.

Procedure:

1. At first, players should perform the drill without the ball.

2. The quarterback places his hands in the proper position to take the snap. Another offensive lineman can take his place if the quarterback is unavailable.

3. As the quarterback's hand comes back and up between the center's legs, the center reaches up with his snapping hand and shakes hands with the quarterback's top hand (figure 3.19).

Coaching points: The center should practice this motion until it is automatic. After the center is comfortable with the motion, the ball can be added.

Figure 3.19 Center snap drill.

SHOTGUN CENTER SNAP

Purpose: To practice consistent shotgun snap technique.

Procedure:

1. Two centers line up 4 to 6 yards apart and work together in the beginning. One player acts as the center, and the other is the quarterback.

2. The center adjusts the ball so that the laces are in the proper location, grips the ball in his passing hand, and looks back between his legs to the quarterback.

3. The quarterback signals the center that he is ready to receive the snap.

4. The center then brings his head up and snaps the ball (figure 3.20, page 66).

5. Players change roles and repeat the drill.

(continued)

Shotgun Center Snap *(continued)*

Coaching points: The center must grip the ball correctly to make the snap. His back should be level, and he must follow through with his snapping hand as he releases the ball. After the snap is consistent, the center should practice the snap while moving forward, back, right, and left.

Figure 3.20   Shotgun center snap drill.

PASS PROTECTION BLOCKING

An offensive lineman faces no bigger challenge than protecting the quarterback on a pass play. Every offensive lineman should take pride in keeping the defense from ever touching the quarterback. For a pass play to be successful, four things must take place:

1. The offensive line must block long enough to give the quarterback the time that he needs to deliver the ball.
2. The quarterback must make an accurate throw.
3. The receiver must run a disciplined pass pattern.
4. The receiver must make the catch.

Pass offense starts with the offensive line protecting the quarterback and giving him time to throw. In pass blocking, the offensive lineman's only job is to keep the defensive player from hitting the quarterback before the quarterback has the opportunity to get rid of the ball. Before a pass play, offensive linemen must try to anticipate the direction that their opponents will charge during the play and adjust accordingly. Pass protection is an aggressive form of blocking.

The proper stance is important in pass protection. An offensive lineman will have difficulty getting a good block if his down hand is too far forward. He will have the same problem if he places too much weight on his down hand. When the offensive lineman has to protect the quarterback, he should put just enough weight on his down hand to allow him to push back. The toe of his back foot, the foot on the side of the down hand, should be even with the middle of the other foot. His back should be straight, his shoulders should be square, and his head should be up (figure 3.21).

To move out of his stance, the offensive lineman pushes off his down hand to start his initial movement back off the line of scrimmage. As his shoulders come up, he takes a short step to the inside with his inside foot. This step puts him in position to stop a hard inside charge by the defender (figure 3.22a). After he takes this step, the offensive lineman bends both knees and lowers his hips. He keeps his back straight and avoids bending forward at the waist. His head is up, and his eyes are focused straight ahead. He brings both elbows in tight against his waist and brings his forearms up so that his hands are in front of his chest. Both hands are up, the thumbs are together, the fingers are spread, and the palms are turned forward.

The offensive lineman has to anticipate the direction that a defender will charge. During a game, the offensive lineman should watch where the defender lines up. If the defender lines up on the offensive line-

Figure 3.21 Pass protection stance.

man's inside shoulder, he probably will go to the inside. If the defender is directly in front of the offensive lineman, he can go inside, outside, or attempt to rush right over the offensive lineman. In either situation, the offensive lineman must protect the inside gap first and then react to an outside rush. When the defender lines up on the offensive lineman's outside shoulder, the defender probably will rush outside. Finally, when the defender lines up way outside the offensive lineman, the defender will start to the outside.

Figure 3.22 Offensive lineman in pass protection: He (a) gets into position to stop the defender's charge and (b) makes contact with the defender and pushes forward.

Offensive linemen should be able to picture each of these rushes coming at them and react accordingly. Wherever the defender lines up, whether on the inside shoulder, outside shoulder, or directly in front of the offensive lineman, the offensive lineman should stay square to the line of scrimmage. He needs to stay directly in front of the rusher because he wants to stay between the rusher and the quarterback.

When the offensive lineman sets up in front of the defensive player, the offensive lineman's first thought should be to stop the defensive player's momentum. The power to stop the defender starts in the offensive lineman's legs and then comes up through his body to the palms of both hands. As the defender comes into him, the offensive lineman uses his leg muscles to explode up, avoiding lunging out at the defender. He strikes out aggressively, hitting the defender in the chest with the palms of both hands (figure 3.22b). He pushes forward with both hands to create space between himself and the rusher, and he flexes his knees, lowering his hips. He brings both hands back into his chest and prepares himself to push forward repeatedly until the pass is thrown or the whistle blows.

When a rusher is definitely going to the offensive lineman's inside or outside, the offensive lineman may not be able to use both hands. In this case, he will have to stop the rusher's momentum by exploding off the leg on the same side as the rush and aggressively hitting into the rusher's chest with the hand on that side. After stopping the rusher, the offensive lineman can try to get more in front of the rusher so that he can use both hands on the second hit. When blocking an outside rusher, the offensive lineman must be careful to not go too far to the outside. If the offensive lineman overextends to the outside, the rusher will quickly change his path and rush inside to the quarterback.

Blocking a defensive rusher who is lined up wide to the outside of the offensive lineman requires a change in technique, usually by an offensive tackle. The offensive lineman will not be able to stay square to the line of scrimmage. To meet and stop this type of rusher, he must turn his body at a 45-degree angle to the line.

To get in proper position to block a wide rusher, the offensive lineman should kick his outside foot back and bring his inside foot back and to the outside in a position turned out at a 45-degree angle (figure 3.23). He needs to set up in a good pass protection stance and establish a position directly between the rusher and the quarterback. The

Figure 3.23   Offensive lineman in position to block a wide rusher.

offensive lineman must be prepared to meet the pass rusher and use the hand on the same side as the rush to stop the rusher's momentum. After initial contact, the offensive lineman separates, sets again, and stays with the rusher until he hears the whistle.

After he is set, the offensive lineman works in a straight line, moving back away from the line as the pass rusher starts to cross his nose. To keep a strong base, the offensive lineman slides his feet as he moves away from the line. He does not cross his feet or bring them too close together because doing so weakens his base. By forcing the defender to rush outside, the offensive lineman will always have the opportunity to push him back behind the quarterback.

PASS PROTECTION

Purpose: To reinforce proper pass protection stance and movement after the snap.

Procedure:

1. **The coach faces the offensive linemen. At first, no defenders are used and one player goes at a time.**
2. **The coach gives the snap count and calls out the cadence to start the drill.**
3. **The offensive lineman gets into the stance for pass protection.**
4. **When the coach calls the snap, the offensive lineman moves out of the stance and into pass protection.**
5. **When all offensive linemen are setting up correctly, the coach can have an entire offensive line get into their stances and drop back together. The center can snap the ball to another player who acts as the quarterback.**

Coaching points: When the offensive lineman is first learning to pass protect, the defender should rush at half speed. Blockers must stay balanced and not lunge forward to stop the defender. The blockers must shuffle their feet and must not cross them during the drill. They must bend at the knees, keep their backs straight and heads up, and keep their hands in position to strike out at the rusher. Eventually a full-speed pass protection drill can be run with one blocker versus one defensive player at a time. Using more than two offensive blockers in a live drill at one time should be avoided because using more than two increases the chance for injury when players run into each other.

Variation: After the players are setting up properly, another offensive lineman can line up in front of each blocker to serve as a defensive rush man.

SCREEN BLOCKING

For an offensive lineman, blocking for a screen pass involves pass protection blocking at the start of the play and then a running drive block to complete the play. For a screen to be successful, the following must take place:

1. The entire offense must sell that the play is a pass.
2. The defense must be invited to rush the passer.
3. The blockers and the player receiving the screen must time their release.
4. Each blocker must focus on blocking a specific player.

On the snap the blocker should set for a normal pass protection block. If possible the blocker should block the rusher for three counts and then invite and direct the rusher up the field by physically pushing the rusher past his body (figure 3.24). After the rusher is clear, the blocker should release to the outside, look for his assigned player, and prepare to use a running drive block similar to the one used when he is pulling and blocking (page 58).

Figure 3.24 Offensive lineman blocking for a screen pass.

SCREEN PASS BLOCKING

Purpose: To perfect offensive line blocking on a screen pass.

Procedure:

1. The coach faces the offensive linemen. A defensive rusher should be in position, and the two players should go at the same time. A blocking bag should be positioned to the outside.

2. The coach gives the snap count, tells the rusher where to rush (inside or outside), and calls out the cadence to start the drill.

3. When the coach calls the snap, the offensive lineman moves out of the stance and into pass protection position, blocking the rusher for three counts.

4. After the third count, the blocker pushes the defender back in the direction of the quarterback.

5. The blocker immediately locates the position of the blocking bag and takes a direct path to be in position to execute a running drive block.

6. After the blocker is doing the drill correctly, a second blocker and rusher can be added so that the two blockers can practice working together to establish a path for the ballcarrier.

Coaching points: The blocker must set up in a realistic pass protection position, hold his block for the proper time, and then direct the rusher back to the quarterback. The blocker must locate and take a good path to the secondary defender. The blocker must keep running as he makes his secondary block and anticipate movement by the defensive man toward the ballcarrier.

Variation: The entire offensive line gets into their stances and drops back together. The center snaps the ball to another player who is serving as the quarterback.

CHAPTER
4

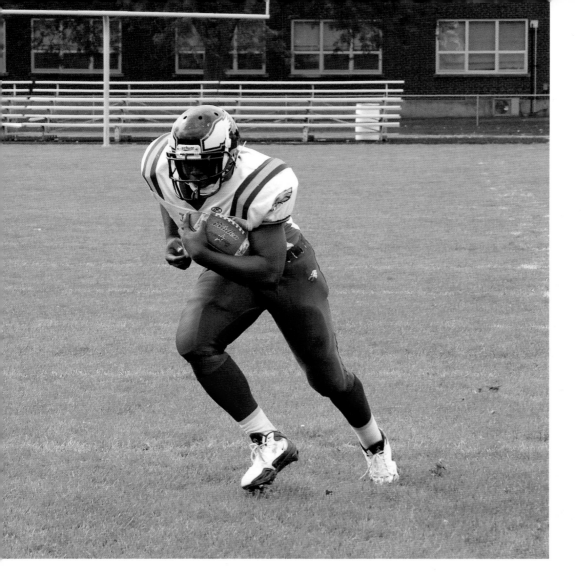

RUNNING BACKS

The running back is in a spotlight position, but he knows that without the blocking of his teammates he would be just another guy out on the field. The running back must run with great desire, but at the same time he must remember to give credit to the blockers who open the way for him.

Contact is guaranteed, so the ballcarrier must expect to be hit. A beginning running back may think that he has no place to run, that he is hit as soon as he touches the ball. He must stay positive, though, because when a hole suddenly opens up, he needs to be ready to burst right through it with the ball.

A successful running back possesses certain key skills. This chapter focuses on the stance and start, securing the handoff, receiving passes, evading defenders, and blocking on running and passing plays. Occasionally a running back may have to pass the ball. Check the section on passing on the move in the chapter about quarterbacks (page 38) for the techniques that a running back needs to master if he is going to pass the ball.

STANCE AND QUICK START

A running back must be able to move quickly and smoothly when the play begins. He needs to be able to drive straight ahead, move forward at an angle, and move laterally right or left. A functional stance allows the running back to move easily in any direction. The three basic stances used by a running back are the four-, three-, and two-point stances. In each stance, he keeps his feet even, shoulders level, head up, and eyes focused straight ahead. Players must not look or lean in the direction that they will be running because either clue helps the defense before the ball is even snapped.

Figure 4.1   Running back's four-point stance.

The four-point stance (figure 4.1) allows forward movement with speed and power. To get in the four-point stance, the running back stands with his feet even. He bends his knees so that he can rest his forearms on his inner thighs, and he reaches forward with both arms. He places both hands on the ground slightly in front of his shoulders, making sure that his shoulders are even. He keeps his back straight, his head up, and his eyes straight ahead. He stays balanced, never leaning to one side or the other. A fullback who mainly charges straight ahead to run and block between the offensive tackles uses this stance.

Figure 4.2   Running back's three-point stance.

A three-point stance (figure 4.2) does not allow as much speed moving forward, but it facilitates movement laterally to the right or left. The running back begins to get into the stance the same way he does for the four-point stance. When both forearms are resting on his thighs, he reaches out with only one arm. He places only a little weight on the fingers of his extended arm as they touch the ground. His down hand is even with his shoulders when the hand reaches the ground. His shoulders are even; he does not lean to the right or left. His back is straight, and his weight is evenly distributed on the balls of his feet.

This standard stance can be used by any running back who is lined up in the backfield because it allows him to move instantly in all directions for any type of play.

The advantage of a two-point stance (figure 4.3) is that it allows the running back to see the defense better. In a two-point stance, the running back gets into his stance as he did before, but he has only a slight bend in the knees. He places both hands on his thighs and has his thumbs on the inside. He keeps his head up, looks straight ahead, avoids leaning either way, keeps his back straight, and has his weight evenly distributed on both feet. A two-point stance is used by a running back lined up in the backfield in I-formation 7 yards off the line and directly behind the quarterback. A running back may also use this stance if he leaves the backfield and lines up wide as a wide receiver before the start of the play.

Starting quickly is one of the most important abilities that a running back can have. After the snap, the running back must instantly be in motion, adjusting his speed for the blocking pattern or the hole being created.

The first step after the snap is crucial. Regardless of which stance the running back uses, he needs to get moving the instant that the ball is snapped. Well-executed footwork is what makes this happen. The first step gets him moving quickly and directs him in a proper path to his running lane. The running back takes his first step with the foot on the side toward which he will be moving (figure 4.4). This step is not a long one; instead, it is a short, forward, directional step that sets the body on a path directly toward the attack. If the running back is going to his right, he takes this short directional step with his right foot. If he is going to the left, he steps with his left foot. This step is the first one that a running back uses any time he executes a play in which he moves forward toward the line of scrimmage, not laterally toward the sideline.

If a play requires the running back to move laterally, a crossover step is the quickest way for him to start after the snap. His first step is with the foot opposite the side of his movement. For example, if he wants to move left, he crosses over with his right foot. After

Figure 4.3 Running back's two-point stance.

Figure 4.4 Running back's first step.

the snap, he leans his body in the direction that he wants to go and brings his leg across his body in a natural motion.

The three- or four-point stance can make the crossover step more difficult. To move laterally out of a three- or four-point stance, the running back starts by leaning with his hips in the direction that he wants to go (figure 4.5a). He then brings his arm back on the side closer to this direction (figure 4.5b). This arm movement turns his shoulders quickly and opens his hips so that his leg can easily come across (figure 4.5c).

Figure 4.5 Running back's crossover step from a three-point stance: He (a) leans with his hips in the direction that he wants to go, (b) brings his arm back to turn his shoulders, and (c) opens his hips and steps across.

A false step can cause the running back to arrive late. When a running back is late getting to the hole or the handoff point, he probably did not get off on the snap or had a poor start. Many running backs do not realize that they are taking a false step when they first step back with one foot rather than step forward or cross over. This false step slows their start.

The body and mind become comfortable with what is practiced. The running back needs to learn the correct start early in his career. This skill will stay with him as he continues to grow as a running back.

RUNNING BACK'S STANCE

Purpose: To reinforce a functional stance for the running back.

Procedure:

1. **Running backs line up in front of the coach.**
2. **On the coach's signal, the running backs move forward and assume the stance (four-, three-, or two-point) called out by the coach.**
3. **The coach observes each stance and provides feedback.**

Coaching points: In each stance, the running back's feet must be even, the shoulders level, the head up, and the eyes focused straight ahead.

RUNNING BACK'S DIRECTIONAL STEP

Purpose: To make sure that running backs are using the correct stepping technique after the snap.

Procedure:

1. **Running backs line up and face the coach.**
2. **The coach calls out the direction in which the running backs should step. In the beginning, one player goes at a time.**
3. **Running backs step in the called direction, and the coach provides feedback on their technique.**
4. **Players can take three or four steps toward the line after taking the correct directional step.**

Coaching points: Running backs should work on the short, directional step to both the right and left and at different angles to the line of scrimmage.

RUNNING BACK'S CROSSOVER FIRST STEP

Purpose: To reinforce proper execution of the crossover step.

Procedure:

1. **The running back gets into a two-point stance.**
2. **He leans his shoulders and hips to the right and steps with his left foot.**
3. **He takes three or four steps toward the sideline after making the crossover step.**
4. **He lines up in the two-point stance and repeats the drill to the left.**

(continued)

Running Back's Crossover First Step   *(continued)*

5. He leans his shoulders and hips to the left and steps with his right foot.
6. He takes three or four steps toward the sideline after making the crossover step.

Coaching points: The running back must not take a false step before the crossover step. After mastering the crossover step from the two-point stance, the running back should practice the crossover step from the three- and four-point stances.

SECURING THE HANDOFF

Chapter 2 covered the quarterback's responsibility in the handoff; this chapter looks at the running back's job in the handoff. One of the most important skills that a running back needs to learn is how to take the ball from the quarterback. All the special skills and ability that he may have as a running back will be wasted if he does not take the handoff cleanly. The quarterback has the job of putting the ball firmly to the running back's belly. After the ball is in his arms, the running back is responsible for securing the ball.

When introducing the running offense, the coach must both show and tell the path that he wants the running back to take on each of the various running plays in the offense. The running back must learn, understand, and practice the exact paths.

The running back and the quarterback must execute the exact footwork to guarantee that they arrive at the handoff point at the same time. If the running back is sloppy in his footwork and path, he will be either too far or too close to the quarterback at the handoff point. When this happens, the handoff will not be clean and may result in a fumble.

Securing the ball is the running back's number one priority. When he receives the ball from the quarterback, when he is running in heavy traffic, or when he sees that he is going to be hit, the running back needs to make certain that the ball is firmly in his grasp.

During the handoff, the running back forms a pocket with his hands and arms to receive the ball from the quarterback (figure 4.6). One arm is above his belly, and one arm is below it, creating a pocket for the ball.

The running back must place the upper arm correctly and in the same position every time he takes the handoff. The arm closer to the quarterback is the upper arm. The running back raises his elbow to just below his shoulders so that the forearm is across his chest. He angles the palm of his hand down slightly so that it can quickly engulf the point of the ball.

The position of the lower arm is just as important as that of the upper arm. The arm away from the quarterback forms the bottom of the pocket. The forearm is slightly below and across the running back's belly, and the palm of the hand is turned up.

After the quarterback puts the ball to the running back's belly, both of the running back's arms grasp the ball (figure

Figure 4.6   **Running back creates a pocket for the ball.**

4.7). He quickly lowers his upper hand and forearm and raises his lower hand and forearm, clasping the ball tightly. A beginning running back should keep two arms on the ball to secure it. A more experienced running back can transfer the ball to one arm while running. But whenever the running back feels that the ball is not secure or when he is about to be hit by more than one tackler, he should not hesitate to get both hands on the ball. Getting the handoff, securing the ball, and protecting it are techniques that must become second nature for running backs.

A technique that can help the running back is visualization. The running back sits quietly with his eyes closed and visualizes taking the handoff for each running play in the offense. He pictures coming to the handoff point and receiving the ball, trying to see in his mind the exact position of his body: The elbow of the near arm is up, the forearm is across the top of his chest, the forearm of his bottom arm is below and across his belly, and his head is up so that his eyes are focused on the blocking. When taking the handoff, he does not have the luxury of looking at the ball. His vision needs to be on the blocking and the hole that is opening up.

TAKING THE HANDOFF

Purpose: To teach the running back to form a pocket with his arms for the ball.

Procedure:

1. **Running backs line up facing the coach. The ball is not used at first.**
2. **On the coach's signal, the running backs move forward for the handoff.**
3. **The coach observes the technique of each running back and provides feedback.**
4. **The quarterback joins the drill, and the actual handoff takes place.**

Coaching points: At the handoff, the running back quickly grasps the ball by raising the bottom hand and forearm and lowering the upper hand and forearm. Beginning running backs should practice running in this position with both hands around the ball. As the running back becomes more experienced, he will know when it is safe to transfer the ball to only one hand.

Figure 4.7 Running back grasps the ball in both arms.

RECEIVING A TOSS OR PITCH FROM THE QUARTERBACK

On certain running plays, a running back will be required to catch a lateral from the quarterback. Based on the type of play, the lateral may be an option toss, in which the quarterback uses a two-handed basketball push toss, or, on a sweep pitch play, an underhanded pitch in which the quarterback uses a reverse pivot to make the pitch.

In both instances, the running back will be moving to the sideline as the ball leaves the hands of the quarterback. The running back should turn his upper body, head, and shoulders back to the quarterback so that he can see the flight of the ball and position his hands to make the catch using the same catching techniques that he would use to make a reception on a forward pass (see chapter 1, pages 7-10).

When the quarterback releases the ball, the running back should reach back with both hands, see the ball and both hands at the moment of the catch, and immediately secure the ball in the arm and hand away from the closest defender.

CATCHING THE OPTION TOSS

Purpose: To teach the running back to receive an option toss from the quarterback and secure it with his hand and arm on the ball.

Procedure:

1. **The running back and quarterback, with the ball, line up facing the coach. A cone or another player can be used to identify the location of the outside defensive player on the line.**

2. **On the coach's signal, both players start in the direction designated by the coach.**

3. **The quarterback moves down the line and simulates his fake handoff to the fullback. As he reaches the cone, the quarterback uses both hands to toss the ball back to the running back.**

4. **The running back should position his body so that he is ahead of the quarterback when the quarterback reaches the cone.**

5. **The running back reaches back with both hands to make the catch, immediately secures the ball, and runs down the field for 10 yards.**

6. **The coach observes the path, location, and technique of each running back and provides feedback.**

Coaching points: The back must run at full speed, turning his upper body, head, and shoulders back to receive the ball. The hand position of the back must be correct for the location of the ball as he makes the catch, and the back must secure the ball right away. The coach should remind the ballcarriers that a lateral is a live ball that, if not caught, can be recovered by the defensive team.

Variation: After the running back and quarterback are successfully executing the toss, a defender can replace the cone and move either toward the quarterback or to the outside to simulate game conditions.

CATCHING THE PITCH

Purpose: To teach the running back to receive a pitch from the quarterback and secure it with his hand and arm on the ball.

Procedure:

1. **The running back and the quarterback, with the ball, line up facing the coach in I- formation position.**

2. **On the coach's signal, the quarterback simulates taking the snap, and the tailback starts in the direction designated by the coach.**

3. **The quarterback executes a reverse pivot and pitches the ball back to the tailback using a two-handed underhand technique.**

4. **At the same time, the tailback uses a crossover step to start, get his body turned, and sprint to the sideline.**

5. On the second step, the tailback turns his upper body, head, and shoulders back to the quarterback so that he can see the ball leave the quarterback's hands.

6. The running back reaches back with both hands to make the catch, immediately secures the ball, and runs down the field for 10 yards.

7. The coach observes the path, location, and technique of each running back and provides feedback.

Coaching points: The back must run at full speed and turn his upper body, head, and shoulders back to receive the ball. The hand position of the back must be correct as he makes the catch, and he must secure the ball right away. The coach should remind the ballcarriers that a lateral is a live ball that, if not caught, can be recovered by the defensive team.

THROWING THE RUN PASS

A running back who successfully executes the pitch play often has the opportunity to throw the ball if he has the ability to make the pass and if the defenders are attacking the line of scrimmage from the secondary. The technique that the running back should use to make the pass is the same technique that a quarterback uses when throwing on the move (figure 4.8).

Figure 4.8 Running back throwing the run pass: He *(a)* takes a crossover step, turns his upper body and head to the quarterback, and reaches back with both hands to make the catch. He then *(b)* takes a path at least 7 yards off the line of scrimmage and toward the sideline; positions his hips, chest, shoulders, and head to face the receiver; steps toward the receiver as he starts the throwing motion; and releases the ball.

EXECUTING THE RUN PASS

Purpose: To teach the running back to receive a pitch from the quarterback and then throw a run pass.

Procedure:

1. The drill starts exactly like the pitch drill, but an additional player lines up wide and runs a slant or corner pass route. The running back and the quarterback, with the ball, line up facing the coach in I-formation position.

2. On the coach's signal, the quarterback simulates taking the snap, and the tailback starts in the direction designated by the coach.

3. The quarterback executes a reverse pivot and pitches the ball back to the tailback using a two-handed underhand technique.

4. The tailback takes a crossover step, turns his upper body, head, and shoulders back to the quarterback, and reaches back with both hands to make the catch.

5. When the running back catches the pitch, he brings the ball up to his chest in both hands, adjusts the ball so that his passing hand is in proper position, looks down the field to see whether a receiver is open, and takes a path slightly back from the line of scrimmage.

6. The running back takes a path at least 7 yards off the line of scrimmage and toward the sideline.

7. The running back must turn and position his body with his hips, chest, shoulders, and head facing the receiver so that he can easily step directly at the receiver as he starts the throwing motion and releases the ball.

Coaching points: The coach should emphasize that the running back must focus on catching the pitch. Only after he secures the ball can he look downfield. The coach should check that the running back has the proper grip on the ball and that he has the ball in the correct position to make the pass. The running back must turn his body so that he can step directly at the receiver with his front foot. The coach needs to remind the running back that if no one is open, he should secure the ball and run up the field.

Variation: To give the running back a more gamelike experience, the same drill can be run with a defender who either drops back to cover the receiver or charges up to the line of scrimmage.

EVADING TACKLERS

Every running back can improve his running skills by working on evasive techniques. No running back can run over defensive players all the time, but at times he will have no choice but to secure the ball, lower his shoulders, and drive for as many yards as he can get.

The defense will occasionally put the running back in a position where he cannot get away. In those instances, the running back should get a good forward lean and try to position himself under the pad level of the potential tackler. He must protect the ball at all costs, using both hands to surround the ball if necessary. Depending on the down and distance, he should be prepared to go to the ground if he has no opportunity to advance the ball.

When the opportunity presents itself to make the defensive player miss, the running back should take it. He has the advantage of knowing the direction in which he is going to cut, whereas the defensive player can only guess. Two running skills that the running back can use to improve his chances of making the tackler miss are the cutting and crossover techniques. When learning these skills, a running back can use a blocking bag or another running back who acts as the defender, standing about 10 yards away.

The running back has to determine which way he is going to cut before starting his forward movement at the defender. When faking to the right, the running back starts the cut with a short step with his right foot to the outside of the defender (figure 4.9a). He needs to move his head and shoulders quickly to the left as his right foot hits the ground. He pushes off his right foot and takes a short change-of-direction step with his left foot (figure 4.9b) that takes him to the outside of the defender (figure 4.9c). He keeps his second step short to keep his feet under his hips. The head and shoulder fake will convince the defender that he is going to the right.

The next technique that the running back can use to make a tackler miss is the crossover step. To use the crossover step, the running back needs to keep space between the defender and himself. When he is 3 to 4 yards away from the defender, if he wants to go to his left, the running back starts the move by taking a short step with his right foot to the outside of the defender (figure 4.10a, page 82). He takes a second step with his left foot directly at the tackler and makes a quick fake to the right with his head. He then leans his upper body to the left as his left foot hits the ground (figure 4.10b). He quickly brings his right leg completely across his body to change the direction and path of his run (figure 4.10c). Leaning the upper body makes it possible for the running back to bring his leg across his body and make the defender miss.

When a running back has to run toward a sideline, he must do everything he can to make sure that the play doesn't create negative yardage. An inside cut technique can help him gain yards. As the running back moves toward the sideline, he must prepare to cut quickly up the field. The running back never wants to be tackled for negative yardage if he can prevent it. He must fake the defender, creating the impression in the defender's mind that he is going to continue to run toward the sideline. Then at the last

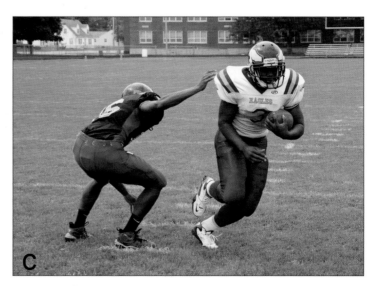

Figure 4.9 Running back fakes right and cuts left: He *(a)* takes a shot step with the right foot, *(b)* takes a change-of-direction step with the left, and *(c)* continues moving left.

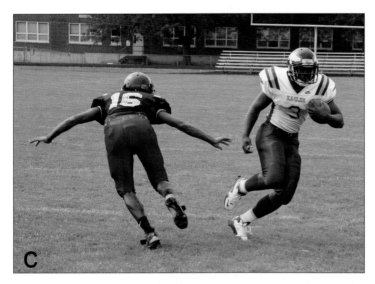

Figure 4.10 Running back's crossover step: He *(a)* takes a short step with his right foot, *(b)* leans to the left, and *(c)* brings his right leg across and moves to the left.

minute, the running back cuts up the field inside the defender's position for positive yardage.

The running back starts in his normal stance with the ball already in his hands. He rolls over the foot in the direction that he is going to run and quickly turns his body toward the sideline (figure 4.11a). As he runs parallel to the line of scrimmage, he picks a point at which the defender will cross the line of scrimmage. He rolls over the foot nearest the line of scrimmage when he is 2 yards from that point and drives up the field as he cuts to the inside (figure 4.11b). When learning this skill a running back should run at half speed at first.

As the running back comes across the formation, he should not angle up toward the line of scrimmage; instead, he should sell the defense on the possibility of a wide run. In a game, the running back has a blocker in front of him leading the way (figure 4.12). The running back times his run with his blocker's run, staying slightly behind his blocker. Just as the blocker makes the block on the defensive player, the running back cuts up the field. The running back should practice running behind all the blockers who might block for him. This group usually includes a guard and fullback and possibly a pulling offensive tackle.

Spinning to avoid a defender is a technique that looks spectacular when it works but is hard to execute properly. When learning this technique, the running back needs the assistance of a coach or another player, who acts as the defensive tackler. The defender's job is to give the running back resistance as he spins.

Beginning running backs who try to spin to avoid being tackled commonly make two errors: Either they begin by leaning back with the upper body or they try to execute the spin when they are too far from the tackler.

When the running back is close enough for the defender to make contact, he steps toward the center of the defender's body with the foot on the same side as his spin (figure 4.13a, page 84). If he is spinning to his right, he steps with his right foot. If he is spinning to the left, he steps with his left foot. He must perform this initial step correctly if he is to avoid the grasp of the tackler. When his foot hits the ground, the running back throws his opposite foot, leg, and shoulder around in one smooth motion. For an

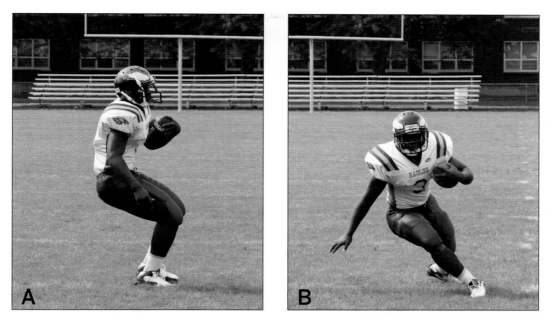

Figure 4.11 Running back makes an inside cut: He *(a)* faces and runs toward the sideline and *(b)* rolls over the foot nearest the line of scrimmage, cuts inside, and drives upfield.

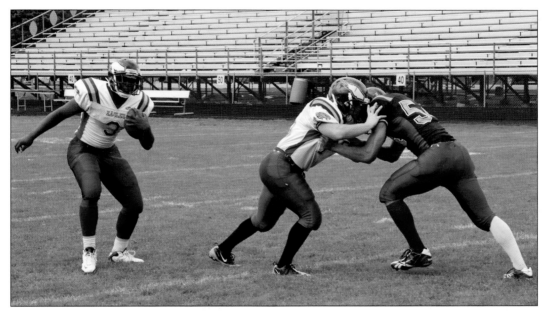

Figure 4.12 Running back makes his cut when the blocker makes his block on the defender.

instant his back is to the tackler as he completes the spin (figure 4.13*b*). This spin move allows him to move quickly away from the tackler. The instant that his leg comes around, he should head upfield again. If he is to escape from the tackler, he must maintain his speed.

When the running back practices spinning, he does not have to worry about being hit by a defensive player. In a game, it's different. The running back needs to get into the habit of securing and protecting the ball. If possible, he should have the ball in the hand that will be farther from the defender after the spin.

Figure 4.13 *(a-b)* Running back's spin move: He steps toward the defender, quickly spins around, and heads away from the defender and upfield.

THE CUT

Purpose: To reinforce proper cutting technique.

Procedure:

1. The coach lines up as a defender about 10 yards in front of the running back.
2. The running back, with the ball secured, approaches the coach and makes a cut to evade him.
3. The coach observes the running back's cut and provides feedback.

Coaching points: To give the running back a feel for the cut and what it will look like in a game, the coach should lean to the side of the running back's first step. The running back should practice the cut to the left and right, beginning at half speed and then increasing the speed of his approach.

EVASIVE CROSSOVER STEP

Purpose: To reinforce the proper technique for using a crossover step to elude a defender.

Procedure:

1. The coach lines up as a defender about 10 yards in front of the running back.
2. The running back, with the ball secured, approaches the coach and uses a crossover step to evade him.
3. The coach observes the running back's crossover move and provides feedback.

Coaching points: The running back should practice the crossover move to the left and right. The running back should start the drill at half speed and then increase the speed of his approach. The movement needs to become automatic for the running back so that he can execute the maneuver without even thinking about it.

RUN TO THE SIDELINE

Purpose: To work on correct technique for running to the sideline to eliminate runs for negative yardage.

Procedure:

1. The coach places a bag to indicate where the running back should cut after running toward the sideline.
2. The running back executes the run toward the sideline and makes the cut as indicated.

Coaching points: The running back should sell the fact that he is going wide to the sideline and not slow down when preparing to cut up the field. The drill should be run to both the right and the left. The running back should accelerate up the field for 10 yards after he makes his cut.

INSIDE CUT

Purpose: To develop the ability to sell the defense on the wide run when making an inside cut.

Procedure:

1. A defensive player sets up opposite a running back with the ball.
2. The defensive player lets the running back get started and then charges across the line to give the running back the feeling of selling the wide run and then cutting up inside.
3. The defensive player can come at the running back from a tight position, from a normal width, or from a wide alignment. The change in width causes the running back to change the point at which he makes his cut up the field.
4. The running back should practice running in both directions.

Coaching points: As the running back becomes comfortable with the move, the coach can add a quarterback. The quarterback can either hand the ball to the running back or pitch it to him. The running back now has to secure the ball and then locate the point of the defensive man.

Variation: A shirt or blocking dummy can be placed on the ground 2 to 3 yards on the offensive side of the line of scrimmage to mark where the defensive back will be in the game.

SPIN TO GET FREE

Purpose: To develop proper spinning technique to avoid defenders.

Procedure:

1. The running back starts 5 or 6 yards away from the defender.
2. The defender pushes the running back in the chest when the running back is within reach. This contact and push by the defender is similar to what the running back will feel in a game when a tackler begins to make contact.
3. The running back keeps a good forward lean with his upper body throughout the drill, especially as he makes contact and executes the spin.

Coaching points: A beginning running back should start at half speed. He can then increase his speed if he is confident that he can execute the technique while running at full speed. The running back must accelerate up the field after completing his spin move.

RECEIVING PASSES

A running back must have the knowledge and techniques necessary to be part of the passing game. Understanding the fundamentals of the passing game, knowing the importance of timing in pass offense, and perfecting the techniques needed to get open and make the catch are three areas in which a running back can improve with practice. The running back should know the proper way to catch the ball. He should always try to have both hands and the ball in his vision when he makes the catch. See chapter 1 for more information about catching technique.

Receivers must understand the importance of running each pass pattern at the proper depth every time. If the running back and quarterback are going to coordinate the passing game, the running back must make certain that he plays his part correctly. When first learning pass routes, the running back should practice without a quarterback and run all pass routes at half speed. After he has a feel for how to run the various routes correctly, he can run them at full speed.

Three Zones

The running back must first understand the different depths of the various pass patterns. The distance that he runs down the field is coordinated with the number of steps that the quarterback takes in his drop, the time that the offensive line has to pass block and protect the quarterback, and the manner of the pass protection blocking. By running his pattern at the proper depth, the running back helps ensure the correct timing of the pass. He should think of the field as being divided into three depths, or zones: short, medium, and deep.

The running back's short zone extends from the line of scrimmage through about 7 yards up the field. Patterns run in this area will be quick. The quarterback may drop three or five steps before delivering the ball. The timing must be exact. The running back will not have time to make elaborate moves; he must run quickly up the field, break sharply into his pattern, and immediately look for the ball.

The running back's medium zone starts approximately 8 yards past the line of scrimmage and goes up to 12 yards. In this zone the running back has the opportunity to get open. Patterns will often be continuous movement routes in which he keeps running before he gets the ball. To pass to this zone, the quarterback uses a five-step drop. The offensive linemen know that they must pass protect for a longer time.

The running back's deep zone extends from the medium zone all the way to the opponent's goal line. Patterns in this area require more time, and the running back often has to run under the ball. The quarterback uses a seven-step drop and should lead the running back, giving him the opportunity to separate from the defender and make the reception.

The running back needs to be able to recognize the various zones as he is on the move. One of the best ways to get a feel for the different depths is to take time every day to run up the field calling out the zone that he is in or saying to himself, "Short, short, short," "Medium, medium, medium," and "Deep, deep, deep," as he travels up the field.

Learning Pass Routes

After the running back understands the depths of the zones, he is ready to learn the various pass routes that he will run in each zone. Learning to run the pass patterns, or routes, is something that running backs can practice on their own. In fact, running backs can practice without a quarterback or ball. When practicing routes, the running back should release quickly, run the routes at the proper depth, break at the proper point, get his head around quickly to see the ball and the quarterback, have his hands in proper position for the catch, and run the route to completion.

Short Pass Routes. In the short zone, the most important thing for the running back to remember is to look quickly for the ball. The three basic pass patterns in the short zone are flat, angle, and wide (figure 4.14). The quarterback might take only a three-step drop before throwing the ball to the primary receiver. If the quarterback drops only three steps, the offensive line will block aggressively and the quarterback will throw the pass quickly.

These three pass patterns must be timed correctly. The running back must get off quickly on the snap count, run hard, break at the proper depth, and look for the ball as soon as possible. Because the running back's initial alignment usually is 4 yards behind the line of scrimmage, he cannot go very far upfield before he makes his break.

In the flat pattern, the running back attacks the line of scrimmage at a 45-degree angle just outside his offensive tackle. After he has gone 1 yard across the line of scrimmage, he rolls over his outside foot and breaks directly toward the sideline. As he continues to run to the outside of the field, he turns his head back toward the quarterback and looks for the ball. He must expect the pass at any height. The ball will often be low and in front, so he will have to adjust his path to make the catch.

When running the angle pattern, the running back starts out exactly as he would if he were going to run a flat route. When he is a yard or two across the line of scrimmage, instead of breaking to the sideline he breaks at a 45-degree angle back into the center of the field. He turns his head back to the quarterback the second that he makes his break and tries to pick out the ball the instant that it leaves the quarterback's hand. In this pattern, the ball travels a short distance and gets to the running back quickly. He must locate the ball and make the catch the instant that he turns back to the center of the field. He should have his hands ready to reach out for the ball.

The wide pattern also is run to the outside of the field, and it is run on the offensive side of the line of scrimmage. The running back starts with a crossover step with his inside foot as he begins to run the route. Because the quarterback will be even with the running back or even slightly in front of him, the running back must angle slightly away from the line of scrimmage with his first few steps. This path allows him to see the ball better and, more important, allows him to be turned up the field when he makes the catch. On a wide pattern, the quarterback throws the ball in front of the running back. The quarterback is going to expect the running back to be turned up the field and running under the pass. If the quarterback is in front of the running back and the running back senses that the pass will be incomplete, he needs to be sure to cover up the ball. The pass may be ruled a lateral, which could be recovered by the defense.

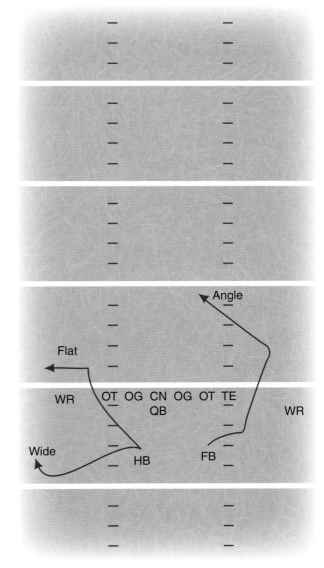

Figure 4.14 Three short pass routes for the running back: flat, angle, and wide.

The receiver must expect to be tackled soon after he touches the ball, especially on short pass routes, so he must secure the ball the instant that it is in his hands. If the hit doesn't happen immediately, so much the better, but the running back must be prepared for the possibility.

Medium Pass Routes. For a medium-zone pass, the receiver operates in an area 7 to 12 yards across the line of scrimmage. A running back therefore has to run 11 to 15 yards before making his final break to catch the ball on any medium pass route.

Because of the distance that he must cover on a medium route, the running back's greatest asset is speed. He cannot afford to come out at half or three-quarter speed. The quarterback will not have time to wait for the running back to make his break. The running back also wants to give defenders the impression that he may be going deep.

Running any pass pattern starts with a good release from the presnap position in the backfield. The running back should try to make the release of all medium or deep routes look the same to the defense. Both the in and out pass patterns are run this way (figure 4.15). The one exception is a stop route, which calls for an angle release and is run at 7 yards.

For the out and in pass patterns, the running back's release should be just wide enough to guarantee that he will clear any offensive blocker or defensive rush man. After he sees that he is clear to the outside, he must immediately turn up the field and make the defense think that he is going deep on his pass route.

On the out route, the running back rolls over his outside foot at 9 yards and breaks directly for the sideline. When the quarterback throws the ball, the running back may need to come back toward the line of scrimmage to make the catch. When catching the pass, the running back turns his shoulders, heads back to the quarterback, and reaches back with both hands to make the catch.

The in route is run off the same release as the out route. The running back runs up the field 10 yards past the line of scrimmage, rolls over his inside foot, and breaks across the center of the field. At the instant that he breaks, his head turns back to the quarterback. He is ready to turn his shoulders to the line to get both hands in position to make the catch. For proper timing, the running back must keep running at full speed after the break.

When running a stop route, the running back must locate the spot where he will make his final cut before the snap of the ball. He must try to run a straight line to that spot. The initial target spot in a stop pattern is 7 yards across the line of scrimmage and 8 yards outside where the offensive tackle lined up. When the running

Figure 4.15 Three medium pass routes for the running back: in, out, and stop.

back nears this spot, he must gather himself and prepare to turn either to the inside or to the outside away from the nearest defensive coverage man. He turns his head back to the quarterback the instant that he makes his stop. He brings both hands up and prepares to make the catch. The quicker the quarterback can get the ball to the running back, the sooner the running back can make the catch, put the ball away, and run up the field.

Deep Pass Routes. A running back may have only two or three chances to run a deep pass pattern during a game. These pass routes take more time—the quarterback needs to hold the ball longer, and the offensive line has to block longer before the ball is thrown. Deep patterns open up when the running back has successfully caught passes in the short and medium zones. Because the running back will have only a few chances to catch a deep pass, he must run his route correctly, run at full speed, get open, and make the reception.

When a running back runs a deep pattern—a flat and up, seam, post, or fan route (figure 4.16)—it helps if the defender thinks that he is running a short or medium route. If the running back can get the defender to commit to a short or medium pattern, the running back can break clear and get in position to make a catch for a long gain. For deep routes the running back's release must be wide enough to guarantee that he will clear any offensive blocker or defensive rush man.

For the flat and up pattern, the running back should look back for the ball as he runs to the sideline. When he is about 6 yards from the sideline, he rolls over the foot nearer the defense, turns, and runs straight up the field. He turns his head back to the inside and focuses on the quarterback, expecting the pass to be lofted to him. He runs under the pass and makes the catch.

The seam, post, and fan pass patterns start exactly as if the running back were running an out or in route in the medium zone. When the defender thinks that the running back is going to break to either the outside or the inside at medium depth, he will slow his coverage, putting the running back in good position to run by him.

When running the seam route, the running back starts up the field just as he would for a medium route. Instead of breaking for the out or in route, he continues running straight up the field. At about 12 yards past the line of scrimmage, the running back begins to angle slightly to the inside. As he runs the seam pattern, he stays on the outside of the hash marks. This is one deep pass pattern in which the pass may be drilled to the running back, not lofted. Because the ball may arrive quickly, the running back must promptly turn his head to the inside and focus

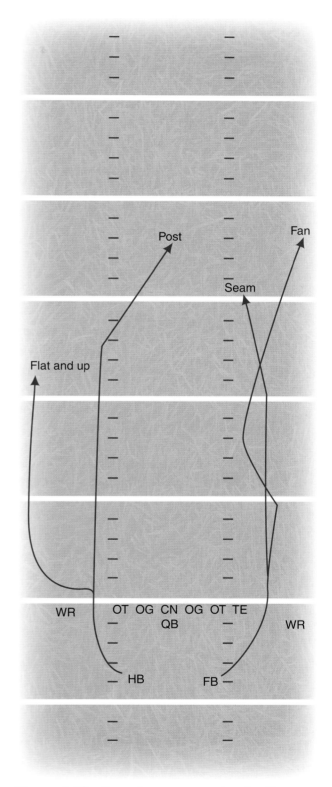

Figure 4.16 Four deep pass routes for the running back: flat and up, seam, post, and fan.

and focus on the quarterback. Ideally, the ball will come over the running back's inside shoulder, but he must be prepared for it to come directly over his head or to the outside.

After the running back has learned to run the seam pattern correctly, he can begin to work on the post pattern. Everything is the same as it is in the seam route except that at 13 yards the running back rolls over his inside foot and runs at a deep angle to the center of the field. He looks back over his inside shoulder and expects to run under the pass.

The fan route is the most difficult to complete. At 8 yards, as the running back runs up the field, he angles slightly to the inside of the field. When he has run 2 or 3 yards at an inside angle, he rolls over his outside foot and breaks at a deep angle up the field toward the sideline. He turns his head over his outside shoulder to look back to the quarterback. He looks for the ball to be lofted over his outside shoulder and is prepared to adjust his path to the path of the ball.

RUNNING PASS ROUTES

Purpose: To give the running back experience in running various pass routes.

Procedure:

1. **The coach lines up in the quarterback's setup position and faces the running back.**
2. **The coach calls out the pass route, and the running back gets into position for the play.**
3. **The coach begins the play by calling out the snap, and the running back runs the pass route.**
4. **The coach offers feedback on the running back's performance.**
5. **In the beginning, the ball is not used in the drill. When players can correctly run each route, a quarterback and ball can be added.**

Coaching points: The running back must start immediately on the snap. The coach should check that the pattern is run at the correct depth, that the running back does not slow down to make his break, and that he turns his head back at the earliest possible moment to look for the ball. Players should run all the patterns to both the right and the left.

BLOCKING

All competent running backs can run with the ball. Good running backs can also catch passes when coming out of the backfield. Great running backs excel at running and catching and have the ability and desire to be outstanding blockers. The combination of these three skills makes the complete running back.

A running back needs to block on running plays when his backfield partner is carrying the ball. On pass plays, he may become part of the pass protection blocking for the quarterback. A running back needs to become skilled in both types of blocking.

Blocking for Running Plays

For running plays, the running back needs to understand that the quicker he can get to the defender, the better he can do his job. He blocks only one side of the defender (figure 4.17). He shortens his stride as he nears the defender. His shoulders are slightly in front of his hips, and his hips are over his feet. He bends his knees, makes contact with his shoulder and forearm at the defender's hip, and keeps his legs driving even after contact. The contact point is at the defender's hip on the side opposite the direction in which the running back wants to block the defender. The running back's head slides to the outside of the defensive man's body. He explodes off the foot on the same side as his block.

A running back may block a linebacker who is lined up on the end of the line or at an inside position. In either situation, the block is at the point of attack, where the ball is being run, and it is crucial to the success of the play. In both instances, the running back must take the most direct route to the linebacker. The quicker he gets to the linebacker, the less time the linebacker has to react and set himself to defeat the block. The running back should practice taking the same path directly toward the linebacker, not changing his path whether he blocks the defender in or out.

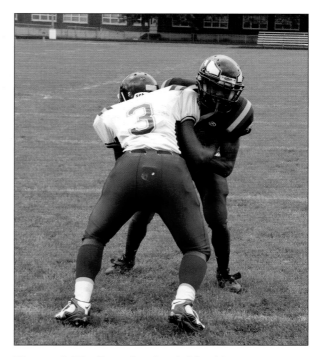

Figure 4.17 **Running back blocking on a running play.**

The running back may be asked to block an outside linebacker to the inside on wide running plays or to the outside on off-tackle plays. The path to the linebacker on both blocks should be the same. The running back uses the same blocking on a defensive back who is coming up on the outside. The difference between the two blocks is the running back's target area. If the running back is blocking the linebacker to the outside, he hits the linebacker's inside hip area. If the running back is blocking the linebacker to the inside, he contacts the linebacker's outside hip. The running back must focus on the target area and make good contact with his shoulder pad and forearm.

When blocking the linebacker to the outside, the running back should explode off his outside foot and make contact with the linebacker's inside hip with his outside shoulder pad and forearm. He should allow his head to slide along the side of the linebacker. The running back then drives the linebacker back and to the outside of his original position.

When the running back blocks the outside linebacker to the inside, his path is the same, except now he aims for the outside linebacker's outside hip. His explosion to start the block comes off his inside foot. He makes contact with the linebacker's outside hip with his inside shoulder pad and forearm. After the running back makes his hit, his goal is to drive the backer back toward the center of the field.

If the play calls for the running back to block an inside linebacker away from the center or back toward the center, he can use the same technique that he uses when blocking an outside linebacker.

The running back may lead block on an inside linebacker. In this type of play, the ball-carrier cuts off (goes opposite) his block. The running back does not know at the start of the play which direction he is going to block the linebacker. The running back should focus on the linebacker's numbers, take a path directly at the linebacker, allow the linebacker to choose a side, and then block him. The technique for the block is the same. The running back has to be ready to decide quickly which side of his body he is going to use to block and which of the defender's hips he is going to attack.

Blocking for Passing Plays

When blocking for the quarterback on pass plays, the running back cannot attack the defender as he would on a run block. Now he must position himself and wait for the defender to rush at him.

Most of the time, the running back needs to block a defender, usually a linebacker or defensive back, who is rushing the quarterback from the outside. At other times, he may block an inside linebacker who is rushing on the inside.

On a pass block, the running back is often unable to stop the defender in his tracks. If the running back knows where the quarterback will be setting up, he may be able to use the defender's momentum and block him past the quarterback. The running back must know how deep the quarterback is going to drop and where he will finally set up to deliver the pass.

To excel as a pass blocker, the running back should know the best way to protect the quarterback. The running back must position his body between the pass rusher and the quarterback (figure 4.18). He keeps his feet parallel and slightly wider than shoulder-width apart. He flexes his knees, keeps his back straight, keeps his head up, and focuses his eyes straight ahead. Both elbows are belt high and close to the side of his body. He bends his elbows so that his forearms come up in front of his numbers. Both hands are in front of his jersey, the palms are up, and the fingers are open. He explodes with his legs and hits aggressively when contact occurs.

An easy way to practice setting up properly is to put a shirt or towel on the ground 7 yards from the line of scrimmage, where the quarterback will be when he is going to pass the ball. The running back lines up to the right or left of this position, in the same place that he would be when he lines up in the backfield. From his normal stance, he can set up to block an outside rusher or an inside rusher.

When he sets up to block an outside rusher, the running back takes a step forward and in with his inside foot. He swings his outside leg and foot back to end up with his feet even and his shoulders square. His body is turned directly toward the sideline in a blocking position.

With his body turned directly toward the sideline, the running back gives the defender only one way to rush—up the field. When the rusher is close, the running back must slow his rush by hitting the center of his chest aggressively with the palm of the hand that is away from the line of scrimmage. He can use the palm of the other hand to hit into the rusher's shoulder and assist in pushing him upfield past the quarterback. After the running back makes contact, he needs to keep shuffling his feet, staying between the rusher and the quarterback.

Blocking an inside rusher starts the same way. The running back takes a good inside and forward step with his inside foot. He then steps up with his outside foot, evens his stance, and looks directly upfield.

When pass blocking an inside pass rusher, the running back sets up to end up inside the

Figure 4.18 Running back blocking on a pass play.

rusher. The running back wants to block him to the outside and direct him past the quarterback. The running back focuses on the rusher's chest. As the rusher nears, the running back bends his knees and prepares to strike him in the chest with the palms of both hands. After he makes contact and stops the rusher, he extends his arms and creates some space between the defender and himself. As he creates this space, he shuffles his feet, brings his arms and hands back to their set position, and again gets between the rusher and the quarterback. During a game, he should continue this hitting and separating until he drives the rusher past the quarterback, the pass is thrown, or the whistle blows.

The hardest pass block comes when an inside rusher is determined to rush up the middle, inside the running back's position. The running back must be certain that the defensive man is really rushing to his inside and not trying to fake him so that he can go past the running back to the outside. When the running back sees the defender's chest cross his nose, he can be fairly sure that the rusher is trying to rush up the middle, not to the outside. When the running back sees the rusher in this position, he steps back slightly with his inside foot and pushes off his inside leg. He strikes the rusher in the chest with the palm of his inside hand and steps quickly with his outside foot toward the defender. He then hits out with the palm of his other hand and drives the rusher across the field.

A running back who is a good pass protection blocker allows the team to run plays from the blocking action. These plays make the defense think that the running back is blocking to protect the quarterback, but the running back then becomes either the ballcarrier or the primary receiver. Success with these plays is based on how well the running back pass blocks.

The draw play (figure 4.19), in which the offense sells the pass and then runs the ball, is an effective play against teams that are trying to rush the passer. On a draw play, the offensive line sets up to pass block, the quarterback drops back as if to pass, and the running back steps inside as if he is going to block an inside pass rusher. The defense sees the play start as if it were a drop-back pass. When all three segments of the offensive team are working together, some of the defensive players will start rushing hard up the field while others will drop back into coverage.

The running back's role in the draw play is important. He moves to the inside to be in position for the quarterback to hand him the ball. When the ball is snapped, the running back steps laterally to the inside with his inside foot and bring his outside foot to the inside so that he has a balanced stance. He bends his knees and keeps his back straight, his head up, and his eyes focused on the offensive line. He positions his arms as if he were taking a handoff. The running back lets the quarterback put the ball to his belly and then secures the ball. He immediately starts upfield through any hole that opens up.

Figure 4.19 Halfback draw.

For the delay route (figure 4.20), the running back steps to the inside and sets up just as he would for an inside pass protection assignment. As he sets up, the quarterback drops back to pass, the offensive line blocks to protect the quarterback, and ideally the defensive linebackers drop off the line to help on pass coverage. As he sets up in his blocking position, the running back mentally counts, "A thousand one, a thousand two, a thousand three." Then he runs downfield between the blocks of the offensive tackle and guard. After he crosses the line of scrimmage, he angles back to the center of the field and turns his head to the inside to find the quarterback. He expects the ball to arrive immediately, 3 to 4 yards downfield. After catching the ball, he secures it and turns upfield, anticipating contact from the linebackers.

The third type of play from the pass-blocking position is the screen pass (figure 4.21). Again the running back sets up in the inside pass-blocking position. Like the delay

Figure 4.20 Halfback delay.

Figure 4.21 Halfback screen right.

pattern, a screen pass requires time for the offensive linemen to block the pass rushers and then move to the outside to block for the running back. As he sets up, the running back counts to a thousand three. He then takes one or two short steps up the line of scrimmage, releases behind the block of his offensive tackle, and moves to the outside. If the defensive player rushes inside the offensive tackle, the running back should move outside the tackle's block so that he has a free path to the outside to receive the screen pass from the quarterback.

After the running back is on the outside of the formation, he turns his head back toward the quarterback and looks for the ball. The pass should come over the shoulder farther from the line of scrimmage. After securing the ball, he yells, "Go!" or another word to alert his offensive blockers that he has the ball.

The running back needs to understand the blocking scheme that the other offensive players will be using. When the receiver on the side of the screen is running deep, the first offensive blocker, usually the offensive tackle or guard if the tackle's assignment is to stay with his man, will try to block the outside defender to the sideline. The second offensive blocker, usually the guard or center, will block back on the first defender reacting from the inside. As the running back makes the catch and turns up the field, he should look for the lane created by the blocks of the offensive players.

When setting up a screen pattern, the running back must stay alert for any blitzing linebacker. If the running back sees that the linebacker is rushing, he should step up and deliver a hit on the backer, stopping his free rush to the quarterback. After the first hit on the linebacker, he can let him go and start moving to the outside on the pass pattern.

The draw, delay, and screen are plays that the running back can practice on his own. Because the setup is the same for all three plays, they can be mentally called and then executed. A running back needs to practice these movements on his own so that they become automatic for him.

BLOCKING THE OUTSIDE LINEBACKER

Purpose: To develop blocking ability on an outside linebacker.

Procedure:

1. **The coach or another back lines up in the defender's position and holds a hand dummy to the side of the block.**
2. **The running back sets up in position. On the coach's signal, the running back approaches the dummy to block it.**
3. **The coach tells the running back which side to block.**

Coaching points: The blocker should take the same path at the defender whether he is blocking him in or out. When blocking a linebacker to the outside, the blocker should take off with his outside foot and make contact on the linebacker's inside hip with his outside shoulder pad. The opposite is true when he is blocking the linebacker to the inside. The blocker should drive the backer for 4 yards after contact.

Variation: This drill is also good for practicing blocking on an inside linebacker. The coach or another running back lines up as an inside linebacker, and the coach calls out the direction of the block.

SCREEN PASS

Purpose: To give the running back experience in running and receiving a screen pass.

Procedure:

1. The coach can line up in the quarterback's shotgun position, and the running back can be in a position to his right or left, depending on the side of the screen.
2. The coach calls out the snap count, and the running back gets into position for the play.
3. The coach begins the play by calling out the snap, and the running back sets up to pass block.
4. The running back counts to three and then releases toward the sideline, turning back to the outside to see the coach and the ball.
5. The running back turns his upper body, head, and shoulders back to the coach so that he can reach back with both hands to make the reception.
6. After he makes the catch, the running back secures the ball and turns upfield.
7. The coach offers feedback on the running back's performance.
8. In the beginning, a ball is not used in the drill. After players can run the screen correctly, a quarterback, the ball, and the lead offensive blockers can be added to the drill.

Coaching points: The running back must set inside to pass block on the snap. He must run the pattern at the correct time, take the proper release path, and turn his upper body, head, and shoulders back at the earliest possible moment to look for the ball. The coach can run the screen to both the right and the left using all backs from various alignments in the backfield and the tight end if he is part of the screen package.

Variation: After the offensive players are successfully running the screen, a defensive end and outside linebacker can be added to the drill so that the running back can experience having to block the blitzing backer before releasing for the screen pass.

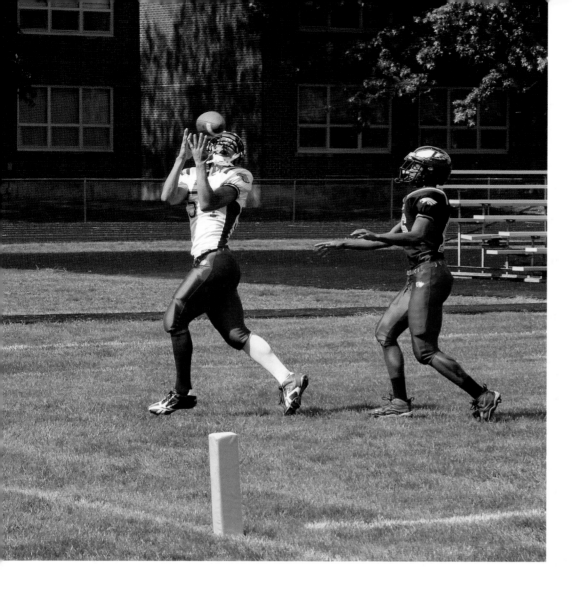

CHAPTER 5

WIDE RECEIVERS

One play by a wide receiver can change the outcome of the game, but consistency is the most important characteristic of a good receiver. Every wide receiver needs to be able to catch the ball. Those who play the position also need the physical skills to get open, and they must do a great deal of work to become truly skilled. Good receivers run more and work harder than anyone else on the offense, and they believe that they can catch every ball thrown to them.

Some of the challenges that the wide receiver faces are shedding the defensive player, going one way and then seeing the ball thrown in another direction, having a ball fly through his hands and land on the ground, and being hit while making the catch. Each of these situations has happened to every wide receiver. Staying positive and not becoming discouraged is important.

This chapter focuses on the techniques and skills that a top wide receiver needs: stance and release, pass routes and timing, and blocking.

STANCE AND RELEASE

Often wide receivers move straight across the line of scrimmage as play begins. Speed and quickness when the ball is snapped are essential for success. Their beginning stance must allow quick forward movement. Which stance to use depends on the team's style of offense. For most offenses, either a three-point stance or an upright two-point stance is appropriate.

In the three-point stance (figure 5.1), the wide receiver starts by standing up with his feet even and hip-width apart. The receiver keeps his back straight and his knees bent, resting both forearms on the inner thighs. From this position, he reaches out with the hand nearer the sideline and steps back slightly with the foot on that side of his body. Keeping his back straight and his head up, he turns his head slightly inside to see the ball when it is snapped. The receiver should be on the balls of both feet, placing more weight on the front foot. This stance allows him to step with the back foot, rolling over the front foot as he moves forward. The hand touching the ground is slightly ahead and slightly to the outside of the front of his shoulders. The back foot is slightly behind the heel of the front foot.

An upright two-point stance (figure 5.2) starts with the feet even and hip-width apart. From this position, the player steps back with his inside foot so that it is a few inches behind his front foot. He adjusts his weight to the front foot, keeping only the toe of his back foot on the ground to maintain balance. The receiver bends forward slightly at the waist as he steps back. He allows his head and shoulders to move in front of his feet and hips. He can either let his arms and hands hang down naturally or raise his elbows and forearms to get into more of a running stance. He turns his head slightly to the inside so that he can see the ball being snapped. He begins his forward movement by quickly stepping forward with the back foot. When leaning forward, the receiver is careful not to go offside.

A wide receiver who can instantly attack the defensive back has a great advantage. Whether he uses an upright two-point stance or a three-point stance with one hand on the ground, the ability to get an instant

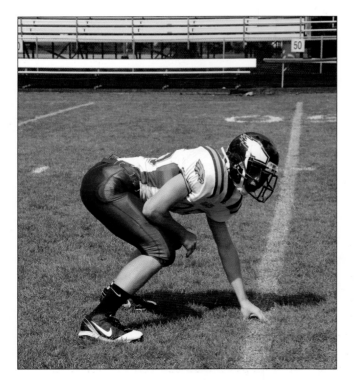

Figure 5.1 Wide receiver's three-point stance.

start is crucial. A wide receiver should release with the same intensity and quickness on every play, whether it is a running play or a passing play. The receiver should not let the defensive player know when he is the primary receiver or when the ball is being run to his side.

When attacking the defender, the receiver's goal is to quickly narrow the distance between himself and the defensive back. He wants the defensive back to turn and begin to run deep. The wide receiver will be able to execute his pass pattern and make the catch while the defensive back is turned and running deep.

Releasing from tight coverage requires skill. When faced with a defender directly in front of him on the scrimmage line, the receiver must adjust his stance. Against this type of press coverage, the receiver places his back foot forward but angled away from the defender instead of stepping straight up with the back foot (figure 5.3a). This stance creates a small space in which to work. He now has the opportunity to bring the arm that is closer to the defensive back up past his shoulder (figure 5.3b). This ripping-up motion is usually enough to get the defensive man's hand off his jersey (figure 5.3c).

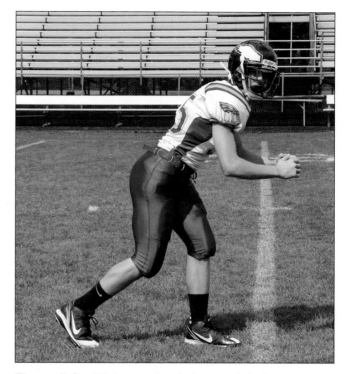

Figure 5.2   **Wide receiver's two-point stance.**

A wide receiver has trouble getting open when he comes off the ball late. The receiver should not step back with his front foot on a release. When the defensive back lines up right in front of him, the wide receiver should drive off the line and not spend time moving only his head and shoulders.

Figure 5.3   **Wide receiver releasing from tight coverage: He *(a)* takes an angle step, *(b)* aligns his shoulder and arm toward the defender, and *(c)* brings the arm and shoulder up to break free from the defender.**

RUNNING PASS ROUTES

Every wide receiver must understand the importance of running each pass pattern at the proper depth every time. If the receiver and the quarterback are to coordinate the passing game, the receiver must do his part. On every pass play, the wide receiver is responsible for running the route at the proper depth and in the correct manner and then catching the ball. The quarterback is responsible for getting the ball to the receiver where the receiver can make the catch. The offensive line and, on occasion, the offensive backs assume the responsibility of blocking the defensive players long enough to give the quarterback time to make the pass. This coordinated effort must be performed correctly for the pass to be thrown and caught; for success, everyone must do his job.

First, the receiver needs to learn the various depths at which to run the pass patterns. Three factors determine the distance that he runs down the field:

1. The number of steps that the quarterback takes in his drop
2. The length of time that the offensive line needs to protect the quarterback
3. The type of blocking used by the offensive line

Running the pattern at the proper depth helps ensure correct timing of the pass. The receiver should think of the field as being divided into three separate depths, or zones: short, medium, and deep.

The wide receiver's short zone extends from the line of scrimmage up the field for 7 yards or so. Patterns run in this zone are quick. The quarterback drops only three steps before delivering the ball. The timing in this area must be exact. The wide receiver must run quickly up the field, break sharply into his pattern, and immediately look for the ball.

The wide receiver's medium zone starts at approximately 8 yards and goes up to about 15 yards. In this zone, the receiver can use all his moves to get open. Medium patterns are often continuous movement routes in which the receiver keeps running before he gets the ball. In this zone, the quarterback uses a five-step drop and the offensive line knows that they must protect for a longer time.

The wide receiver's deep zone extends from the far edge of the medium zone all the way to the opponent's goal line. The patterns run in this zone require more time, and often the receiver has to run under the ball. The quarterback tries to give the receiver the opportunity to separate from the defender and make the reception.

A receiver must be able to recognize the three zones when on the move. One way to get a feel for the different depths is to take time every day to run up the field calling out the zone or mentally saying, "Short, short, short," "Medium, medium, medium," and "Deep, deep, deep." After the receiver understands the depths for each zone, he is ready to learn the various pass routes that he will run in each zone.

Short Routes

A team often uses the short passing game to get the passing attack started. The short passing game can quickly move the ball, neutralize a blitzing defense, and allow the quarterback to get into a passing rhythm.

Because the quarterback takes only a three-step drop before throwing the ball, timing is the number one priority for the short passing game. The wide receiver's contribution to the timing of the short passing game involves three actions. First, he must run each of the short patterns at the proper depth, making it possible for him and the quarterback to time the pass properly. Second, he must run every short route at a constant speed, which must be full speed. Any slowing down on the break or coming out of the break usually results in an incomplete pass. Third, the receiver must be prepared to catch the ball immediately. The receiver has to turn his head and focus his eyes on the quarterback the instant that he makes his break. He prepares to position his hands to make the catch (figure 5.4). The three major short pass routes are the quick out, the hitch, and the slant (figure 5.5). Each is run differently, but the timing relies on the same three actions by the wide receiver.

Quick Out. When running a quick-out pass pattern, the receiver must drive hard off the line to sell the defensive back on the idea that he is going deep. At 4 yards, the wide receiver rolls over his outside foot and redirects his momentum toward the sideline. The receiver may run 6 or 7 yards before the pass arrives.

As he runs toward the sideline, the receiver needs to be prepared to come back toward the line of scrimmage to make the catch. He should expect the pass to be low because the quarterback is throwing at a sharp angle to the outside. The receiver should have his hands below his waist, and his little fingers should be together to form the catching pocket.

Hitch. The hitch pattern is more difficult. The receiver's momentum has to stop completely, and he has to come back for the ball. He wants to run full speed to sell the defensive back on the idea that he is going deep. At 4 or 5 yards, he plants his outside foot to stop his forward movement. After he plants his outside foot, he sits back slightly and turns his body back to the inside to face the quarterback. Because the ball should be there almost as he turns, he must have his hands even with his numbers and his thumbs together, ready to make the catch.

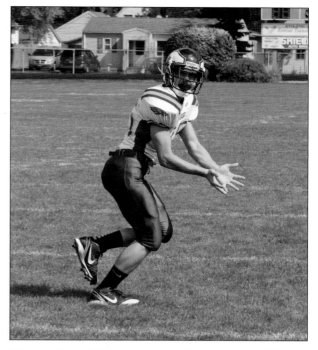

Figure 5.4 Wide receiver's hands in position to catch a low pass.

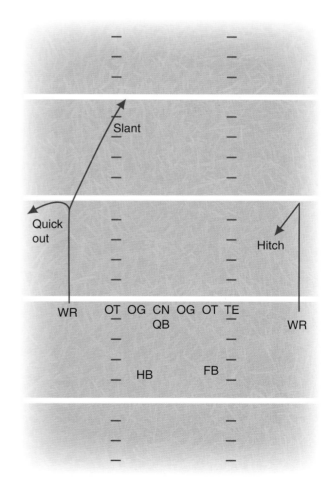

Figure 5.5 Short routes for the wide receiver: quick out, hitch, and slant.

Slant.   The third short pass pattern is the slant pass. During the slant route, the receiver redirects his upfield run. Again, he comes off the line of scrimmage at full speed. When he reaches 4 yards, he rolls over his inside foot and redirects his momentum to run at a 45-degree angle into the center of the field. When running a slant route, the receiver expects the quarterback to lead him, so he continues up the field a few yards before the ball arrives. The slant pass can arrive at any height, so the receiver must be ready to position his hands quickly to make the catch. His head and eyes must turn to the quarterback the instant that he starts his move to the inside.

On all three short pass routes, the receiver must prepare to be hit immediately. He should concentrate first on making the catch and securing the ball. Running with the ball comes after he does those two things.

Basic Medium Routes

All good wide receivers must learn and master the proper techniques for running medium pass routes. While running these patterns, the receiver repositions the defensive back by altering the path that the receiver takes as he moves up the field.

The three basic medium pass routes are hook, in, and out (figure 5.6). All three have a 10- to 12-yard breaking point. On these passes, the quarterback uses a five-step drop to move away from the line of scrimmage. If the receiver runs at full speed, the receiver and the quarterback should be able to time the pass correctly.

Hook.   When running the hook, the wide receiver must make the defensive back believe that he is going deep. The receiver comes off the line in a full sprint straight up the field, forcing the defensive back to turn and run at full speed toward his own goal line. As the receiver nears the 12-yard area, he lowers his hips slightly and stops his momentum by stepping with his outside foot. He quickly turns his body to the inside and faces the quarterback when his outside foot hits the ground. When playing on a wet or slick surface, the receiver can stop his momentum by taking three quick steps, allowing him to keep his feet under his hips at all times.

In the hook pattern, the ball may be on the way as the receiver turns back to the inside. His hands must be up, his chest high, and his eyes looking for the ball. If the quarterback is late, the wide receiver should continue moving back toward the ball.

Out and In Patterns.   The out and in pass patterns are run identically. The in pattern goes toward the center of the field, and the out pattern goes toward the sideline. Both pass patterns start with a hard drive straight up the field. During this drive, the receiver needs to see where the defender is in relation to where the

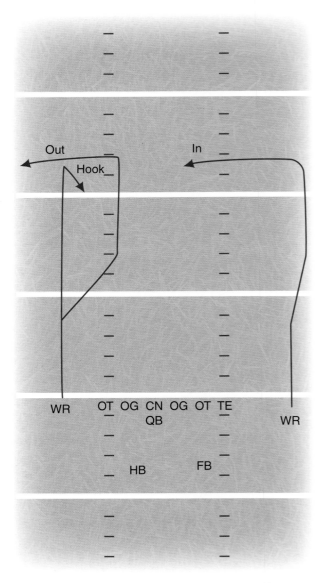

Figure 5.6   Basic medium pass routes for the wide receiver: hook, in, and out.

receiver wants to go. If the defender is where the receiver wants to go, the receiver should angle in the opposite direction and take the defensive back out of the area. If the defensive back is opposite where the receiver's pattern will take him, the wide receiver should drive at an angle directly toward the defender and make him move farther away from the receiver's final cut (as illustrated in the out pattern shown in figure 5.6).

After relocating the defensive player, the receiver sprints straight up the field again and sells the fact that he is going deep. As he nears the 12-yard area, the receiver prepares to make his final cut into the pattern.

Both of these pass routes must be run at full speed. The receiver has to roll over the foot in the direction in which he is headed and not stop his momentum. If he is going to his outside on an out route, he leans his upper body to the outside and rolls over his outside foot. For an in pattern, he leans his upper body to the inside and rolls over his inside foot.

Using this technique to run these pass routes may cause the player to round off the pattern, but he will be going at full speed. As he takes the second step to the inside or the outside, he may have to adjust his pass route slightly back toward the line of scrimmage. This adjustment gives him a chance to create greater separation from the defender, brings him back toward the ball, and decreases the chance of an interception. A slight adjustment back toward the line of scrimmage is especially important on an out route, because the quarterback throws the ball a greater distance than he does on an in route.

The receiver must keep coming across the field on the in route, because the quarterback may come to him late. He should make certain that he is at least 12 yards from the sideline when he breaks in an out pattern so that he has enough room to make the reception and turn up the field before going out of bounds.

Special Medium Routes

Besides the three basic medium pass routes (in, out, and hook), three additional pass routes are run at medium depth. Because of the time required to run these routes, the quarterback has to take a five-step drop.

These three routes—cross, delay, and quick post (figure 5.7)—are all run with the timing of a medium pass route. Each requires special adjustments and comes into the inside of the field.

Cross. The cross, a variation of a short pattern, is the pattern that all good receivers run with success. When running the cross, the receiver sprints up the field for 4 yards and then angles to the inside, just as he would when running a slant route. At about 8 yards, he rolls over his inside foot and heads directly across the field. He continues to run at full speed so that the

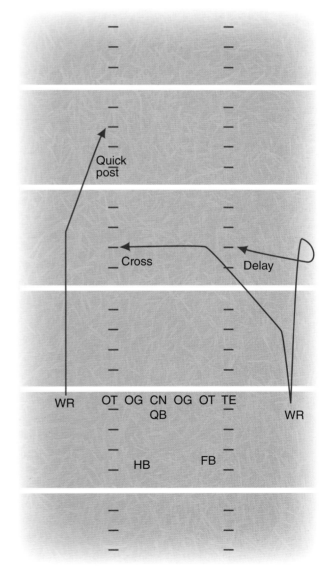

Figure 5.7 Special medium pass routes for the wide receiver: cross, delay, and quick post.

quarterback can accurately lead him with the ball. He turns his head around and focuses on the quarterback, preparing to catch the ball at any time.

As he comes across the field, he may find that his path angles slightly farther from the line of scrimmage. He should try to stay within 8 yards of the line of scrimmage and not allow himself to get so deep that he is running directly into coverage.

Delay.   The delay pattern is run at the same 8-yard depth. At the start of this pattern, the receiver sprints off the line at a slight angle to the outside of the field and gives the defensive player the idea that he is going deep. When he reaches 7 yards, the receiver stops his momentum upfield with his inside foot and spins back into the inside. As he spins, he momentarily turns his back on the defender. After he comes out of the spin, he runs just as he would on a cross.

One major difference between the delay and the cross is that in the delay, the player expects the pass to come to him on his third or fourth step toward the center of the field. The angle release to the outside and the spin to the inside take additional time, which is why this pattern is run with medium pass timing.

Quick Post.   The quick post pattern requires no special move and is based solely on speed. The receiver comes straight off the line with as much speed as possible. At 8 yards, he breaks to the center of the field and continues up the field at a slight angle to the inside. The angle must keep him on the outside of the hash marks. The angle should be just enough to get some separation from the defensive back. The receiver must be alert for the ball at any time after running 5 yards from the breaking point.

Deep Routes

Short and medium routes are the bread and butter for every wide receiver. Deep pass patterns are the icing on the cake. A wide receiver always feels a special thrill and a little boost in adrenaline when called on to run a deep pass pattern.

The timing of these patterns takes longer. To give the receiver time to run his deep route, the quarterback drops seven steps before delivering the ball. The offensive line has to block a few seconds longer on this type of pass. If the pass is complete, a touchdown often results.

The two basic deep patterns are the up and the post patterns (figure 5.8a). Both are run in the deep zone and break 12 or more yards up the field from the line of scrimmage.

To be successful, the receiver must run at full speed for the entire duration of these pass patterns. The post and up routes are pass routes in which the receiver runs under the ball and may have to stretch to make the catch. He should always try to see his fingers and the ball at the same time as he attempts to make the reception.

Up and Comeback Routes.   Before releasing off the line of scrimmage, the receiver must observe where the defender is playing. If the defender is inside, the receiver wants to keep him there. If the defender is outside, the receiver wants to move him away from the sideline as he comes off the line. In this situation, the receiver uses a slight angle to the inside to position the defensive back where he wants him to be.

Ideally, on an up route the receiver has at least 5 yards between himself and the sideline so that he has some room to adjust to the pass. When running the up pattern, the receiver must drive hard off the line of scrimmage and angle to position the defensive back where the receiver wants him. He must get to full speed and burst straight up the field, attacking the defender.

At 12 yards, he angles slightly to the outside to get clear of the defender. He sprints past the defensive back and heads straight up the field. He looks over his inside shoulder without breaking stride to pick up the flight of the ball as soon as possible, and he

Figure 5.8 Deep routes for the wide receiver: *(a)* the basic up and post routes; *(b)* the specialty comeback (off the up pattern) and corner (off the post pattern) routes.

adjusts to the flight of the ball. He must be prepared to make the catch on his inside, directly in front, or, if the pass is perfectly thrown, over his outside shoulder away from the defender. In some instances, he may have to dive to make the catch.

The comeback (figure 5.8b) is a deep pass route that comes off the up pattern. A receiver usually does not run the comeback pattern until he has had success running the up route. When the defensive back is worried that the receiver is going to run by him on the up pattern, the receiver is free to complete the comeback route.

At first, the comeback pattern is run the same as an up route. The difference comes at 15 yards. To run the comeback properly, the receiver needs to get the defensive back turned and running up the field with him. At 15 yards, the receiver lowers his hips. At about 17 yards, he plants his inside foot to stop his momentum and quickly turns to the sideline. He comes back toward the line of scrimmage at an angle and turns his head around to focus on the quarterback and the ball. He expects to make the catch at about 14 yards.

After he makes the catch and secures the ball in his outside arm and hand, the safest thing for the receiver is to turn to the outside of the field and make as many yards as he can. If he turns back into the center of the field, he will run directly into defenders who are reacting to the pass.

Post and Corner Patterns. The post is run into the center of the field away from the sideline.

The receiver looks to see where the defender is before the start of the play. If the defender is lined up and playing to the inside, the receiver angles slightly toward the sideline to get the defender to come with him as he sprints up the field, opening up the inside of the field. If the defender plays the receiver to the outside, the receiver should be able to sprint straight ahead for 12 yards before breaking to the inside. In short, the receiver comes off the line quickly, angles to position the defender if necessary, and bursts straight at the defender. At 12 yards, he rolls over his inside foot and runs at a 45-degree angle toward the center of the field.

The receiver must expect to run under the pass. This pattern is not like the quick post, a medium pattern in which the quarterback tries to drill the ball. On the deep post pattern, the quarterback lofts the pass and the wide receiver must keep running to make the catch. As soon as he makes his break and heads toward the center of the field, the receiver turns his head back to the quarterback and prepares to pick up the ball as it leaves the quarterback's hand. He may have to adjust his path slightly to make the catch. Often the receiver will need to reach out as he runs to catch the pass.

A wide receiver may have only one or two opportunities in a game to make a reception on a deep pass. The receiver must do everything possible to get open, concentrate on the ball, look it into his hands, and secure it before running for the score. When a defensive back is worried that the receiver will go deep, the short and medium passing routes open up.

The wide receiver may use the corner route if the defensive back is playing way inside to stop the post pattern. The corner (figure 5.8b) is a deep route that comes off the post pattern. A receiver will have difficulty running the corner route until he has success running the basic post route. To begin the corner route, the receiver sells the post pattern. The defensive back must be convinced that the receiver is going to run the post. The receiver must turn the defender around and have the defender running as hard as he can to keep the receiver from going to the center of the field to make the catch. To help convince the defender, the receiver runs the first part of the corner pattern just as he would the post pattern.

After driving five or six hard steps toward the center of the field, the receiver leans his upper body to the outside and rolls over his outside foot. He breaks at a 45-degree angle to the corner of the field, keeping his speed and momentum as he breaks. He looks back over his outside shoulder to focus on the quarterback and pick up the flight of the ball.

On a corner pattern, the ball may hang in the air for a long time. The receiver may have to run 12 yards or more after breaking for the corner before he has a chance to make the catch. Ideally, the ball comes to the receiver over his outside shoulder, away from any defensive backs. This placement allows the receiver to make the catch, secure the ball, and run up the sideline. Because the corner is a difficult pass to throw, however, the receiver should watch for the ball and prepare for it to be anywhere. The pass may come directly over his head or to the inside. The receiver needs to see the ball early in its flight so that he can turn his head to the correct side and position his hands where can see both the ball and his hands as he makes the catch.

SHORT PASS ROUTES

Purpose: To give the wide receiver experience running short pass routes.

Procedure:

1. The coach lines up 10 yards in front of the wide receiver.
2. The coach calls out the short pass route, and the wide receiver gets into position for the play.
3. The coach begins the play, and the wide receiver runs the pass route.
4. The coach offers feedback on the wide receiver's performance.

Coaching points: When learning any pass route, the receiver must have a good stance, take a forward step, and threaten to go deep on each route. He should break his route at the proper depth, use good technique when changing direction, and turn his head back to the quarterback at the earliest possible moment.

Variation: This drill is also good for practicing medium and deep pass routes. For medium routes, the coach lines up 20 yards in front of the wide receiver. For deep routes, the coach lines up 10 yards away and faces the wide receiver. The coach can vary his position from inside to outside.

OUT AND IN PATTERNS

Purpose: To give the wide receiver experience running out and in pass routes.

Procedure:

1. One wide receiver lines up as a defensive back inside or outside the other wide receiver, 8 yards off the line.
2. The play starts on the coach's command, and the wide receiver runs the route.
3. The other wide receiver drops back as if he were a defender reacting to the wide receiver's movements.
4. The coach offers feedback on the wide receiver's performance.

Coaching points: The receiver angles his run to position the defender. On his break, he must maintain his speed and momentum.

SPECIAL MEDIUM ROUTES

Purpose: To give the wide receiver experience running cross, delay, and quick post pass routes.

Procedure:

1. The coach stands 20 yards away and faces the wide receiver. A defensive back sets up to cover the wide receiver.
2. On the coach's command, the wide receiver runs the called route. The coach observes his moves.
3. The defensive back drops straight back as the wide receiver runs each route.

Coaching points: The receiver must come off the line at the proper angle to run each route. He must get up to speed soon after making his break and look for the ball as soon as possible.

CORNER AND COMEBACK

Purpose: To give the wide receiver experience running the corner and comeback routes.

Procedure:

1. **The coach lines up 20 yards away and faces the wide receiver.**
2. **On the coach's command, the wide receiver runs the specified route.**
3. **The coach observes the wide receiver's movements and provides feedback.**

Coaching points: The receiver must sell the deep patterns that these two patterns build on. He must run the base pattern hard before making the break on either of these patterns.

GOAL-LINE PASS ROUTES

Because of the limited area available to run pass routes when a team is near the opponent's goal line, one or two special routes should be designed specifically for this area.

Routes that can be effective in this area are the fade route and the pivot in or pivot out pass.

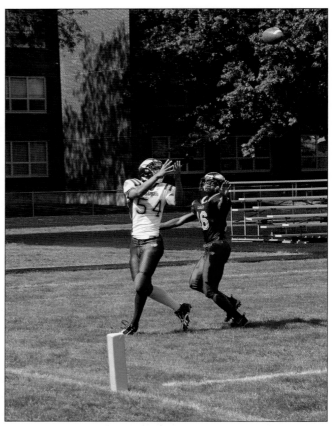

Fade Route. A fade pass is thrown to the back corner pylon of the end zone. The receiver needs to line up far enough from the sideline so that he has room to release outside the defender and take a path to the pylon. The quarterback should loft the ball, and the receiver should run under it while making certain that he stays inbounds as he makes the reception. Ideally, the ball should come over the receiver's outside shoulder, but the receiver must be prepared to adjust to the flight of the ball. This route is especially good for a tall receiver who can go up and make the catch (figure 5.9).

Figure 5.9 Wide receiver running a fade route.

FADE ROUTE

Purpose: To give the wide receiver experience executing the fade route.

Procedure:

1. **The coach lines up in the quarterback position and calls for a fade route.**
2. **The receiver lines up on the 5-yard line and adjusts his position so that he is at least 8 to 10 yards from the sideline.**
3. **On the coach's command, the wide receiver takes an outside release and angles toward the pylon in the corner of the end zone.**
4. **As he moves to the pylon, the receiver must look back, locate the ball, and determine where the ball will be when it reaches his hands.**
5. **The coach observes the wide receiver's movements and provides feedback.**
6. **A quarterback can throw the ball after the receiver understands and can run the route correctly.**

Coaching points: The receiver must line up so that he has room to run the route. He must look back to locate the flight of the ball as soon as he is moving to the pylon. Because this is a spot timing route, the quarterback and receiver will need to get a lot of repetitions to refine the play.

Pivot Routes. To execute a pivot route, either to the inside or the outside, a receiver needs to convince the defender that he is going to run the original route and continue on his original path. This route is effective against an aggressive defender who will try to jump the initial move.

For a pivot in pass, the receiver starts on a quick out route. After taking two steps, he plants his upfield foot, pivots back, leans his body back to the inside, and comes back to the quarterback. The receiver should look for the ball the instant that he turns back to the inside of the field.

For the pivot out pass, the receiver starts on a slant route. After taking two steps, he plants his outside foot, pivots back, leans his body back to the outside, and runs to the sideline (figure 5.10). The receiver should look for the ball the instant that he turns back to the outside of the field.

Figure 5.10 Wide receiver running a pivot out route.

PIVOT IN AND PIVOT OUT ROUTES

Purpose: To give the wide receiver experience executing a pivot in and pivot out route.

Procedure:

1. **The coach lines up in the quarterback position and calls for a pivot route.**
2. **The receiver lines up on the 5-yard line and adjusts his position so that he is at least 8 to 10 yards from the sideline.**
3. **On the coach's command, the wide receiver takes an outside release and starts his initial pass route.**
4. **After two steps on his initial pass route, the receiver pivots back in the opposite direction and immediately looks for the ball.**
5. **The coach observes the wide receiver's movements and provides feedback.**
6. **A quarterback can throw the ball after the receiver understands and can run both routes correctly.**

Coaching points: The receiver must line up so that he has room to run both phases of the route. The coach should check that the receiver immediately looks back to the quarterback when he comes out of his pivot. Because this is a timing route, the quarterback and receiver will need to get a lot of repetitions to refine the play.

RECEIVING A BUBBLE SCREEN

More teams are now using a form of screen pass to the outside to one of their receivers. The goal is to get the ball quickly into the hands of a gifted athlete and have blockers in position to block for him. Usually this type of screen is run from some form of spread formation that has at least two receivers on the same side. One player blocks, and the other catches the screen.

This type of pass is usually thrown to a player who is lined up off the line of scrimmage. On the snap, the receiver takes one step forward and then steps back and turns his body to the inside so that he is facing the quarterback. As he turns to the inside, he brings his hands up in position to make the catch (figure 5.11).

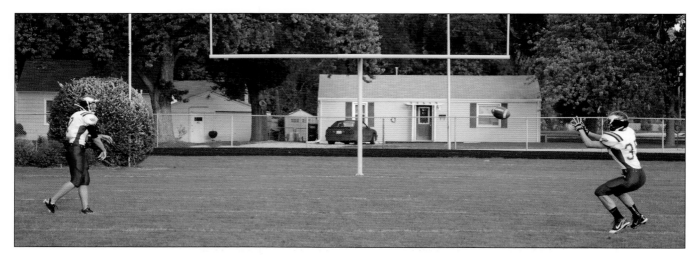

Figure 5.11 Wide receiver making the catch on a bubble screen play.

The player receiving the screen must understand the blocking that is taking place on the play and where his potential running lanes may be. After he receives the pass, he should immediately turn up the field and gain as much yardage as possible (figure 5.12).

Figure 5.12 In a bubble screen play, the wide receiver follows the blocking to move up the field.

PERFECTING THE BUBBLE SCREEN

Purpose: To give the wide receiver practice in running a bubble screen.

Procedure:

1. **The coach lines up in the quarterback position and calls for a bubble screen route.**
2. **Two receivers line up on one side of the coach; the inside receiver is on the line, and the outside receiver is off the line. A blocking dummy can be placed 8 yards downfield in front of the outside receiver.**

(continued)

Perfecting the Bubble Screen *(continued)*

3. On the coach's command, the wide receiver on the outside takes a step forward and then steps back, turns, and faces inside with both hands up and his chest high, ready to make the catch.

4. The inside receiver should sprint and block the dummy.

5. The wide receiver should simulate making the catch and immediately turn and run up the field.

6. The coach observes the wide receiver's movements and provides feedback.

7. The coach or a quarterback can throw the ball after the receiver understands and can run the route correctly.

Coaching points: The receivers must line up so that they have the room to run the route. The receiver must immediately look back to the quarterback and move his hands up to make the catch. Because this is a timing route, the quarterback and receiver will need to get a lot of repetitions to refine the play. The quarterback should practice throwing the bubble screen to both sides of the formation and to all possible receivers.

Variation: Instead of turning and waiting for the ball, the receiver can be instructed to move directly toward the quarterback and catch the pass on the run. This type of action often allows offensive linemen to release downfield to the outside and become potential blockers. This action can be difficult for the quarterback and the receiver because the quarterback seldom throws this type of pass.

RECOGNIZING AND UNDERSTANDING DEFENSES

Adjusting or changing pass routes on the move based on the play of the defense is an advanced skill that requires total coordination between the receiver and the quarterback. Both players must see and interpret the movement by the defense in the same way. Adjusting pass routes can be of particular benefit versus blitzing players and zone defenses.

These adjustments should only be made when the players have had time to walk through the situation and practice it live versus a defense.

Man-to-Man Defense.   Receivers need to be reminded that in man-to-man pass defense, one player will be running with them for the entire play. Getting open requires making moves or running away from the coverage person. Versus man-to-man pass coverage, receivers need to use feints, fakes, and flat-out speed to create separation from the defender. Medium routes may include an in or out route based on the location of the defender, and the receiver will break in the opposite direction.

Zone Defense.   A zone defense assigns defensive players to certain areas of the field. Defenders allow a receiver to move freely from one area of the field to the other. On certain pass routes, a receiver may want to run between two defenders to be open for the ball. This adjustment is often effective for an in or crossing route. A receiver often sees immediately whether the defender near him moves to an area of the field and is not mirroring the movement of the receiver. When a receiver identifies a zone pass coverage, instead of running full speed he can run more under control and be prepared to slow down when he reaches an area that is void of a defender. With practice, the quarterback and receiver can adjust an up route to a comeback when they see that the deep zone is covered.

Blitz Defense.   A receiver may see a defensive back or linebacker lined up in front of him or to his inside move inside and run a blitz. Blitz coverage may involve press coverage or man-to-man alignment and coverage. When this happens, the quarterback may see the blitz and signal orally or by hand to the receiver to break off any deep or medium route and instead run a slant route to the inside. This route provides the quarterback with a receiver who can be thrown to quickly to avoid a sack.

READING THE DEFENSE

Purpose: To give the wide receiver an opportunity to learn to differentiate between various forms of defense.

Procedure:

1. **The coach lines up behind a receiver, and another player lines up in front of the receiver to act as the defender.**
2. **The coach tells the receiver the pass route to run and then signals the defender to cover the receiver, to drop wide to the outside, or to blitz to the inside of the field.**
3. **On the coach's command, the wide receiver starts his initial pass route, and the defender makes his appropriate move.**
4. **As the receiver sprints up the field, he should call out the coverage that he sees as quickly as possible.**
5. **The coach listens for the wide receiver's call and provides feedback.**
6. **Because this drill is designed to teach identification, no route adjustment by the receiver is necessary and the ball should not be used.**
7. **Each receiver should have the opportunity to observe each situation, and the drill should be repeated as quickly as possible.**

Coaching points: The receiver must be able to call out the different defenses quickly before moving on to adjusting the route called. The quarterback and receiver should practice all adjustments before moving on to implementing them in a team drill. Because they must coordinate these changes, the more repetitions that the quarterback and receiver get in practicing the route adjustments together, the better they will be able to implement them in a game.

Variation: After the receiver demonstrates that he understands the different defenses, can make adjustments on the move, and can consistently run the correct route against each defense, the coach or a quarterback can throw the ball.

Defensive setup:	Adjustment by receiver:
blitz	run a slant route
zone	run a hook route
man-to-man	execute the in route as quickly as possible

BLOCKING

Most offensive football teams with a strong running game have wide receivers who have the desire and know-how to block. When a running play results in a touchdown, the wide receiver on the side of the play probably executed a good block on one of the defensive backs. Wide receiver blocking for running plays is 60 percent desire and 40 percent technique. When a receiver has the desire to block, he can easily learn the proper techniques.

Blocking downfield is as satisfying for a wide receiver as tackling is for a defensive player. To block effectively, a wide receiver must have a burning desire to get the job accomplished and the drive to succeed. Size is not the issue. A number of small wide receivers today block effectively on every running play. The player who wants to become a complete wide receiver must work on blocking with complete focus.

A wide receiver who is blocking positions himself between the defender and the ballcarrier. The receiver must think in terms of maneuvering his body into that position. The goal is to force the defensive player to come through the receiver to reach the running back and make the tackle.

If the receiver's blocking assignment is the defender lined up directly in front of him, the receiver must drive off the line and create indecision in the defender's mind. If the defender keeps backing up or covering a deep zone, then the receiver should continue his drive and use the glide part of his release, the run after his start, from 5 to 12 yards, to position himself.

The instant that the defender stops his backpedal and focuses on the ballcarrier, the receiver must shorten his stride and bring his body under control. The closer he comes to the defender, the more he widens his base. He keeps his feet moving in short, choppy steps as he positions himself between the defender and the ballcarrier. As the defender comes closer, the receiver focuses on the middle of the numbers on the defender's jersey. In preparation for the block, the receiver bends at his knees but not his waist, keeping his back straight and his head up (figure 5.13a).

Figure 5.13 Wide receiver block: He (a) focuses on the defender's jersey and positions himself for the block and (b) makes contact, pushing hard on the defender's chest.

At the point of contact, the receiver keeps his elbows close to the sides of his body (figure 5.13b). His forearms are up and angled into the center of his chest. Both hands are open, the fingers are up, and the palms are facing the defender. The receiver hits the defender in the chest with the heels of both hands with as much force as he can generate. He generates power for the block first with the big muscles in the legs and then with the up and out motion of the hands and arms.

After making the initial contact, the receiver needs to keep his balance, gather himself, and hit the defender repeatedly until the whistle blows. If the defender fails to make the tackle, the receiver has done an outstanding job even if he never knocks the defender down.

When blocking downfield, the receiver must anticipate that the defender will try to avoid the block and go to one side or the other. By shortening his stride and widening his base, the receiver will be able to react easily to any attempt by the defensive player to go around him to the ballcarrier.

REACTING TO THE DEFENDER

Purpose: To give the wide receiver practice blocking a defender.

Procedure:

1. **The coach or another wide receiver, holding a dummy, lines up 8 yards from the wide receiver.**

2. **When the wide receiver releases, the coach or other wide receiver backs up 6 yards and then steps up, allowing the wide receiver to block.**

3. **The wide receiver blocks on the dummy.**

Coaching points: The drill should run at half speed initially. Speed can be increased as the wide receiver becomes proficient in blocking. Ultimately, the drill is run at full speed. The receiver should know where the ball is going to be run so that he can position himself to the right or left of the defender.

TIGHT ENDS

Playing tight end involves using a combination of the skills needed to play offensive lineman, wide receiver, and running back. No other position on the team requires such a mix of abilities. On one play a tight end may make the key block to spring the running back, and on the next play he may jump high in the air to make a catch. This chapter focuses on the skills needed to be a top tight end, including stance, blocking, and pass routes.

STANCE

The tight end has to block like an offensive lineman, but at the same time he has to release off the line and run pass routes like a wide receiver. He must have a balanced stance that allows him to accomplish both tasks.

Figure 6.1   Tight end's three-point stance.

The tight end uses the basic three-point stance (figure 6.1). To get into the three-point stance, the tight end stands with his feet even and shoulder-width apart. His toes point straight ahead. He lowers his body by bending his knees, keeping his back straight. He rests both forearms on his inner thighs and reaches out with one hand. He then takes a small step back with the foot on the same side as the down hand.

The down hand extends straight out and down and contacts the ground just in front of the shoulders. The toes of the back foot are even with the middle of the front foot. His weight is evenly distributed on both feet, especially if the first step changes with each play.

After he has put his hand down and adjusted his back foot, the tight end needs to focus on keeping his back straight, his shoulders even, and his head up. He must not lean to one side or the other. Leaning or looking anywhere but straight ahead gives the defense a good idea where the tight end is going and whom he will block.

BLOCKING

The main challenge to playing tight end is learning to be an effective blocker. To be a good blocker, the tight end must have good technique, understand how defenders will play against him, and possess the desire to complete the block successfully.

Run Blocking

A tight end must understand that during a running play he becomes an additional offensive lineman. On every wide running play to his side, the tight end's block is at the point of attack.

Tight ends can learn run blocks by using a blocking bag or blocking sled, but they must remember that the real defender will be in motion, not stationary. The techniques and drills for each of the blocks that a tight end may use during the game on running plays—drive, hook, angle, running drive, double team, and combination—are covered in chapter 3, beginning on page 50. Refer to that chapter for detailed information on technique. This section focuses on the tight end's blocking role in each of the blocks.

The tight end uses the drive block against a defensive lineman or a linebacker who is playing directly in front of him. The goal of the drive block is to move the defender back off the line of scrimmage. A good drive block starts with getting out of the stance instantly on the snap. The tight end must focus on the defender because he may stunt to one side or the other. When he makes contact, the tight end drives forward with both arms and hands. To get maximum leverage and force, he keeps his elbows close to his ribs. The palms of both hands contact the middle of the defender's body in a strong, forceful manner.

Although he makes contact with his hands, his legs do most of the work. The instant that he makes contact, he pushes his hips forward and up, gathering his legs under him while driving his feet with short, choppy steps. For most tight ends, this last step is the most difficult. The tendency is to stop moving the feet at the moment of contact. When the forward thrust stops, getting started again is extremely difficult, and the tight end usually ends up just leaning against the defender. The tight end should pick a spot 2 to 3 feet past the defender and keep driving until he reaches that spot. This approach enables the tight end to finish the block successfully.

The tight end uses the hook block against a defensive player who lines up in front of him or on his outside shoulder. The hook is a difficult block. Trying to hook a linebacker or defensive lineman lined up on the tight end's outside shoulder is the hardest of all. The primary objective of the hook block is to prevent the defender from coming across the line of scrimmage and to stop his pursuit. After he is in this position and has stopped the defender's movement across the line, the tight end needs to continue driving with his feet, using short, powerful steps as he would in a drive block.

On an angle block, the tight end blocks a defender who lines up opposite an offensive player to the tight end's right or left. The defensive lineman is focused on the offensive player in front of him when the play begins, so his reaction to the tight end and his block is secondary. Because the goal is to block the defender before he is able to react, the tight end must execute the angle block with speed and quickness. Another reason to be quick is that the tight end must stop the defender's penetration. The defender will be charging straight ahead, so the tight end must anticipate the block. The tight end should practice the angle block to both his right and his left until he can execute it correctly in either direction.

With the variations in defensive alignment, the tight end may block a linebacker who is not on the line of scrimmage. To get this done, the tight end must be familiar with the running drive block, which he uses to block a linebacker who is playing off the line of scrimmage directly in front of him or to his inside. Moving in the right path is essential when blocking an opponent who is not on the line of scrimmage. The tight end's quick start is crucial to his success when blocking a linebacker on the run. The tight end must keep a wide base and stay low as he comes off the line. If the linebacker is inside the tight end or in front of the tackle, the tight end must be sure that he takes his first step with his inside foot. He must always anticipate that the linebacker will charge straight ahead on a blitz. The tight end's goal is to drive the linebacker off the line of scrimmage back toward his own goal line.

For the double-team block, the tight end works with another offensive player to block one defensive player (figure 6.2, page 120). This block requires practice to perfect, but the results are well worth the effort. Both players must work in unison and toward the same goal as they learn this block. The double team is not just one block, but a combination of two blocks. When executing the block, the offensive player directly in front of the defender uses a drive block. The offensive player who blocks from the side of the

Figure 6.2 Tight end helping with a double-team block.

defender uses a modified angle block. Based on the type of offense that the team runs, a tight end may be part of a double-team block with either an offensive tackle or with an offensive player who lines up in the wing position outside the tight end. When working with the tackle, the tight end is the angle blocker. When working with the wing, the tight end is the drive blocker.

In combination blocking, the tight end and offensive tackle are responsible for blocking two defensive players (figure 6.3). The two players to be blocked are usually a defensive lineman who is lined up on the offensive tackle and a linebacker who is lined up off the line. Players use a combination block against stunting or slanting defenses, defenses in which the defensive linemen move quickly into a gap on the snap of the ball. The combination block starts with an attack on the defensive player on the line of scrimmage. The defensive end is lined up on the line of scrimmage directly in front of the tackle, and the outside linebacker is in front of the tight end. The play is run to the opposite side of the formation. The goal is to keep both defensive linemen from pursuing down the line of scrimmage. Players may also use a combination block on an outside wide running play versus a defense in which the defensive lineman is in front of the tight end and the linebacker is in front of the offensive tackle. The roles of the tight end and the offensive tackle are reversed. Both players take their first steps with their outside feet.

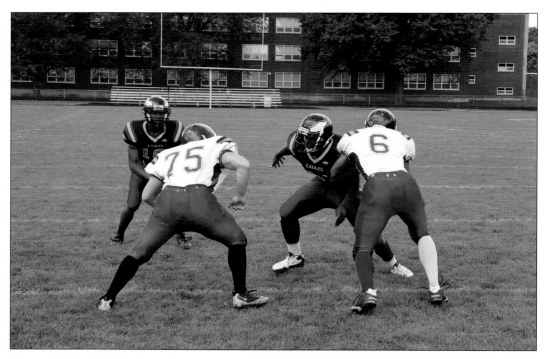

Figure 6.3 Tight end and offensive tackle executing a combination block on a defensive lineman and a linebacker.

Pass Blocking

During the course of a game, a tight end may be required to pass block in unison with the offensive line and running backs. This situation often occurs when the defensive team is blitzing an outside linebacker or a defensive back.

The proper stance is important in pass protection. A tight end will find it difficult to get a good block if his down hand is too far forward. He will have the same problem if he places too much weight on his down hand. When the tight end has to protect the quarterback, he should put just enough weight on his down hand to allow him to push back. The toe of his back foot, the foot on the side of the down hand, should be even with the middle of the other foot. His back should be straight, his shoulders should be square, and his head should be up.

To move out of his stance, the tight end pushes off his down hand to start his initial movement back off the line of scrimmage. As his shoulders come up, he takes a short step to the inside with his inside foot. This step puts him in position to stop a hard inside charge by the defender. After he takes this step, the tight end bends both knees and lowers his hips. He keeps his back straight and avoids bending forward at the waist. His head is up, and his eyes are focused straight ahead. He brings both elbows in tight against his waist and brings his forearms up so that his hands are in front of his chest. Both hands are up, the thumbs are together, the fingers are spread, and the palms are turned forward.

When a tight end is asked to pass block, his first thought should be to stop the defensive player's momentum. The power to stop the defender starts in the tight end's legs and then comes up through his body to the palms of both hands. As the defender comes into him, the tight end uses his leg muscles to explode up, thus avoiding lunging out at the defender. He strikes out aggressively, hitting the defender in the chest with the palms of both hands (figure 6.4). He pushes forward with both hands to create space between himself and the rusher, and he flexes his knees, lowering his hips. He brings both hands back into his chest and prepares himself to push forward repeatedly until the pass is thrown or the whistle blows.

When a rusher is definitely going to the tight end's inside or outside, the tight end may not be able to use both hands. In this case, he will have to stop the rusher's momentum by exploding off the leg on the same side as the rush and aggressively hitting into the rusher's chest with the hand on that side. After stopping the rusher, the tight end can try to get more in front of the rusher so that he can use both hands on the second hit. When blocking an outside rusher, the tight end must be careful not to go too far to the outside. If he overextends to the outside, the rusher will quickly change his path and rush inside to the quarterback.

After he is set, the tight end works in a straight line, moving back away from the line as the pass rusher starts to cross his nose. To keep a strong base, the tight end slides his feet as he moves away from the line. He does not cross his feet or bring them too close together, because doing so weakens his base. By forcing

Figure 6.4 Tight end pass blocks a defender in front of him.

Figure 6.5 Tight end pass blocks a wide rusher.

the defender to rush outside, the tight end will always have the opportunity to push him back behind the quarterback.

Blocking a defensive rusher who is lined up outside the tight end requires a change in technique. The tight end will not be able to stay square to the line of scrimmage. To meet and stop this type of rusher, he must turn his body at a 45-degree angle to the line (figure 6.5).

To get in proper position to block a wide rusher, the tight end should kick his outside foot back and bring his inside foot back and to the outside in a position turned out at a 45-degree angle. He needs to set up in a good pass protection stance and establish a position directly between the rusher and the quarterback. The tight end must be prepared to meet the pass rusher and use the hand on the same side as the rush to stop the rusher's momentum. After initial contact, the tight end should separate, set up again, and continue blocking the rusher until he hears the whistle.

PASS PROTECTION

Purpose: To reinforce proper pass protection stance and movement after the snap.

Procedure:

1. **The coach faces the tight end. At first, no defenders are used and players go one at a time.**

2. **The coach gives the snap count and calls out the cadence to start the drill.**

3. **The tight end gets into the stance for pass protection.**

4. **When the coach calls the snap, the tight end moves out of the stance and into pass protection.**

5. **The coach checks that the tight end is setting up correctly.**

Coaching points: When the tight end is first learning to pass protect, the defender should rush at half speed. Blockers must stay balanced and not lunge forward to stop the defender. The blockers must shuffle their feet and must not cross them during the drill; they must bend at the knees, keep their backs straight and heads up, and put their hands in position to strike out at the rusher. Eventually, a full-speed pass protection drill can be run with one blocker versus one defensive player at a time. Using more than two offensive blockers in a live drill at one time is not advised because using more than two increases the chance for injury when players run into each other.

Variation: After the players are setting up properly, another tight end can line up in front of the blocker to serve as a defensive rush man.

PASS PLAYS

In a pass play, the tight end must have a good release off the line of scrimmage. He must quickly move from his starting position into the defensive secondary. Most tight ends use a three-point stance, although some may use an upright two-point stance, especially when flexing away from the offensive tackle. No matter the stance, the ability to get off the line quickly is vital to the passing game.

The tight end's release is more difficult when a defender lines up directly in front of him, which is usually the case. The tight end's defender may be a linebacker, a defensive lineman, or, in some situations, a defensive back. The first step is crucial when releasing off the line. With a defender in front of him, the tight end needs to take an angle step with his back foot to the side of his release (figure 6.6a). This step must be forward, one that starts the tight end moving up the field. If the right foot is back and he releases to the right of the defender, the tight end should step slightly to the right as he brings the back foot up. When releasing to the left from the same stance, the tight end needs to bring the back foot up and slightly across his body to create a path to the left of the defender.

This first step creates a small separation from the defender, giving the tight end time to move the arm that is closer to the defender forward and swing it forcefully up and in front of his own shoulder (figure 6.6b). This ripping-up motion, if done with force and determination, is usually enough to get the defender's hands off the tight end's jersey.

The tight end must stay low and come off the ball hard. Spending time trying to fake the defender at the line of scrimmage only slows the release and prevents the tight end from getting into his pass pattern.

Short and Medium Pass Routes

After the tight end has learned the stance, start, and release, he is ready to learn to run short and medium pass routes.

Figure 6.6 Tight end releases off the line: He *(a)* takes an angled first step and *(b)* swings his arm up to clear the defender's grip on him.

Quick-Release Short Routes. For many short routes of 7 yards or less, the tight end goes directly from his release into his route. Timing is crucial on these routes. For short routes such as a look-in or short-out pattern (figure 6.7, page 124), the tight end does not have time to move the defensive back where the tight end would like him to be when he makes his final cut. On all short routes, the quarterback takes a short three-step drop and delivers the ball. The offensive line blocks aggressively for only a short time, so every short pass must be thrown quickly to be successful.

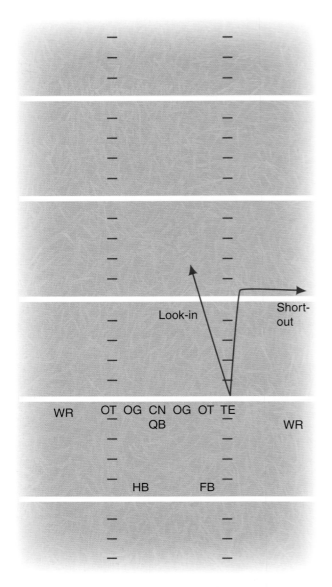

Figure 6.7 Short pass routes for the tight end: short-out and look-in patterns.

Distance and momentum are important in short routes. As he releases up the field on a short route, the tight end needs to know the distance that he should run before he breaks. If he is going to the outside at 5 yards, a short-out pattern, he rolls over the foot in the direction that he is going. He does not plant and step because doing so will only stop his momentum. If he is coming to the inside on a look-in pass, again the tight end must know the distance that he needs to go and then redirect his body to the inside. In both of these short patterns, the tight end bursts into his final move and brings his head around quickly. He establishes good vision of the quarterback and gets his hands into position to catch the ball. The tight end has to stay alert. The ball comes to him quickly, and he probably will be hit the instant that he makes the catch, so he must make certain that the ball is secure.

Block and Release Short Routes. A tight end runs other types of short pass routes after he initially pass blocks. Two of these routes are the delay and the drag. On both routes, the tight end sets up and pass blocks any outside rusher for two counts. On the delay, the tight end pushes the rusher to the outside after two counts and then releases to the inside at a 45-degree angle to the center of the field. In the drag route, the tight end makes the same initial movement, but after pushing off the rusher, he releases straight down the line of scrimmage toward the sideline. Because the tight end is often an outlet receiver for the quarterback on both pass routes, he must look back for the quarterback and the ball the second that he clears the pass rusher.

The third type of pass that a tight end runs after making a pass block is a screen pass. For the screen, the tight end pass blocks for three counts, allows the rush to get by him, and then releases to the outside, moving off the line of scrimmage. After the tight end is on the outside of the formation, he turns his head back toward the quarterback and looks for the ball. The pass should come over the shoulder that is farther from the line of scrimmage. After securing the ball, the tight end yells, "Go!" or another word to alert his offensive blockers that he has the ball.

The tight end needs to understand the blocking scheme that the other offensive players are going to use so that he can take advantage of the opportunities that they create. When the wide receiver on the side of the screen is running deep, the first offensive blocker, usually the offensive tackle or the guard if the tackle's assignment is to stay with his man, tries to block the outside defender to the sideline. The second offensive blocker, usually the guard or center, blocks back on the first defender, reacting from the inside. As the tight end makes the catch and turns up the field, he should look for the lane created by the blocks of the offensive players.

Medium Routes. For medium routes of about 8 to 12 yards, the tight end adds two more elements to his pattern. As he releases up the field, he determines how the defensive back is playing him. Is the defender on his inside or outside? The tight end can influence the position of the defensive back and get open by angling his route slightly away from the direction that he wishes to go in his final cut.

When running an in pattern after going straight up the field for 3 yards, the tight end angles to the outside for 5 yards (figure 6.8). This slight adjustment in his route makes the defender leave the area where the tight end wants to go. If the defender is inside the tight end, the defender will come with the tight end. If the defender is outside, he will go even wider, trying to stay outside the tight end. After the tight end sees that the defender is moving with him, he again directs his pattern straight up the field. This move should convince the defender that the tight end is going deep. Ideally, the defender will turn and start running toward his own goal line.

After sprinting up the field for 5 more yards, the tight end is ready to make his final cut. He keeps his speed and momentum by leaning his upper body to the inside and rolling over his inside foot. The tight end may feel as if he is rounding off the turn, but the important thing is to maintain speed.

After he is in the burst of the final turn, the tight end needs to turn his head and focus on the quarterback. The quarterback may be under pressure and not see the tight end the instant that he makes his cut, so the tight end must continue his burst and keep moving across the field until the ball is thrown.

When running an out pattern, the tight end first angles to the inside and then sprints up the field before making his cut to the outside. The tight end should practice running all four paths until he feels comfortable with them. Only by getting open will he ever have the opportunity to make a catch.

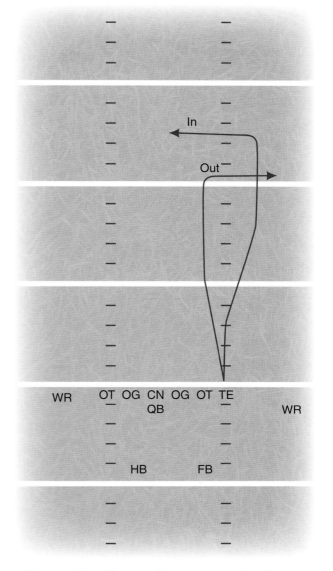

Figure 6.8 Two medium pass routes for the tight end: in and out.

When running the hook route (figure 6.9, page 126), the tight end must drive straight up the field and not worry about positioning the defender. His goal is to make the defender think that he is running deep. When he reaches 10 yards, he shortens his stride, lowers his hips, and stops his forward momentum by planting his outside foot. He quickly turns back to the inside and faces the quarterback, moving both hands up to the center of his chest. He immediately looks for the ball and moves toward the ball to make the catch.

A cross route is not run as deep as the other medium routes are, but it requires the same timing. When running a cross route, the tight end takes an inside release off the line of scrimmage if possible and drives up the field, as he does for a look-in route. The tight end rolls over his inside foot at 6 yards and starts running across the field at full speed. He increases his depth slightly as he runs across the field, although he never goes

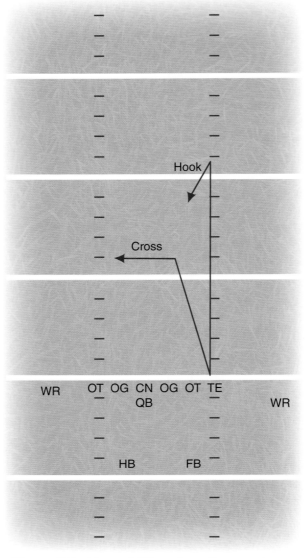

Figure 6.9 Two additional medium routes for the tight end: hook and cross.

deeper than 10 yards. He turns his head and focuses on the quarterback. He expects the pass any time after he passes the offensive center. The tight end often runs this route when the play requires the quarterback to move out of the pocket to throw the ball.

Deep Pass Routes

Deep patterns take longer to develop, so the timing of these patterns takes longer. To allow time for the receiver to run the deep route, the quarterback drops seven steps before delivering the ball. The offensive line has to block a few seconds longer for a deep pass. When successful, the deep pass often results in a touchdown.

The three basic deep pass routes—seam, post, and corner—all require speed (figure 6.10). All are run in the deep zone, 12 or more yards up the field from the line of scrimmage. To have success with these three patterns, the tight end needs to run at full speed for the entire length of the pass pattern. For the post, corner, and seam pass routes, the tight end runs under the ball and often has to stretch to make the catch. The tight end should try to see his fingers and the ball at the same time when attempting to make the reception.

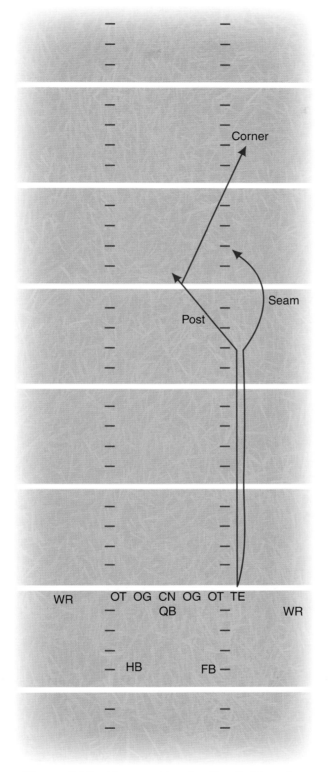

Corner

Seam

Post

| WR | OT OG CN OG OT TE | WR |
| | QB | |

HB   FB

Figure 6.10   Deep routes for the tight end: seam, post, and corner.

The first deep pattern is the seam pattern. Before the start of the play, the tight end should determine the alignment of the safety on his side of the field. Trying to position the defender is OK, but the tight end must never sacrifice speed to move a defender. When running the seam pattern, the tight end tries to release outside any defensive

Figure 6.11 Tight end looks back and makes the catch over his shoulder while running a seam route.

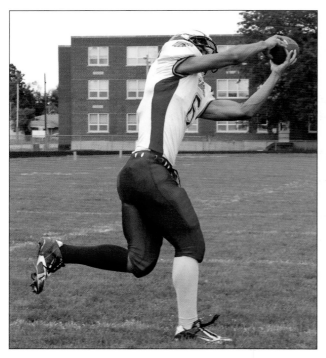

Figure 6.12 Tight end looks back and reaches out to make the catch while running a post pattern.

man in front of him. He immediately gets his speed and momentum going straight up the field. At 12 yards, he bends to the outside while still going up the field. He gets into a position that allows him to run up the field 5 to 7 yards outside the hash marks. At about 15 yards, he comes slightly back to the inside and establishes a sight path to the quarterback and the ball. He picks up (locates) the ball as soon as it leaves the quarterback's hand by looking over his inside shoulder. He does not break stride. He may need to adjust to the flight of the ball, and he should expect to make the catch on his inside, directly in front, or over his outside shoulder (figure 6.11). Speed is crucial for the entire time. Regardless of where the defender is, the tight end cannot slow down. He needs to keep his momentum going up the field at all cost. At times, he may have to dive to catch the ball.

The second deep pass pattern is the post route. The post pattern is run into the center of the field away from the sideline. The tight end looks to see where the defender is before the start of the play. If the defender is lined up and playing the tight end on the inside, the tight end angles slightly toward the sideline to entice the defender to come with him, opening up the inside of the field. If the defender is playing the tight end on the outside, the tight end probably will be able to sprint straight ahead for 12 yards before making his break to the inside. When running the post, the tight end releases to the outside, comes off the line quickly, angles to position the defender if necessary, and bursts straight at him to 12 yards. At 12 yards, the tight end rolls over his inside foot and directs his path at 45 degrees into the center of the field. He expects to run under the pass. On this pattern, the pass will be thrown with loft and the tight end must keep running to make the catch. As soon as he makes his break and heads toward the center of the field, the tight end turns his head back to the quarterback, ready to pick up the ball as it leaves the quarterback's hand. He may have to adjust his path slightly to make the catch. Often he will make the catch in front by reaching out as he runs (figure 6.12).

The third pattern, the corner route, is run off the post pattern. To run the corner route successfully, the tight end must sell the post pattern to the defender. The tight end runs up the field exactly the same way he does for the post and cuts to the inside. After running 3 or 4 yards toward the center of the field, bringing the defensive back with him, the tight end makes a second cut. This cut is on a 45-degree angle back to the corner of the field. He keeps his momentum by rolling over his outside foot as he goes to the corner of the field. In this pass pattern, the ball is in the air for a long time. The tight end must run hard and expect to travel at least 15 to 20 yards before making the catch. He looks back over his outside shoulder to pick up the quarterback and the ball. He may need to adjust his route as he heads for the ball.

A tight end will have only one or two opportunities, at most, to make a reception on a deep pass in a game. He must do everything possible to get open, concentrate on the ball, look it into his hands, and secure the ball before running for the score. For a receiver, there is no better feeling than running deep, seeing the ball spiraling his way, making the catch, and running into the end zone.

SOLO PATTERN PRACTICE

Purpose: To give the tight end experience in running basic pass routes by himself.

Procedure: The tight end can practice all the basic patterns alone by following this procedure:

1. **Decide which pattern to run.**
2. **Get into a good stance.**
3. **Execute a proper release.**
4. **Picture where the defensive man is going to be.**
5. **Run the route quickly.**
6. **Face the quarterback at the right time in the pattern.**
7. **Visualize the path of the ball.**
8. **Go through the motions of making the catch and securing the ball.**

Coaching points: The coach should check that the tight end is making his break at the proper depth for each pass route. The tight end should keep his momentum during the entire route and turn his head back to the quarterback as soon as he can.

RUNNING SHORT ROUTES

Purpose: To give the tight end experience running short routes.

Procedure:

1. **The coach lines up 10 yards downfield. A tight end and a linebacker line up as if they are on the line of scrimmage. A tight end can take the place of the linebacker if a linebacker isn't available.**
2. **The coach calls a short route and signals the start of the play.**
3. **On the coach's signal, the tight end releases around the linebacker and runs the short route.**
4. **The coach observes the tight end's release and pattern and offers feedback.**

Coaching points: In all these drills, the coach should make certain that the tight end is stepping forward with his first step, that he is releasing on the correct side of the defensive man, and that he is moving at full speed as soon as possible. On medium pass routes, the tight end should adjust his route to position the defender away from his final cut.

Variation: The same setup is helpful for practicing medium routes, including the in, out, and hook routes. The coach should line up 20 yards downfield.

RUNNING SHORT ROUTES AFTER PASS BLOCKING

Purpose: To give the tight end experience running short routes after pass blocking a rusher.

Procedure:

1. The coach lines up 10 yards downfield. A tight end and a linebacker line up as if they are on the line of scrimmage. A tight end can take the place of the linebacker if a linebacker isn't available.
2. The coach calls a short route and signals the start of the play.
3. On the coach's signal, the tight end sets up to pass block, and the linebacker blitzes to the outside.
4. After pass blocking for the appropriate time, the tight end releases and runs the pass route called by the coach.
5. The coach observes the tight end's pass block, release, and pass route and offers feedback.

Coaching points: The tight end must set up correctly off the line and execute a proper pass block before releasing on his pass route. He must immediately locate the quarterback and get in position to make the reception.

Variation: An offensive tackle, a second rusher, and a quarterback can be added to provide the tight end with a more realistic situation.

RUNNING DEEP ROUTES

Purpose: To give the tight end experience running deep routes.

Procedure:

1. For the seam route, the coach lines up 10 yards downfield and outside the tight end. A tight end and a linebacker line up on the line of scrimmage. A tight end can take the place of the linebacker if a linebacker isn't available.
2. The coach calls the seam route and signals the start of the play.
3. On the coach's signal, the tight end releases around the linebacker and runs the seam route.
4. The coach observes the tight end's release and pattern and offers feedback.

Coaching points: The coach should check the tight end's release and his drive up the field. The tight end should break on each pattern at the correct depth. On the corner route, the tight end must sell the post before breaking to the outside.

Variation: The same setup can be used to practice other deep routes. For the post and corner patterns, a defensive back or another tight end should line up 8 yards down the field inside or outside the tight end's original position.

CHAPTER 7

DEFENSIVE LINEMEN

Defensive linemen make contact on every play, guaranteed. They are in the middle of the action, colliding with the offensive players who are trying to block them. Unlike their teammates, who may be lined up off the line of scrimmage, defensive linemen instantly experience action. Defensive linemen need to stay focused to see and understand what is taking place.

The challenge for the defensive lineman is to defeat the offensive blocker on every play and then attack the ballcarrier. Learning to play this physically demanding position can be frustrating, especially when starting out. A defensive lineman doesn't know who is blocking him or who has the ball. He will begin to see more of what is happening as he gains experience.

To become a good defensive lineman, a player must learn the following techniques: using the proper stance, moving on the ball, defeating and separating from blocks, and rushing the passer. Each of these techniques helps players become better and more successful defensive linemen.

STANCE

The defensive lineman's stance depends on the type of block that he faces and any adjustments that he needs to make based on down and distance. The closer the defensive lineman is to the ball before the play begins, the greater the number of players who will be there to block him. As the lineman moves to the outside, he may see several blockers, but he usually has a little time to see what is happening. His beginning stance must allow him to react to the wide variety of blocks that he will face.

The stance depends on the style of defense that the team is using. Beginning players typically use a four-point stance, whereas more experienced players may use a three-point stance. Defensive linemen who are facing a running team should use a balanced stance, whereas defensive linemen who are facing a passing team may need to use a more staggered stance.

To get into a three- or four-point stance, the player begins by standing with his feet even and about shoulder-width apart. The coach should check to see that the defensive lineman's toes point straight ahead. While keeping his head up and back straight, the defensive lineman starts bending his knees until he can rest his forearms on the inside of his thighs. From this position, the player can reach forward and down with both hands and arms for the four-point stance (figure 7.1a). He places his hands on the ground slightly in front of his shoulders. In this position, the player's weight is distributed evenly over both hands and both feet. To get into a three-point stance, all he has to do is lift one hand off the ground, rest the forearm and hand on the knee briefly, and then bring the forearm forward and up. The palm of the hand no longer on the ground should be open with the fingers spread and pointing up (figure 7.1b).

On a passing down or when he is playing on or outside the offensive tackle, the defensive lineman should stagger his feet slightly. He steps back with his inside foot so that the toe is slightly behind the heel of his other foot. In a three-point stance, the hand on the ground and the back foot are on the same side of the player's body. The heel of his back foot should be off the ground. See the section on rushing the passer for more about the staggered stance (page 142).

In a good stance, the defensive lineman's head is up and his eyes look straight ahead. He needs to keep his shoulders even and his back straight. He should feel ready to react to a block from the right, left, or straight ahead.

Figure 7.1 Defensive linemen's stances: *(a)* four-point stance and *(b)* three-point stance.

MOVING ON THE BALL

Although offensive players have the snap count to tell them when the play begins, the ball and any movement on the offensive line serve as the sign for defensive linemen to move. Because of the nearness of the offensive blockers, if the defensive lineman hesitates, the blockers will probably defeat him. A successful defensive lineman has the ability to get off the ball quickly and into position to defeat offensive blockers.

Regardless of the stance, the defensive lineman must condition himself to concentrate on moving the instant that an offensive lineman or the ball moves. On his first step, he must stay low and not rise to look for the ballcarrier. A defensive lineman has to charge straight ahead, take a control step to his right or left, or take a crossover step to his right or left. With each of these movements, his first step must be quick.

If playing a control technique—one in which he does not penetrate across the line of scrimmage—the defensive lineman's first step is a quick lateral step. The foot that he steps with depends on the defense called and the gap that is his responsibility. He always takes the control step with the foot on the side of the direction in which he will move. The defensive lineman should practice stepping in both directions.

For a penetrating start with fast movement into a gap between two offensive players, the defensive lineman may need to use a crossover start. Instead of stepping laterally with the near foot as he did in a control start, he takes his first step across his body with the opposite foot. If he is moving to his right, his first step is with his left foot. If he is attacking the gap to his left, his first step is across his body with his right foot. The crossover start may bring his shoulders up more than when he charges straight ahead or uses a control step, but on all three starts, the defensive lineman should stay as low as possible with his shoulders square to the line of scrimmage.

DEFEATING BLOCKS

Because the offensive man in front of the defensive lineman is in position to be the first to block him, the defensive lineman must concentrate on this offensive lineman and look for the drive or hook block (figure 7.2). The next offensive player in position to block the defensive lineman is the offensive player to his immediate right or left. After these two players, the near back, if there is one, or the offside guard may be secondary blockers.

When beginning to play defensive line, the defensive lineman must think in terms of a blocking progression. He should ask himself which offensive player can block him, when the offensive player can block him, and what type of block the offensive player will use. After he knows the answers to these questions, he is on his way to becoming a top-flight defensive lineman.

If he is playing in front of the offensive center, in a nose tackle position, the defensive lineman must be aware of the blocking triangle formed by the center and both guards. Any one of these three offensive players may be the initial blocker, or any two of them can work together in a combination or double-team block. Because of the close proximity of all three blockers, the nose tackle must be prepared to react to and defeat each block.

Figure 7.2 Blocking progression for defensive linemen: *(a)* defensive end and *(b)* defensive tackle.

Drive Block

One of the first offensive blocks that a defensive lineman must learn to expect, recognize, and defeat is the drive block. In this block, the offensive lineman directly in front of the defensive lineman tries to drive the defensive lineman off the line of scrimmage.

As the blocker moves toward the defensive lineman, the defensive lineman must start his momentum toward the offensive blocker (figure 7.3a). To meet and defeat the blocker's power, the defensive lineman must have a wide base and take only short power steps.

At contact the defensive lineman keeps his shoulder pads even with or slightly below the blocker's shoulder pads (figure 7.3b). With his shoulder pads in this position, the defensive lineman will be able to keep the blocker from getting underneath him and driving him off the line of scrimmage.

As he steps forward and his shoulder pads make contact with the offensive blocker, the defensive lineman slides his helmet to the side of his gap responsibility. The defensive lineman should always make contact with the blocker with his pads, not his helmet. The defensive lineman is responsible for one side of the drive blocker or the other unless he is responsible for the running lanes on both sides of the blocker (two-gap responsibility).

The instant that the defensive lineman makes contact with his shoulder pads, he extends his arms so that the palms of both hands make contact at the numbers of the offensive blocker's jersey (figure 7.3c). From this point, he can straighten his arms, get separation from the blocker, and be in position to throw the blocker aside and move to attack the ballcarrier.

If he takes a lateral or crossover step to secure a gap, the defensive lineman moves directly to one side of the blocker or the other on the snap of the ball. In this style of defense, the defensive lineman must fight back into the blocker and not let the blocker use the defensive lineman's own momentum to drive him out of the hole.

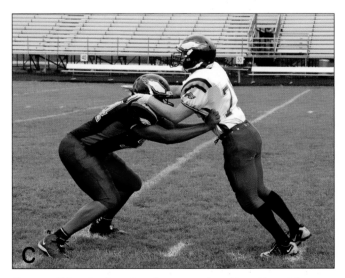

Figure 7.3 Defensive lineman beating the drive block: From a wide base, he *(a)* moves toward the blocker, *(b)* keeps his pads below the blocker's pads at contact, and *(c)* extends his arms to get separation.

Hook Block

Like the drive block, the hook block is used by a blocker who lines up directly in front of the defensive lineman. The goal of the drive block is to keep the defensive lineman from penetrating across the line of scrimmage and to move him back toward his own goal line. The objective of the hook block is different: The offensive player wants to stop the defensive lineman's penetration and force him to move to either his right or his left.

When the play begins, the defensive lineman needs to see immediately that the blocker is moving laterally to his right or left and not coming directly at him. The blocker will try to get his helmet outside the defensive lineman's shoulder pad so that he can drive the shoulder away from his movement into the defensive lineman's belly and hip.

As the defensive lineman takes his first short step forward, he sees the blocker's helmet and shoulder pads moving to the right or left. The defensive lineman quickly extends both arms into the blocker. He tries to make contact with the palms of both hands on the blocker's shoulder pads (figure 7.4). If he can get his hands and arms extended quickly enough into the blocker, he will have greater power at the moment of contact. The blocker's momentum may still be lateral, not forward. As his hands make contact, the defensive lineman continues to take short power steps to drive the blocker back across the line of scrimmage into the offensive backfield.

In this position, the defensive lineman is able to keep the blocker from using his legs or shoulder pads to get into the defensive lineman's body. The defensive lineman should keep his head up. After he locates the ballcarrier, he sheds the blocker and tries to get in on the tackle.

Figure 7.4   Defensive lineman defeating a hook block.

Angle Block

One of the most difficult blocks that a defensive lineman faces is the angle block. The difficulty comes from the closeness of the blocker and the fact that the blocker is not lined up directly in front of him. The defensive lineman must focus on the offensive lineman directly in front of him, and at the same time he must see in his side vision the offensive linemen to his right and left, men in position to attack him. The challenge in defeating the angle block is that the defensive lineman must start forward first toward the player in front of him and then quickly redirect his momentum to the right or left.

When defeating an angle block, the defensive lineman's goals are to redirect his momentum into the blocker, stop the blocker's momentum, and prevent the blocker from driving him off the line of scrimmage. If the defensive lineman is ever in a situation in which he thinks that he is losing this battle, he should drop down to his hands and knees to create as big a pile as possible.

The offensive blocker using an angle block comes at the defensive lineman from the side. The defensive lineman cannot turn and meet this block squarely as he did when playing the drive or hook block. The second that he sees that the offensive player in front is not going to block him, the defensive lineman must see whether the offensive player on his right or left is coming at him. The instant that he determines which blocker is coming at him, he needs to take a short step at the blocker with the foot on the same side as the block (figure 7.5*a*).

The defensive lineman will be able to make contact with the offensive man with his near shoulder pad only (figure 7.5*b*). Keeping his knees bent, he redirects as much of his momentum as possible into the blocker. As his shoulder pad makes contact, the defensive lineman tries to lift his forearm on the side of the block into the chest of the offensive blocker (figure 7.5*c*).

As he makes contact, he continues to drive his legs using short, choppy power steps as he works to defeat the blocker. Continuing his leg drive and staying low are two important techniques when reacting to this block. After the defensive lineman has stepped into the blocker, made contact with his shoulder pad, and struck a blow with his forearm, he can try to turn his entire body into the blocker. As his far shoulder comes around, he tries to strike the blocker's shoulder pad with the palm of his far arm. He may be able to get under the shoulder pad and knock the blocker off balance.

Scoop, or Combination, Block

Now that the defensive lineman knows how to defeat one offensive blocker who is attacking him, he can focus on defeating blocks in which two offensive players attack him.

The first block of this type is the scoop, or combination, block. In the scoop block, the offensive player directly in front of the defensive lineman fires out at the defensive lineman in a way that makes him think that the blocker is trying to hook block him. The defensive lineman's natural reaction is to defeat the hook block. All his attention is directed at the offensive player in front of him, and his first instinct is to put both hands on the first blocker.

As the defensive lineman makes contact, he will feel that the blocker is not really trying to hook him but instead is trying to stop his pursuit. The offensive blocker's job is to stop the defensive lineman's penetration and lateral movement for a moment. The blocker is setting up the defensive lineman for the final block by the offensive lineman opposite the first blocker's movement.

After the first blocker has stopped the defensive lineman, he pushes off the defensive

Figure 7.5 Defensive lineman defeating an angle block: He *(a)* takes a short step to the blocker, *(b)* makes contact with his near shoulder pad, and *(c)* pushes with his forearm and uses his body to drives the blocker back.

lineman, releases on the side of the fake hook block, and continues up the field to get in position to block a linebacker. After the initial blocker releases, the second blocker tries to position himself directly in front of the defensive lineman. Then he tries to work his way around the defensive lineman, just as he does in a hook block. The second blocker's job is not to drive the defensive lineman off the line of scrimmage but to position himself so that the defensive lineman cannot pursue down the line to tackle the ballcarrier. The second blocker steps laterally down the line, fighting to get a head-up position on the defensive lineman. The second blocker is most vulnerable when he is moving down the line and not attacking the defensive lineman directly.

The defensive lineman must quickly recognize this block as the play begins. He should notice that the offensive player in front of him is not as low as he would be on a normal hook block. Instead of seeing his shoulder pads, the defensive lineman sees the numbers on the offensive blocker's jersey. This picture should alert the defensive lineman that the blocker is faking a hook block, so he must be prepared for an attack by another offensive blocker.

As soon as the defensive lineman senses that the offensive player in front of him is not a true blocker but is only setting him up, he must charge straight up the field and try to engage the second blocker (figure 7.6). The second blocker, the scoop blocker, will not come at the defensive lineman with much power in the beginning, so the defensive lineman should quickly try to get both hands into the second blocker's chest. He must keep a good defensive position with his head up, back straight, and knees bent, using the large muscles of his legs to push the blocker back to the offensive side of the ball.

From this position, the defensive lineman works his head and body to the side of the first blocker's release and fights down the line. The defensive lineman must never let the scoop blocker cut off his lateral movement. He should get into the pursuit path that will take him to the ballcarrier.

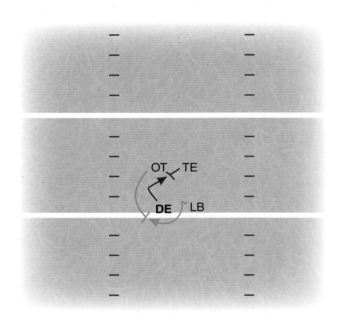

Figure 7.6 Defensive lineman defeating a combination block by engaging the second blocker.

Double-Team Block

A defensive lineman faces no greater challenge than fighting off a double-team block. For most of the game, only one offensive player blocks the defensive lineman. During a scoop block, two offensive linemen block him but not at the same time. On a double-team block, all that changes. Two offensive players block the defensive lineman for the entire play, so he has to defeat the combined power and weight of two blockers instead of one.

A double-team block is an offensive block executed in unison by the offensive player directly in front of the defensive lineman and an adjacent offensive blocker to the right or left. For a defensive end playing in front of an offensive tackle, the double-team block usually comes from the offensive tackle and the tight end just to the outside. If the defensive lineman lines up in front of one of the offensive guards, the double-team block comes from the offensive guard and the offensive tackle or the center. When the defensive lineman is in the middle of the action and lines up in front of the center, he can expect the center and either guard to be involved in the double team.

The double-team block is not one block but a combination of two blocks. The offensive blocker in front of the defensive lineman executes the drive block, and the offensive player coming at the defensive lineman from the side executes the angle block. Combining the angle and drive blocks results in a double-team block. The objective of these two offensive players who are working together is to drive the defensive lineman off and down the line of scrimmage. They want to stand him up and then, shoulder to shoulder, drive him out of the hole.

The defensive lineman first reacts to the offensive blocker in front of him, so he works to stop the drive block. To do this, the defensive lineman places both hands on the drive blocker and concentrates on defeating the drive block (figure 7.7a). The instant he sees that he is the target of a double-team block, the defensive lineman must prepare for the angle block that is coming from the side. He lowers his body and directs as much weight as he can into the angle blocker (figure 7.7b).

Seldom will the defensive lineman have the strength or power to defeat both blockers. If he can just create a pile at the site of the block, he will have effectively defeated the double-team block and won the battle. Staying as low as the blockers or lower is important if he is to win the battle. He directs his weight into the angle blocker and is prepared to turn his back to the angle blocker. He can go to the ground on the side of his body nearer the angle blocker to create a pile in the running lane.

If the defensive lineman ever thinks that the two blockers are beginning to drive him back, he must drop the side of his body nearer the angle block to the ground and turn sideways between the two blockers. This maneuver causes the two offensive players to block each other. The angle blocker blocks the defensive lineman's back, and the drive blocker blocks the defensive lineman's front. The defensive lineman's body is wedged between the two blockers, and the energy of the block is reduced. From this position, the blockers are unlikely to move the defensive lineman out of the hole.

A

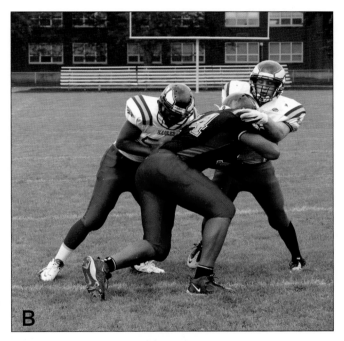

B

Figure 7.7 Defensive lineman defeating a double-team block: He *(a)* confronts the drive block and *(b)* drops the side nearer the angle blocker to direct his weight into the angle blocker.

Trap Block

In the previous blocks, the defensive lineman was blocked by one or two offensive linemen who were either in front of him or to his right or left. In his stance, he could see the blockers and react immediately to their blocks. In a trap block, none of the blockers in the defensive lineman's sight block him. If the defensive end is lined up in front of the offensive tackle and sees the tackle and guard block to the inside, he immediately

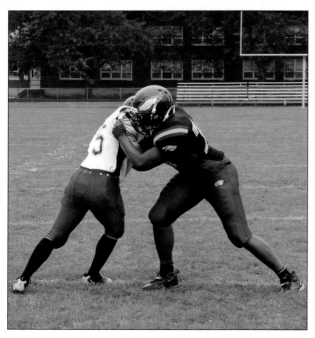

TE OT OG CN **OG** OT

LB **DE** LDT   RDT   DE

ILB

Figure 7.8 Trap block on the defensive end.

Figure 7.9 Defensive lineman defeating a trap block.

thinks that the tight end is going to angle block. But the tight end is not blocking the defensive end; instead, he's blocking straight ahead on the linebacker. The instant that the defensive end reads this play, he should think trap block and turn back to the inside toward the center. He attacks the line of scrimmage and tries to locate the trap blocker. He faces the blocker and moves toward him (figure 7.8).

After the defensive lineman has turned his body toward the center of the field and located the blocker, he is in position to defeat the block. At the moment of contact, he brings his outside arm and forearm hard across the blocker's chest and face. He keeps his knees bent, his back straight, and his head up. His shoulder pads should be at the same height as the blocker's pads (figure 7.9). He redirects the blocker's body back into the hole.

Every defensive lineman must understand that he can and will be trapped. When playing in front of an offensive guard, he must stay alert for the guard or tackle on the other side of the center who may try to trap block him. The nose tackle lined up in front of the offensive center has a more difficult job. When the center or guards aren't blocking him, he must look to both the right and left, because either offensive tackle may be coming to trap block him.

When beating the trap block, the defensive lineman must remember that it will take longer for the blocker to get to him. He should stay on or just across the line of scrimmage and not go upfield.

Lead Block

Many defensive linemen have trouble defeating the lead block. An offensive back, not an offensive lineman, executes this block. Like the trap block, the lead block does not happen the instant that the ball is snapped. The blocker needs time to reach the defensive lineman.

The challenge comes when the defensive lineman who is not blocked by any offensive linemen begins to look into the backfield. Automatically his eyes seek out the ballcarrier. He focuses on the running back with the ball and does not see the other running back coming in to block him from the side. The defensive lineman is usually bigger and stronger than the running back trying to block him. The blocker understands this, so he won't drive into the defensive lineman like an offensive lineman would. Instead, the blocker will try to block the defensive lineman at the hip with his shoulder pads.

Stopping this type of block is different because of the size of blocker and the method that he uses to block the defensive lineman. To defeat the lead block, the defensive lineman must recognize that a back will be blocking him and that the blocker will need time to reach him. He then has to locate the back who is going to block him. If necessary, he turns his body to face the blocker (figure 7.10a). He keeps his shoulder pads even with the blocker's shoulder pads. He stops the momentum of the block by hitting out with the palms of both hands, directing both palms into the top of the blocker's shoulder pads. He pushes the blocker's head, shoulders, and chest into the ground away from his own feet, legs, and body (figure 7.10b).

If the defensive lineman stands up and looks into the backfield for the ballcarrier, the other running back will be into his body before he can react to the block. The defensive lineman needs to stay low and not help the blocker.

Lead blockers will attack any defensive lineman, so all defensive linemen should be prepared for running backs who will try to block them. This block usually comes from a fullback who is lined up to one side of the center or directly behind the center and quarterback. The defensive lineman who is playing in front of the center must look out for a block

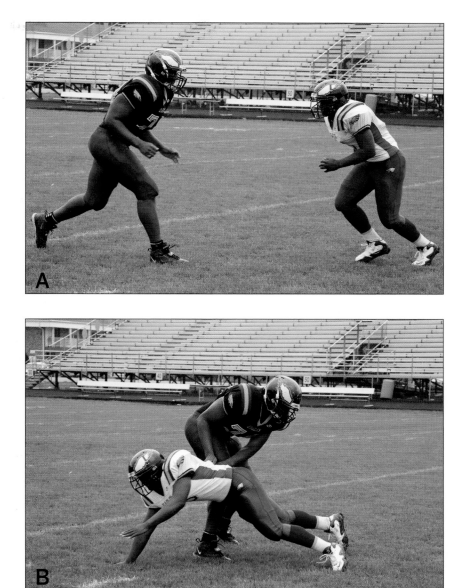

Figure 7.10 Defensive lineman defeating a lead block: He *(a)* turns his body to face the block and *(b)* pushes the blocker away and to the ground.

from his outside by a fullback who may be lined up directly behind the offensive tackle.

Speed is essential in stopping a lead block. The defensive lineman must get rid of the blocker as quickly as possible. Good ballcarriers understand that the running back will not be able to block for long, so they often run right behind the blocker. The defensive lineman will have only a moment to push off the blocker, locate the ballcarrier, and reach out to make the tackle.

Learning to defeat each type of block and understanding blocking progression is essential to becoming a top defensive lineman. As a player continues to develop as a defensive lineman, he will be able to sit back, relax, close his eyes, and visualize how each block will come, who will do the blocking, and how he will defeat it.

RUSHING THE PASSER

For a defensive lineman, no emotion can surpass the thrill that results from tackling a quarterback and getting a sack. When playing the defensive line against a running play, the defensive lineman reacts to the block being used by the offense. This circumstance changes when the offensive lineman sets up to pass block. In this situation, the defensive player is in control. He is the one making the moves, and the offensive lineman has to react to the defensive lineman.

A pass rusher must anticipate when the offense is going to try to pass the ball. He adjusts his stance when he anticipates a pass and concentrates on the ball. He starts moving forward the instant that the center moves the ball. Any time the defense thinks that the offense is going to pass the ball, defensive linemen need to decide before the play begins what pass-rush move they will use. They attack the target area and make the offensive blockers react to them. They pressure the passer, force the quarterback to hurry the throw, bat or deflect any pass they can get to, and tackle the quarterback every chance they get.

The defensive lineman uses a balanced stance when defending a running play. He has a wide base and can react to his right or left. When the defensive lineman thinks that the offense is going to pass, he changes his stance so that he can rush the passer. He narrows the distance between his feet and moves one foot back, bringing the front foot directly under his hip. He places one hand on the ground in front of his helmet, shifting most of his weight to the front foot and the hand on the ground. He raises his hips above his shoulders and focuses his eyes on the ball. He thinks about exploding forward and coming up as he moves across the line.

Getting a sack is not the only way to defeat a pass play. Making the quarterback move or leave the pocket can cause a poor pass or at least force the pass to only half of the field. A defensive player can also rush the quarterback and force him to throw the ball before a receiver gets open. Another way to influence a pass play is for the defensive player to anticipate when the quarterback is going to throw and then reach up and deflect or redirect the ball. Any of these actions helps a team defend the pass. Each action can result in an incompletion, which is just as good as stopping a running play for no gain.

Defensive linemen use several pass-rush techniques. The key is to find the one or two that are best suited to the size of the individual player. Regardless of the technique, the defensive lineman must always have an idea where the quarterback will set up to throw (the target area). He must remember that his ultimate goal is to influence the quarterback, but he needs to defeat the blocker first. He must keep moving forward and keep his legs and feet moving toward the quarterback. He needs to be aggressive for the entire play. If these movements become second nature to the defensive lineman and his feet, legs, hips, upper body, arms, and hands move together smoothly, he is on his way to becoming a great pass rusher.

Straight-Ahead Bull Rush

The first pass-rush technique is the straight-ahead bull rush. In this play, the defensive lineman quickly comes off the ball and drives forward to the target area, where the quarterback will set up to throw.

In this pass rush, the defensive lineman's goal is not to get around the blocker but to drive the offensive blocker right back into the quarterback. If he can drive the blocker into the quarterback, he can interrupt the quarterback's throwing motion and possibly force the quarterback to throw before he is ready, interrupting the pass timing. This type of rush is effective against a blocker who backs away from the line of scrimmage.

On the snap of the ball, the defensive lineman explodes off the line in a low charge (figure 7.11*a*). He keeps his shoulders below the blocker's shoulders and bends his arms, keeping his elbows close to his body. His palms are up, his fingers are open, and his thumbs are close together.

As the defensive lineman reaches the blocker, he drives the palms of his hands into the armpits of the blocker (figure 7.11*b*). He pushes his arms forward and up, raising the blocker up and back (figure 7.11*c*). He drives the blocker into the quarterback with short, quick steps, and he keeps driving until he reaches the quarterback, the pass is thrown, or the whistle blows.

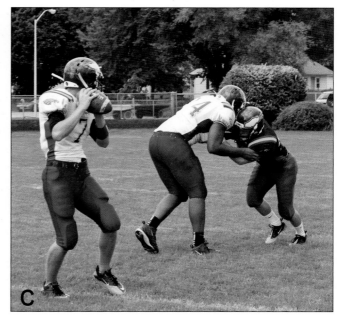

Figure 7.11 Defensive lineman executing a straight-ahead bull rush: He *(a)* explodes off the line, *(b)* makes contact with the blocker, and *(c)* drives the blocker into the quarterback.

Figure 7.12 Defensive lineman executing the bull and jerk: He (a) grabs the blocker's jersey and jerks the blocker to the side and (b) steps across and drives to the target area.

Bull and Jerk

The bull and jerk is a variation of the normal bull rush that should be taught right along with the bull rush. Often when the defensive lineman is successful in pushing the blocker into the quarterback, the blocker sets his feet and lunges at the defensive lineman. The defensive lineman must be alert to this possibility as he charges at the blocker. The lineman can use the blocker's forward thrust to help pull the blocker out of the way.

When the defensive lineman sees the blocker set and lunge, he grabs the front of the blocker's jersey in both hands and jerks or pulls the blocker's body to the side (figure 7.12a). He steps across the blocker's body with the foot on the same side that he pulled the blocker to and drives past the blocker to the target area (figure 7.12b).

Rushing to the Outside

Two techniques are used for rushing to the outside shoulder of a blocker. The first works for a defensive lineman who is shorter than the offensive blocker. The second is helpful for a defensive lineman who is the same height as or taller than the offensive blocker.

The shoulder-club and arm-slip pass rush is an ideal pass-rush technique for a shorter player to learn and perfect. In this technique, the defensive lineman steps quickly with his inside foot, takes a long step with his outside foot, and gets in position to touch the blocker. He takes his outside hand and arm and hits hard under the blocker's shoulder pad, lifting his shoulder and arm up. He steps to the outside of the blocker with his inside foot while dropping his inside shoulder and driving it under the armpit of the blocker. He bows and pushes back his neck and back. He drives his hips up and past the blocker and keeps moving to the quarterback (figure 7.13).

The wrist-club and arm-over pass rush begins the same way. Instead of pushing the blocker's shoulder and arm up, now the defensive lineman directs them down and into the blocker's chest. As the defensive lineman's second step hits, he uses his outside forearm to drive down on the blocker's outside forearm and wrist (figure 7.14a). The defensive lineman drives the blocker's arm and hand down and into his chest. He reaches over the blocker's outside shoulder with his inside arm and drives his elbow into the blocker's back. He drives his inside leg to the outside and past the offensive blocker (figure 7.14b). He keeps moving forward and attacks the quarterback.

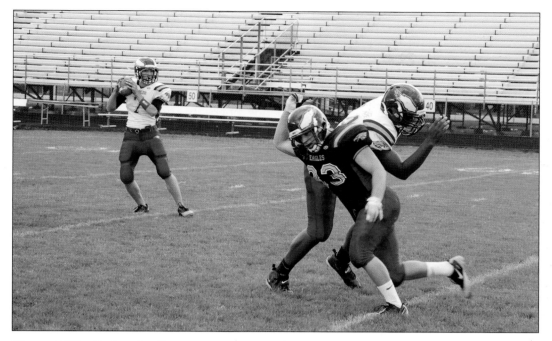

Figure 7.13 Defensive lineman executing the shoulder-club and arm-slip pass rush: He gets in position to make contact under the blocker's shoulder pad, drives his shoulder into the blocker, and drives past him.

Figure 7.14 Defensive lineman executing the wrist-club and arm-over pass rush: He *(a)* pushes the blocker's arms down with his forearm and *(b)* brings his arm over the blocker's shoulder and drives past him.

Figure 7.15 Defensive lineman executing the rip and run pass rush: He *(a)* drops his outside shoulder and drives it toward the blocker's armpit and *(b)* brings his outside arm up and back and drives toward the quarterback.

Rushing to the Inside

The defensive lineman uses the rip and run pass-rush technique to take an inside path to the quarterback. The defensive lineman attacks the inside of the offensive blocker with a rip and run. Often this technique uncovers the shortest and quickest path to the quarterback. The technique is unique in that the defensive lineman commits to an inside rush on the snap of the ball and only the rip arm comes in contact with the offensive blocker. The instant that the center moves the ball, the defensive lineman takes a long step with his outside foot forward and across the blocker's body, allowing his outside shoulder to drop (figure 7.15a). The defensive lineman tries to drive his outside shoulder under the blocker's inside armpit. He propels himself past the blocker by bringing his outside arm up and back. He drives his feet and hips toward the quarterback (figure 7.15b).

Reacting Off a Pass Rush

A defensive lineman needs to practice reacting to two offensive plays as he makes a pass-rush move to the quarterback. These two plays are a draw play and a screen pass. In both instances, the defensive lineman should react to the direction of the ball and ballcarrier.

On a draw play, the quarterback starts his drop and then hands the ball to a running back who is setting up to pass block. The play is designed to be run between onrushing defensive players. After a defensive player sees that the play is a draw, he should immediately stop his rush, turn, and take the same path back toward the line of scrimmage that he took as he rushed the passer. He needs to follow the back with the ball and be part of the tackle.

On a screen pass, the quarterback often drops back 7 yards, sets up, and then begins to drop again. Recognition of the screen pass begins with the defensive player's realization that the offensive blocker has allowed him to get past his block and freely move to the quarterback. Next comes the realization that the quarterback is inviting the defender to continue his rush and follow him away from the line of scrimmage. If the defender is near the quarterback, he should continue the rush, hurry the throw, and raise his arms to try to deflect the ball as it leaves the quarterback's hand. If the defender recognizes that the offensive player assigned to block him sets up, hits him once, and then begins to move to the outside, the defender should stop his rush, turn, and follow the offensive player. As the defender moves to the outside, he should try to locate the eligible receiver, move to him, look for the ball, and be ready to make an interception or the tackle if a catch is made.

DEFENSIVE LINEMAN DRILLS

Before they take on live offensive blockers, defensive linemen should practice getting off the ball and hitting with their shoulder pads and hands against a big bag or sled. When working on any of these techniques, the defensive lineman can go through the motions without having an offensive player blocking him. Without a blocker, players can repeat the movement many times and won't become as fatigued or go through the pounding that comes with contact.

INSTANT MOVEMENT ON THE BALL

Purpose: To improve the reaction time of defensive linemen to the snap of the ball.

Procedure:

1. **The coach lines up at the offensive center's position on one knee with a ball on the ground.**

2. **Defensive linemen move into their positions.**

3. **When the coach snaps the ball, the defensive linemen charge straight ahead.**

Coaching points: When defensive linemen are practicing the start, someone should make a movement like the center's snapping of the ball. If the defensive lineman is charging straight ahead, he takes a quick forward step with his back foot, keeping his back straight, shoulders low and square, and his head and eyes up. The important thing is to attack the line of scrimmage.

Variations: This drill is also good for practicing control steps and crossover steps. To practice the control step, the coach calls out the direction of the first control step when he snaps the ball. To practice the crossover step, the coach calls out which foot to use in the crossover when he snaps the ball.

FACING THE DRIVE BLOCK

Purpose: To give defensive linemen experience defeating the drive block.

Procedure:

1. **The coach stands to the side of the defensive lineman. Another defensive lineman serves as the offensive blocker and lines up opposite the defensive lineman. The coach tells the defensive player the side of main gap responsibility.**

2. **The coach calls out the snap count to start the drive. The blocker executes the drive block.**

3. **The defensive lineman reacts to the drive block.**

Coaching points: The defensive player should move the instant that the blocker starts forward. He should keep his shoulder pads below the blocker's pads. At contact his head should slide to his gap responsibility, his arms should extend, and he should separate from the blocker. He should continue to drive the blocker for four or five steps until the coach blows a whistle.

Variation: This drill is good for working on the hook block as well. For the hook block, the defensive lineman serving as the blocker lines up to the side of the defensive lineman.

PLAYING THE ANGLE BLOCK

Purpose: To give defensive linemen experience defeating the angle block.

Procedure:

1. The coach stands to the side of the defensive lineman. The defensive lineman sets up on the line, and two offensive linemen line up, one in front of the defensive lineman and one to the side.
2. The coach calls out the snap count to start the drive.
3. The defensive lineman reacts to the angle block from the side. The offensive lineman who lined up opposite the defensive lineman is not blocking and can step to the inside.

Coaching points: The defensive player must start forward on the movement of the offensive blockers. He must lean into the angle block as it develops. Against the scoop block, he needs to direct his charge into the second blocker and push him back into the offensive backfield. Against a double team, he must play both blockers and go to the ground by dropping the side of his body that is nearer the angle blocker to keep from being driven off the line.

Variations: This drill can also be used to work on the scoop block and the double-team block. When working on the scoop block or the double-team block, the offensive lineman who lines up opposite the defensive lineman does block. The defensive lineman must correctly defeat the block.

BLOCKER IN THE HOLE

Purpose: To give defensive linemen experience defeating the trap block.

Procedure:

1. The coach lines up in the offensive backfield with an offensive lineman, a tight end (or another offensive lineman), and a trapping defensive lineman.
2. The coach calls the snap count to start the play. The offensive player in front of the defensive man blocks to the inside, the tight end blocks straight ahead, and the trapping lineman pulls and tries to trap the defensive player.
3. The defensive lineman sees and reacts to the trap block.

Coaching points: Against a trap block, the defensive player should take short steps to protect against a drive or angle block. He then should stop his charge, look inside, and turn to face the trapping lineman. At contact he should bring his outside forearm across the blocker's face and chest.

Variation: This drill also works for the lead block. For the lead block, an additional blocker sets up in the backfield and lead blocks the defensive lineman.

ATTACKING THE TARGET AREA

Purpose: To give the defensive lineman practice sprinting to where he thinks the quarterback will set up.

Procedure:

1. A shirt or dummy is placed directly behind the ball 7 yards off the line of scrimmage to mark the target area. The coach stands behind the target area to observe the defensive linemen.
2. The defensive linemen form one line. The first defensive lineman gets into his normal stance on the line.
3. The defensive lineman can start the play on his own or react to someone simulating the snap.
4. The defensive lineman takes a quick charge and runs to the target area as fast as he can.

Coaching points: When attacking the target area, defensive linemen should move from one side of the ball to the other. The defensive lineman should change his stance from a running-defense stance to more of a pass-rush stance. After the defensive lineman is coming off the ball on the snap and attacking the target area, the coach can begin to teach the pass-rush techniques to defeat an offensive blocker. The coach should walk through each technique, making certain that the player's movements and steps are correct. Then players can speed up their movements in preparation for actual blockers.

STRAIGHT-AHEAD BULL RUSH

Purpose: To reinforce proper technique for a straight-ahead bull rush.

Procedure:

1. The coach stands to the side of the defensive lineman. The defensive lineman lines up in front of the offensive lineman, who is set up to pass protect.
2. On the coach's snap count, the defensive lineman rushes using a straight-ahead bull rush to get past the offensive lineman.
3. The coach provides feedback.

Coaching points: In any pass-rush drill, the defensive lineman needs to move forward in a low charge on the snap and slowly come up as he nears the blocker. The drill should continue until the defensive man reaches the target area or the coach blows a whistle. The pass rusher or the coach should determine before the snap which rush technique to use.

Variations: This drill is useful for practicing other pass-rush technique as well. For the bull and jerk, the offensive lineman lunges at the defensive lineman. For the shoulder-club and arm-slip pass rush and the wrist-club and arm-over pass rush, the defensive lineman lines up on the outside shoulder of the blocker. For the rip and run pass rush, the defensive man lines up directly in front of the blocker.

REACTING OFF A PASS RUSH

Purpose: To reinforce proper reaction technique to a draw or screen play.

Procedure:

1. The coach stands to the side of the defensive lineman. The defensive lineman lines up in front of the offensive lineman, who is set up to pass protect. A running back is in a split-back position, and the quarterback is in a shotgun position with a ball.

2. The coach indicates to the offensive players whether the play will be a draw or a screen.

3. On the coach's snap count, the defensive lineman rushes, using a straight-ahead bull rush to get past the offensive lineman.

4. The offensive players execute the play called, and the defensive player reacts.

5. The coach provides feedback.

Coaching points: In any pass-rush drill, the defensive lineman needs to move forward in a low charge on the snap and slowly come up as he nears the blocker. The drill should continue until the defensive man reaches the ballcarrier or the coach blows the whistle. Initially, the coach should walk through the drill so that the defensive player gets a picture of each offensive action. The defender must rush hard and must not stand up to see whether the play is a draw or a screen. The defensive player must be alert for the opportunity to cause a fumble when coming from behind an offensive ballcarrier to make a tackle.

Variations: The coach tells the defender which play is going to be run so that he has the proper reaction. The coach can also add a true drop-back pass play so that the defender must really rush. Finally, the drill can be run under gamelike conditions: The offensive players huddle up, the quarterback gives them the play call and snap count, and the defensive player must recognize and react to the play in full speed.

LINEBACKERS

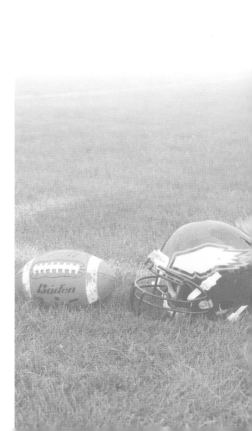

inebacker may be the most difficult position on the defensive side of the ball. On a single play, the linebacker may defeat a blocker, tackle the ballcarrier, and stop a running play. On the next, he may have to read the pass play, react to his coverage assignment, and play pass defense.

Being a linebacker is demanding from both a physical and mental standpoint. A linebacker has a great deal to learn and do, but the position can be a lot of fun. Most linebackers have a real love of football and have fun both in practice and during games. Often they set the tempo at practice, liven up drills, and make the practice time pass quickly.

Linebacker is a challenging position to learn, and players should not become discouraged if playing the position is difficult at first. To be an outstanding linebacker, a player must use the proper stance, understand who can block him, move on the ball, defeat various kinds of blocks, drop into man-to-man or zone coverage as needed, and blitz to reach the quarterback.

STANCE

The linebacker's stance varies depending on whether he plays inside or outside. The initial stance must allow him to react to a variety of blocks and permit easy movement into his pass defense responsibility. The stance used by a linebacker depends on the style of his team's defense. Both inside and outside linebackers should bend at the knees and not at the waist, keep the back straight, and keep the head up and the eyes focused straight ahead.

An inside linebacker starts with his feet even, pointing straight ahead and about shoulder-width apart. He bends a little at the knees and brings his shoulders forward slightly, in front of his feet. Keeping his elbows in against his body, he lifts his forearms up and out so that they extend in front of his body. His hands are open, and his fingers are spread (figure 8.1).

An outside linebacker's stance is much like an inside linebacker's stance, but it varies depending on whether the outside linebacker has a blocker in front of him. When an outside linebacker lines up in front of an offensive tackle, he uses the same stance as an inside linebacker does. When he lines up in front of a tight end, he moves his outside foot back slightly until it is even with the middle of his inside foot (figure 8.2a). He keeps his hands up to react to the tight end's block. An outside linebacker who has no one in front of him can drop his outside foot so that the toe is slightly behind the heel of his inside foot (figure 8.2b). When playing in this position, the outside linebacker can narrow his stance and allow his hands and arms to hang at his side in a relaxed manner. A linebacker should not change his stance when blitzing so that the offense won't be able to tell that he is rushing until the ball is snapped.

Figure 8.1 Inside linebacker's stance.

Figure 8.2 Outside linebacker's stances: *(a)* lined up opposite a tight end and *(b)* lined up with no opponent in front of him.

MOVING ON THE BALL

The offense has the advantage of knowing when the play will start. To neutralize this advantage, the linebacker must concentrate on the ball and be prepared to move the instant that the center begins the snap.

The linebacker position requires quick movement in many directions. A linebacker must move in a quick, decisive manner. Whether attacking straight ahead to defeat a blocker, coming on a blitz, moving in pursuit, or dropping for pass coverage, the linebacker needs to move with instant quickness. He must start moving with the snap of the ball.

Each move requires a different start. The body and mind become comfortable and respond to what is practiced, so learning the proper start and steps is important. When moving forward, the linebacker should step up with short, choppy, powerful steps that keep him balanced and allow him to engage an offensive blocker aggressively. He needs to practice the first step with both feet, because the foot used for the first step depends on the path of the blocker.

On a blitz, the linebacker rolls over the foot in the direction that he is going and takes a quick step up with the other foot. An outside linebacker uses a long stride to cover a great deal of ground. An inside linebacker uses a shorter first step so that he can be ready to take on blockers. When moving in pursuit, the linebacker first takes a shuffle step in the direction that he wants to go. He then slides his trailing foot until it is under his hips. The starting movement and steps must be quick and decisive.

When dropping into zone pass defense, the linebacker first takes a crossover step. He turns slightly, leans, and rolls over the foot in the direction that he wants to go. He quickly steps with the opposite foot, bringing his foot and leg across his body. He should now be moving to his zone. When going into man-to-man coverage, the linebacker's first movement is a step back away from the line of scrimmage. He must keep his hips and shoulders square to the line of scrimmage. He can adjust his movement after the offensive blocker makes his move.

DEFEATING BLOCKS

Every defensive player must understand that he has to defeat at least one blocker before he will be in position to tackle the ballcarrier. The first step to becoming a great linebacker is to know the order in which different blockers come. Some blockers get to the linebacker quickly, and he has to react instantly. Other blockers take longer to get to him, giving him time to position himself properly.

Blocking Progression

When linebackers know the order in which blockers will come at them, they can more easily stay calm, get into position to defeat the block, and move to the ballcarrier. They start by focusing on the first blocker and then move from one blocker to the next in a relaxed, controlled progression. To understand block progression, linebackers must know in what order the blockers will come, what type of block each blocker will use, how to defeat each type of block, and how to locate the ballcarrier and be part of the tackle.

Against any offensive running play, after the ball is snapped the linebacker must follow these actions in precise order. The linebacker first determines who is trying to block him and then analyzes what type of block is going to be used. He defeats the block, locates the ballcarrier, and makes the tackle.

Let's first look at the inside linebacker playing in front of the center. Most likely, the center is the first to attack the inside linebacker. Next, one of the offensive guards attacks the inside linebacker, most likely the guard opposite the direction of the center's block. Third, one of the offensive tackles blocks the inside linebacker, usually the tackle to the side of the backfield movement. Fourth, any lead back may block him, and the tight end may follow (figure 8.3).

When an inside linebacker is playing in front of the offensive guard, the first blocker he must concentrate on is the guard. If the guard blocks to the inside on the nose

Figure 8.3 Inside linebacker's blocking progression.

tackle, the inside linebacker's next blocker is the offensive tackle to the linebacker's side. After looking for the offensive tackle, he needs to look to the guard from the other side of the formation, then any lead back, and finally the tight end to his side (figure 8.4).

An outside linebacker who is playing in front of an offensive tackle to the tight end side first looks to the offensive tackle. If the offensive tackle blocks to the inside or pulls to the outside and does not block the outside linebacker, the linebacker must locate the tight end. After looking for the tight end, he looks for the offensive guard on his side and then the near back who may be leading through the line. The final blocker is the offensive guard from the opposite side of the formation (figure 8.5).

An outside linebacker who lines up in front of an offensive tackle on the open side can eliminate the tight end as a blocker. The order of his blocking progression is the offensive tackle in front of him, the offensive guard on his side, an offensive back who can be a lead blocker, and finally the offensive guard from the other side of the offensive center.

For an outside linebacker who lines up in front of an offensive tight end, the tight end is his first blocker, and the offensive tackle on his side is number two. The order of the rest of the blockers is the same as if he were playing in front of the offensive tackle (figure 8.6, page 156).

When playing in open space, the order of the blockers changes for an outside linebacker. The first blocker to focus on is the offensive guard on his side. Next is any lead

Figure 8.4 Inside linebacker's blocking progression.

Figure 8.5 Blocking progressions for an outside linebacker lined up on an offensive tackle on the tight end side and on the open side.

back lined up on his side, and third is the offensive guard from the opposite side of the formation. Besides looking for these three blockers, he must know whether he is facing a team that pulls the center to block on the linebacker or uses an outside wide receiver to crack block on him (figure 8.7).

Figure 8.6 Blocking progression for an outside linebacker lined up in front of a tight end.

Figure 8.7 Blocking progression for an outside linebacker lined up in open space.

Beating Drive Blocks

A drive block on a linebacker comes from an offensive blocker lined up directly in front of the linebacker. The blocker comes straight at the linebacker and tries to drive the linebacker back off the line of scrimmage. The linebacker starts his momentum toward the blocker (figure 8.8a). He must have a wide base and take short, powerful steps to meet and defeat the block.

The linebacker should try to make first contact (figure 8.8b). He should keep his shoulder pads slightly below the blocker's shoulder pads. In this position, the linebacker will be able to keep the blocker from getting under him and driving him off the line of scrimmage.

Unless the linebacker is responsible for plugging the running lanes on both sides of the blocker (two-gap responsibility), he is responsible for only one side of the drive blocker. As he steps forward and his shoulder pads make contact with the offensive blocker, he slides his helmet to the side of his gap responsibility (figure 8.8c). The linebacker should use his pads, not his helmet, to make contact with the blocker.

The instant that the linebacker's shoulder pads make contact, he extends his arms so that the palms of both hands make contact at the numbers of the offensive blocker's jersey (figure 8.8d). He then straightens his arms, separates from the blocker, throws the blocker aside, and gets ready to attack the ballcarrier.

If the linebacker is blitzing through a gap, he moves directly to one side of the blocker on the snap of the ball. In a blitz defense, the linebacker must fight back into the blocker and not let the blocker use the linebacker's own momentum to drive him out of the hole.

Figure 8.8 Linebacker defeating a drive block: He *(a)* moves to the blocker, *(b)* makes contact with his shoulder pads below the blocker's pads, *(c)* slides his helmet to the side of his gap responsibility, and *(d)* extends his arms for separation and moves the blocker aside.

Beating Hook Blocks

An outside linebacker has to face and defeat hook blocks. A tight end often uses this block on wide running plays to his side. The tight end's objective when using the hook block is to block the linebacker's penetration across the line and stop him from moving to the right or left down the line of scrimmage. Tight ends are more agile and quicker than offensive linemen. The hook block does not require a great deal of power; instead, it relies on the speed of the blocker to get into position on the linebacker.

Defeating this block starts with understanding the block progression. First, the linebacker focuses on the tight end lined up directly in front of him. His focus stays on the tight end until he is certain that the tight end is not attacking him.

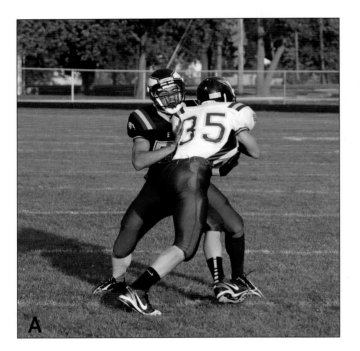

Recognition of the block is the key to stopping it. When the play begins, the linebacker will see the tight end move laterally rather than directly at the linebacker. The tight end will try to get into a position in which his helmet is outside the linebacker's shoulder pad so that he can drive his shoulder away from his movement into the linebacker's belly and hip. As the linebacker takes his first, short step forward, he sees the tight end's helmet and shoulder pads move laterally. He quickly extends both arms into the tight end, trying to make contact with the palms of both hands on the front portion of the tight end's shoulder pads (figure 8.9a).

If he extends his hands and arms into the tight end quickly enough, the linebacker will have the greater power at the moment of contact. The tight end's momentum may still be lateral rather than forward, which will help the linebacker reposition the tight end

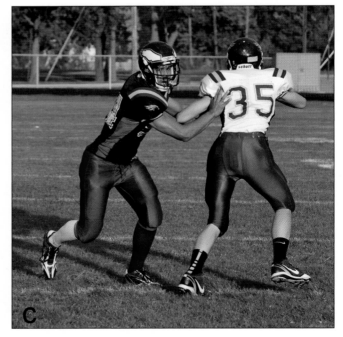

Figure 8.9 Linebacker defeating a hook block: He *(a)* extends his arms to the tight end's shoulder pads, *(b)* drives the tight end into the backfield, and *(c)* sheds the tight end and moves to the ballcarrier.

(figure 8.9b). As the linebacker's hands make contact, he continues to take short power steps and drives the tight end back across the line of scrimmage into the offensive backfield. In this position, the linebacker is able to control the tight end, preventing him from using his shoulder pads to get into the linebacker's legs or body. After the tight end is under control, the linebacker should look up and locate the ballcarrier. Based on the path of the ballcarrier, the linebacker will know the direction that he wants to move. He sheds the blocker in the opposite direction (figure 8.9c) and quickly moves to get in on the tackle.

Beating Angle Blocks

All linebackers need to learn to recognize the angle block quickly. This block is used mostly against inside linebackers, but it can also be used against outside linebackers. The outside linebacker who lines up in front of the tight end may be angle blocked by a wingback blocking from the outside or by an offensive tackle blocking from the inside.

The instant that the offensive player lined up in front of the linebacker blocks to one side, the linebacker should be alert for an angle block. The angle block will come from the opposite side of the movement of the blocker directly in front of the linebacker. If the blocker in front of the linebacker moves right, the angle blocker will come from the left. This block comes the instant that the ball is snapped. Usually the linebacker does not have time to turn and face the angle blocker as he does when contending with a drive or hook block.

As he sees the angle blocker moving toward him, the linebacker quickly steps at the blocker with the foot on the same side as the block (figure 8.10a). He meets the blocker with the shoulder pad on that side. As the shoulder pad makes contact, the linebacker strikes with his arm and forearm. He leans into the blocker to stop the blocker's momentum. He drives the palm of his other hand into the blocker's shoulder pad and attempts to knock the blocker off balance, pushing him back where the ballcarrier wants to run (figure 8.10b).

Figure 8.10 Linebacker defeating an angle block: He (a) steps to the blocker, leading with his shoulder pad and (b) leans into the blocker and pushes him into the hole.

The linebacker's goal is to hold his ground and not let the offensive blocker drive him off the line of scrimmage. The quicker that he reacts to the block, the faster he can stop the blocker's momentum. If the linebacker can create a pile using himself and the angle blocker, the running back will be forced to run somewhere else, where other defensive players can make the tackle.

Beating Trap Blocks

Both inside and outside linebackers must be prepared to face the trap block. This block does not come at the linebacker the instant that the ball is snapped. It takes time for the play to develop and for the blocker to get to the linebacker.

Usually the trap blocker is at least two players removed from the linebacker when he lines up. For an outside linebacker, the trap blocker is either of the offensive guards. For an inside linebacker, the trap blocker is the guard or tackle on the other side of the offensive center. If neither the guard nor the tackle comes to trap block, the inside linebacker should immediately look to the outside for the tight end. The trap block may come from the outside on the tight end's side of the ball.

The trap blocker's goal is to knock the linebacker out of the hole to create a path for the ballcarrier. The trap blocker counts on two things to happen. First, he hopes that the linebacker will come across the line of scrimmage. Second, he hopes that the linebacker will be focusing on the ballcarrier and therefore will not see the trap blocker coming to block. The trap blocker will come with momentum, so the linebacker must brace himself for the block (figure 8.11a). His reaction must be quick and decisive. He turns to face the

Figure 8.11 Linebacker defeating a trap block: He *(a)* braces for contact, *(b)* brings his shoulder and forearm across the blocker, and *(c)* drives the blocker into the running lane.

blocker. He then bends his knees and brings his outside shoulder and forearm across the blocker's helmet and chest (figure 8.11b). He pushes the blocker into the hole and uses his body to block the running lane (figure 8.11c).

The inside linebacker's first read is the offensive player in front of him. If the offensive player blocks to his left, the inside linebacker looks at the offensive player to his left to make sure that the offensive player is not angle blocking him. If neither offensive player blocks him, the linebacker looks for the trap block.

The inside linebacker's first response is to attack toward the offensive side of the ball. As the inside linebacker comes up, he looks across the center to the other side of the ball to try to determine whether the guard or tackle is trying to trap block him. After he identifies the blocker, the linebacker slows his forward movement and prepares to attack the blocker. When taking on the trap blocker, he uses the same technique as the outside linebacker does, bringing his outside forearm across the blocker's helmet with as much force as he can. The goal is to put the blocker into the ballcarrier's running lane.

Both outside and inside linebackers must remember to keep their shoulders even with the blocker's pads. The linebacker's head must be up, his back straight, and his knees bent. He explodes into the blocker with the large muscles of the legs and with his forearm.

Beating Lead Blocks

All the types of blocks discussed so far have come from either an offensive lineman or a tight end. The lead block is different because the running back is the potential blocker. Both inside and outside linebackers must be prepared to take on the running back's block. A running back may not have the bulk or strength of most offensive linemen and some tight ends, but he will have quickness and explosive power, which he can incorporate into the block.

Often a bigger back, such as a fullback who is used as a lead blocker, may come at the linebacker with the technique that an offensive lineman uses on a trap or running drive block. Because of their size, smaller, quicker backs may hesitate to hit a linebacker high and will instead try to block the linebacker at the hip.

When a linebacker looks into the backfield, he often focuses on the man with the ball. The running back assigned to block him is counting on that—he wants the linebacker's concentration on the ballcarrier, not on him. For this reason, the linebacker needs to focus on the blocker. Before the snap of the ball, the linebacker should locate the position of any running back who is a potential blocker. He concentrates on the man in front of him, but he should be aware of the possibility that a running back may block him.

When a running back lines up behind the offensive tackle to the outside linebacker's side, the outside linebacker must be aware that the running back is a possible blocker. An inside linebacker must be alert for the possibility of a lead block when he sees any I-formation or offset I-formation. In either case, the linebacker must locate the running back the instant that he determines that he is not being blocked by an offensive lineman or tight end. When he sees the back coming at him, the linebacker must move forward to meet the blocker at the line of scrimmage.

If the running back is coming high, the linebacker can play the blocker as he would play a trap block. An outside linebacker can bring his outside arm across the blocker's head and shoulders and force the blocker's body into the hole where the ballcarrier wants to run. When a running back comes at the linebacker high, the linebacker needs to keep his head on the side of his gap responsibility. He must always play to one-half of the lead blocker so that he can quickly get off the block and make the tackle. He can use the forearm and shoulder away from his gap responsibility to deliver a blow on the running back if the running back tries to block the linebacker high.

If the running back's shoulders start to dip and angle to the ground, the linebacker should recognize this as a sign that the running back will try to block him at his hip. The linebacker should extend both hands hard into the top of the running back's shoulder pads. As the linebacker pushes the blocker's head and shoulders down into the ground, he straightens his arms, keeping his feet and legs away from the blocker. An inside linebacker plays the lead block the same way, using his hands and arms to keep the blocker away from his legs.

BLITZING

Rushing across the line of scrimmage to blitz the quarterback or ballcarrier is tremendous fun for a linebacker. He gets to be the aggressor and go after the quarterback or the ballcarrier instead of reacting to offensive blocks or dropping into pass coverage.

A linebacker may run a blitz when the offense runs or passes the ball. When attacking the line of scrimmage against a running play, he should use the same block progression reads that he uses from his normal alignment (pages 154-156). With the momentum of the blitz, he should use the techniques described in the previous sections to defeat the various blocks. Blitzing against a running play can disrupt the blocking of the play and force the ballcarrier to alter his path, often resulting in a tackle for a loss.

Blitzing linebackers must understand that getting a sack is not the only way to defeat a pass play. Forcing the quarterback to leave the pocket and run can cause a poor pass or at least force the pass into only half of the field. Rushing a quarterback who does not run may force him to make the throw before the receiver becomes open. Another way that a linebacker can influence a pass play is to anticipate when the quarterback is going to throw the ball. As the quarterback starts to throw, the linebacker stretches his arms up to deflect or redirect the ball. All three actions can result in a successful pass defense.

Blitzing means that the usual roles are reversed. When a linebacker plays against a running play, he must react to the block being used by the offense. When the offensive lineman or running back sets up to pass block and the linebacker is on a blitz, the linebacker is the one making the moves and the offensive blocker is in the position of reacting to what the linebacker decides to do. As he gets ready to blitz, the linebacker needs to anticipate when the offense is going to try to pass the ball. He concentrates on the ball and starts moving forward the instant that the center moves the ball. He identifies and defeats the offensive pass blocker and then accelerates to the quarterback.

Before working on pass-rush technique, the linebacker should work on getting off and sprinting to the target area, the place where he thinks that the quarterback will set up. When practicing attacking the target area, the linebacker should rush from both sides of the ball. After he is coming off the ball on the snap and attacking the target area well, he can begin to learn pass-rush techniques to defeat offensive blockers. The linebacker should walk through each technique, making certain that his movements and steps are correct. After he has mastered the correct form, he can speed up his movements in preparation for working against a blocker.

When coming on a blitz, the linebacker must be prepared to be blocked by a big offensive lineman or a smaller offensive back. The linebacker should try to determine immediately who is assigned to block him as he moves on the snap of the ball. He must focus on defeating the blocker before going after the quarterback or the ballcarrier.

When the Running Back Blocks

When the linebacker sees that a running back has been assigned to block him on a pass play, he should determine how to defeat the running back. If the running back is short, one of the most effective ways to get around him is the arm-over technique. The linebacker immediately squares himself with his blocker, turning his chest to face the blocker's chest. He takes a short inside step and moves his head to the inside (fakes) when he is two steps away from the blocker. The linebacker uses his outside arm and hand to hit the blocker's shoulder pads, driving his shoulder and arm toward the blocker's chest. The linebacker steps to the outside and brings his inside arm up and over the blocker's shoulder. He drives his elbow into the blocker's back and sprints past the blocker to the quarterback.

The goal of the bull rush is not to get around the blocker but to drive the blocker back into the quarterback. By forcing the blocker into the quarterback, the linebacker interrupts the quarterback's throwing motion, possibly forcing the quarterback to throw before he is ready. As the linebacker reaches the blocker, he drives the palms of both hands into the blocker's armpits (figure 8.12*a*). He pushes his arms forward and up, raising the blocker up and back. He uses short, quick steps to drive the blocker back into the quarterback (figure 8.12*b*). The linebacker keeps driving the blocker back until he reaches the quarterback or the whistle blows. This type of rush is effective against a

Figure 8.12 Linebacker executing a bull rush: He *(a)* drives his hands into the blocker and *(b)* pushes forward and up, driving the blocker back into the quarterback.

Figure 8.13 Linebacker executing a bull and jerk rush: He *(a)* grabs the blocker's jersey, *(b)* jerks the blocker to one side, and *(c)* steps across and drives to the quarterback.

running back who backs up toward the quarterback and never gets set to stop the charge.

The bull and jerk rush is a variation of the normal bull rush and should be practiced right from the start. If the linebacker is successful in pushing the blocker into the quarterback, the blocker may set his feet and try to lunge or fire out at the linebacker. The linebacker must be ready for this as he charges straight at the blocker, using the blocker's forward thrust to pull the blocker out of the way. When the linebacker sees the blocker set and his chest and helmet come at the linebacker, the linebacker grabs the front of the blocker's jersey in both hands (figure 8.13*a*). He jerks or pulls the blocker's body to one side (figure 8.13*b*). He steps across the blocker's body with the foot on the same side as the jerk and drives past the blocker to the target area (figure 8.13*c*).

When an Offensive Lineman Blocks

If an inside linebacker is going to blitz directly over an offensive guard or if an outside linebacker sees an offensive lineman moving out to block him, they must be ready to get around these bigger players to reach the quarterback.

If the guard is the same height or shorter, the linebacker can use the arm-over blitz technique covered in the previous section. The arm-over technique is more difficult to complete if the offensive blocker is taller than the linebacker is. When going against a taller offensive blocker, the linebacker may want to use the arm-under blitz technique. This pass-rush technique is ideal for a shorter player to learn and perfect. The linebacker steps quickly with his inside foot. He takes a long step with his outside foot, putting himself in position to touch the blocker (figure 8.14*a*). He uses his outside hand and arm to hit hard into the under part of the blocker's shoulder pad, lifting the blocker's shoulder and arm (figure 8.14*b*). The linebacker steps to the outside of the blocker with his inside foot and drops his inside shoulder, driving it under the blocker's outside armpit. The linebacker pushes back, or bows, the blocker's neck and back. He drives his hips up and past the blocker and keeps moving to the quarterback (figure 8.14*c*).

Figure 8.14 Linebacker executing the arm-under blitz technique: He (a) takes a long step to meet the blocker, (b) hits the under part of the blocker's shoulder pad, and (c) drives his shoulder into the blocker, lifting him up and back and drives to the quarterback.

MAN-TO-MAN COVERAGE

When asked to cover a receiver man-to-man, usually the linebacker covers a running back coming out of the offensive backfield. The linebacker begins 7 to 8 yards away from the man he is assigned to cover. Often he covers the running back all by himself, but sometimes he and another linebacker work together to cover the running back. Man-to-man coverage requires great concentration, good technique, and an understanding of what the running back may do to get open.

In man-to-man coverage, a linebacker backpedals, adjusts his backward run from a straight line to an angle (angle backpedal), shifts out of his backward run into a forward run without losing momentum (rolling over), and recognizes the pass pattern being run by the running back. After he learns these four techniques, the linebacker is ready to line up and cover any offensive back as he comes running out of the backfield to catch the ball.

For successful man-to-man coverage, the linebacker needs to use proper technique, recognize pass routes, roll over the foot in the direction of the coverage, and sprint to the running back. He must look back for the ball only when he can touch the running back and is in position to see the running back and the ball at the same time. He keeps his body between the receiver and his goal line. If the receiver does make the catch, the linebacker must be in position to make the tackle.

Footwork

For the backpedal, the linebacker begins in his normal stance. He pushes off his inside foot and steps back with his outside foot to begin the backpedal. After taking the first step, he narrows the distance between his feet to no more than hip-width apart. He leans forward slightly with his shoulders just ahead of his hips. He allows his hands and arms to swing in normal running motion. With each step, he reaches back and does not push his body with his feet (figure 8.15). He continues running in this manner for 10 yards.

Not every running back is going to run straight down the field. To get around the offensive linemen, the running back will have to release out of the backfield at an angle. The linebacker must adjust his backpedal to mirror the action of the running back. If the running back angles to the outside, the linebacker needs to backpedal at an angle to the outside; if the running back angles to the inside, the linebacker does the same.

When changing the angle of the backpedal, the linebacker must not cross his feet. He must keep a smooth backward run and keep his head and shoulders in front of his hips. After backpedaling straight back for 5 yards, the linebacker angles to his left by swinging his right leg around to change direction. To return to a straight backpedal, he swings his left leg around to change direction. To angle backpedal to the right, he changes the direction of his backpedal by swinging his left leg back and around.

During any pass play in which the linebacker is in man-to-man coverage, he may need to shift out of the backward run and into a forward run. This occurs when he recognizes the pass route being run by the

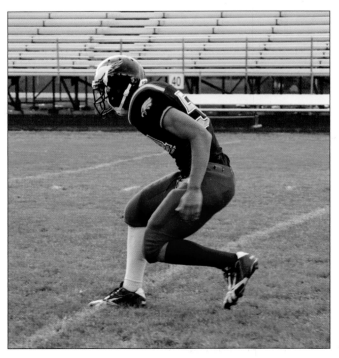

Figure 8.15 Linebacker's backpedal.

back or when the back gets within 3 yards of him. Going from a backward run to a forward run is a vital part of man-to-man coverage. The key is to maintain momentum, keeping the feet under the hips and always rolling over the foot in the direction that he desires to go. Learning this skill and understanding exactly what path to take to get to the interception point will make him a much better linebacker.

The linebacker quickly shifts from his backward run into a forward run at a 45-degree angle. To angle left, he leans his upper body back and to the left, rolling over his left foot. As he leans, his shoulders turn to the left. He will feel his right foot come across the front of his body as he continues to run.

When the linebacker rolls over his foot in the direction that he wants to go, he maintains his momentum and is able to run at top speed. He keeps both feet directly under his hips, allowing him to adjust to any double-move pass routes, such as a corner pattern.

Recognizing Pass Routes

After the linebacker can backpedal, angle backpedal, and roll over into a forward run with ease, he is ready to learn to recognize pass routes. He starts by learning the three areas on the field in which various pass routes will be run. The short zone is up to 6 or 7 yards from the line of scrimmage, the medium zone is from about 8 to 12 yards, and the deep zone is more than 12 yards.

The linebacker should think in terms of the three zones. When the running back is in the short zone, the linebacker only has to think about the pass routes that the running back can run in that area. As the running back moves to the medium zone, the linebacker looks only for medium routes. After the running back goes past the medium zone, the focus is on deep pass routes.

The running back will run three basic patterns in the short zone. The flat and wide routes are run to the outside. The angle route brings the running back across the center of the field (see figure 4.14, page 87). In the medium zone, the running back may run a stop route, usually at about 7 yards, or an in or out route at 10 yards (see figure 4.15, page 88). In the deep zone, the running back can run a flat and up, seam, post, or fan pass route. For a linebacker, these four deep pass routes are the most difficult to cover. The linebacker has to run farther, the ball is in the air longer, and the offense has a chance for a long gain (see figure 4.16, page 89).

When in man-to-man coverage, the linebacker must stay to one side of the running back as the running back comes down the field. If an inside linebacker is covering the running back by himself, he should try to keep his outside shoulder even with the running back's inside shoulder. An outside linebacker is in the opposite position—his inside shoulder should be even with the running back's outside shoulder. If the linebacker gets directly in front of the running back, the running back will be able to cut either way without difficulty.

When playing man-to-man coverage, the defender should remember that an incompletion is just as good as stopping a running play for no gain. The linebacker should never take himself out of coverage by guessing the pass route, reaching behind the receiver to deflect the ball with only one hand, or looking back for the ball for an interception. He must stay with the running back and make an interception only when he is certain that he can make the catch.

When a linebacker has a running back in man-to-man pass coverage and the running back sets up to pass protect block, the linebacker must continue to focus on the man he has in coverage until the play is over. The linebacker should set up in a position 5 yards off the line of scrimmage and 2 yards outside the position of the man he has in coverage.

From this position, the linebacker can see the quarterback hand the ball to the running back on the draw play, quickly attack the running lane that the ballcarrier is trying to use, and make the tackle.

If the running back sets for two counts and then releases to the outside for a screen pass, the linebacker must instantly go to him before any potential blocker has the opportunity to release and block for the running back. The linebacker should drive for a position where he can either intercept or deflect the screen pass or instantly tackle the running back after he makes the reception.

Both reactions can take place only if the linebacker maintains a constant focus on the running back and does not allow himself to drop deeper than 5 yards or look for other receivers coming into his area.

ZONE COVERAGE

Playing zone pass defense is the opposite of playing man-to-man pass defense. In man-to-man coverage, the focus is on the running back. The linebacker allows the receiver whom he is covering to tell him where to go by running a route, and the linebacker runs all over the field to cover the receiver for the entire length of the play. In zone defense, the linebacker is assigned to a specific area of the field. He reacts to any pass thrown in that area regardless of who is trying to make the catch. When playing zone defense, the linebacker must recognize the pass play, go immediately to his zone, get as deep in his zone as he can before the quarterback sets to throw, focus on the quarterback and the ball, and react to the pass. The ball directs the linebacker to the receiver.

First, the linebacker should learn the zones that he will cover. The coach should outline the names and zones that will be used in the defense. On each zone pass defense, the linebacker is assigned one of the zones. Figure 8.16 shows one way to divide the medium zones on the field.

The technique that the linebacker uses to drop into his zone depends on how wide he has to go from his original position to get into the zone. The wider he has to go, the more he will have to sprint. When he sprints, the linebacker rolls over the foot in the direction that he needs to go and runs as fast as he can to his area. He should constantly look back over his shoulder to the quarterback.

After he reaches his zone, he swings his inside leg around and begins to backpedal. As he starts to backpedal, he focuses on the quarterback. When he sees that the quarterback is ready to throw, he stops his backpedal but keeps running in place, moving his feet in short, choppy steps. He prepares to move to either his right or his left when he sees the quarterback start to throw. The linebacker breaks to the ball by rolling over the foot in the direction that he needs to go.

One challenge that a linebacker faces when playing zone defense is keeping his eyes on the quarterback and not looking at a receiver running into his zone. The linebacker may want to come up to cover the receiver before the ball is thrown, but he must resist this temptation. He

Figure 8.16 Linebacker's zone coverage in the medium zone.

must practice going to his zone, looking at the quarterback, backpedaling, and then reacting to the right or left based on the throw. He should let the quarterback and the ball take him to the receiver. Focusing on the quarterback and the ball gives him a great chance to make an interception.

When playing zone pass coverage, the reaction of the linebackers to a draw or screen pass will be different in that they must first concentrate on moving to their assigned zones rather than focus on one offensive player.

The linebacker will likely be moving away from the line of scrimmage when he recognizes that the offense is running a draw or screen pass play. An inside linebacker can help defeat the draw play if he backpedals for the first few steps until the quarterback is past the running back and not in position to hand him the ball. With this technique, the linebacker can keep his shoulders square to the line of scrimmage and quickly come up if he sees the draw play being run.

To react to the screen pass from zone pass coverage, the linebacker usually has to avoid the offensive blocker coming from the inside. Because of his depth off the line, the linebacker will not normally reach the running back until after the back has made the reception.

When the linebacker has a defensive back in the zone to his outside, he should go to the inside of the lead blocker, taking a path between the offensive tackle and guard or guard and center (figure 8.17a). When the linebacker is assigned to the outside zone on the side of the screen pass, he must stay outside the first blocker and make certain that the running back is forced to the inside of the field toward the other defensive players (figure 8.17b).

An inside linebacker reacting to a screen pass must be alert for the second blocker releasing to the outside and trying to turn back on him using a running drive block. If the running back is to his outside, the inside linebacker should try to go in front of this second blocker, move to the outside, and not give the running back a free lane up the field.

Figure 8.17 Linebacker's coverage for the screen pass.

LINEBACKER DRILLS

Linebackers should practice getting off the ball and hitting with the shoulder pads and hands against a big bag or sled before taking on offensive blockers. Of course, a bag or sled does not attack the way that an offensive lineman will.

STARTING FORWARD TO THE BLOCKER

Purpose: To improve quickness getting off with the snap.

Procedure:

1. The coach sets up at the center's position on one knee with a ball on the ground. Linebackers line up in their normal alignment on the defensive side of the line of scrimmage.
2. When the coach moves the ball, the linebacker moves.
3. This drill is good for fine-tuning starts from many positions.

Coaching points: Players should go one at a time. They should line up in their normal stance before the movement of the ball. The focus is on the first two or three steps of each movement.

Variation: This drill is also good for practicing the start on a blitz. The coach should clearly define the start that they are working on. To use the drill to practice starting in pursuit by moving laterally to the ballcarrier, the setup is the same except that the coach calls out the direction of the pursuit after moving the ball. To practice starting when dropping into zone coverage, the setup is the same except that the coach raises the ball into the air to alert the linebacker to drop. To practice starting when dropping into man-to-man coverage, the setup is the same except that the coach calls out man coverage before moving the ball.

BEATING THE DRIVE BLOCK

Purpose: To reinforce proper technique when defeating the drive block and shedding the blocker.

Procedure:

1. The coach stands to the side of the linebacker. Another linebacker serves as the blocker.
2. To start the drill, the coach calls out the snap count and the linebacker's gap responsibility.
3. On the snap, the linebacker moves to defeat the drive block. The drill should be run at half speed at first. The tempo can increase as the defensive man masters the proper technique.

Coaching points: The linebacker needs to move forward to meet the blocker. His head should always end up on the side of his gap responsibility.

DEFEATING THE HOOK BLOCK

Purpose: To reinforce proper technique when defeating a hook block and separating from the blocker.

Procedure:

1. The coach stands to the side of the outside linebacker. The outside linebacker lines up in front of a player in the tight end position. Another outside linebacker can serve as the tight end.
2. The coach calls out the snap count to start the drill.
3. On the snap, the linebacker moves to defeat the hook block.

Coaching points: The drill should begin at half speed and later work up to full speed. The linebacker needs to get both hands on the blocker while he is still moving laterally.

DEFEATING THE ANGLE BLOCK

Purpose: To reinforce proper technique for defeating the angle block.

Procedure:

1. The coach lines up to the side of the linebacker. The linebacker and two offensive linemen get into position at the line of scrimmage.
2. The coach calls the snap count to start the play.
3. The linebacker should look at the offensive lineman in front of him and react to the angle block.

Coaching points: The linebacker must step at the angle blocker and lean into his block. The hand opposite the block needs to be driven into the shoulder pad of the blocker to knock him off balance. Initially the drill should be run at half speed.

DEFEATING THE TRAP BLOCK

Purpose: To reinforce proper technique for defeating the trap block and escaping the blocker.

Procedure:

1. The coach lines up in the offensive backfield with a tight end or offensive lineman and a trap blocker on the other side of the formation. An offensive blocker lines up directly in front of the linebacker. The trap blocker comes from the opposite side of the formation.
2. The linebacker lines up in his position.
3. The coach calls the snap count to start the play.
4. The linebacker reads the man in front of him blocking to the inside and then reacts to the trap block.

Coaching points: The linebacker should turn to face the trap or lead blocker. He must attack the blocker and not sit and wait. The drill should be run at half speed until the linebacker has learned the technique.

Variation: Inside linebackers can also use this drill to practice reading blocks and looking for the blocker. To use this drill to practice defeating the lead blocker, the setup is the same except that another blocker is added to the backfield. This second blocker lead blocks the linebacker.

FINDING THE TARGET AREA

Purpose: To train blitzing linebackers to go to the target area.

Procedure:

1. A shirt or dummy is placed directly behind the ball 7 yards off the line of scrimmage.
2. The coach lines up on the offensive side behind the target area. The linebacker lines up in his normal stance.

(continued)

Finding the Target Area *(continued)*

3. To start the drill, the linebacker moves on his own or someone simulates the snap.
4. The linebacker takes a quick charge and runs to the target area as fast as he can.

Coaching points: The linebacker must take a forward step as he starts his blitz. He should stay low on his charge and attack the target area as quickly as he can.

ARM-OVER RUSH

Purpose: To teach proper arm-over rushing technique.

Procedure:

1. The coach sets up outside the linebacker, even with the running back.
2. On the coach's signal, the linebacker pass rushes. The running back moves to block the rush.
3. The linebacker uses the arm-over technique to get past the running back and to the quarterback area.
4. The linebacker immediately squares himself with his blocker, turning his chest to face the blocker's chest.
5. He takes a short inside step and moves his head to the inside (fakes) when he is two steps from the blocker.
6. The linebacker uses his outside arm and hand to hit the blocker's shoulder pads, driving his shoulder and arm toward the blocker's chest.
7. The linebacker steps to the outside and brings his inside arm up and over the blocker's shoulder.
8. He drives his elbow into the blocker's back and sprints past the blocker to the quarterback.

Coaching points: Both inside and outside linebackers should participate in this drill and practice blitzing from both sides of the ball. The drill should begin at half speed and then increase in tempo as the linebacker masters the technique.

Variation: This drill is also helpful for practicing bull rush techniques against a running back. When using the drill to practice the bull and jerk rush, the running back lunges on the block. To practice the arm-under blitz technique, an offensive lineman sets up to block the linebacker.

BACKPEDALING

Purpose: To practice proper footwork when backpedaling.

Procedure:

1. The coach lines up in front of the linebacker.
2. On the coach's command, the linebacker starts to backpedal.
3. To practice angle backpedaling, the coach points for a change in direction as the linebacker moves back.

Coaching points: The linebacker should step back with each step, keeping his shoulders in front of his hips and swinging his arms in a normal manner. When changing to an angle backpedal, he should not cross his feet.

ROLLING OVER

Purpose: To give linebackers a sense of what it feels like to roll over when changing direction.

Procedure:

1. The linebacker stands on the sideline, facing the field. His feet are even and hip-width apart.
2. Without turning his body, the linebacker leans his head, shoulders, and upper body to the right.
3. As his body moves over his right foot, his left leg automatically comes across the front of his body. He takes a step in the direction of the lean.
4. The linebacker repeats steps 2 and 3 in the opposite direction, leaning to the left and rolling over the left foot.

Coaching points: The linebacker must roll over the foot in the direction that he is to go and must start the movement by leaning his upper body.

Variation: To practice rolling over on the move, the coach points out the direction for the linebacker to roll over.

BACKWARD TO FORWARD RUN

Purpose: To practice switching from a backpedal to a forward run.

Procedure:

1. The linebacker lines up on the line of scrimmage.
2. The coach calls the snap count to start the play. The linebacker backpedals into his coverage. He begins his backward run at half speed.
3. At 10 yards, the linebacker quickly shifts from his backward run to a forward run at a 45-degree angle deep to his left. He leans his upper body back and to the left, rolling over his left foot. As he leans, his shoulders turn to the left.
4. His right foot comes across the front of his body as he continues to run.
5. He rolls over to his right.

Coaching points: When the linebacker is comfortable rolling deep to his left and right, he can gradually increase the speed of his backward run. He should keep his momentum throughout the drill, and his feet should always be under his hips.

LEARNING PASS ROUTES

Purpose: To learn to recognize pass routes.

Procedure:

1. The coach lines up with an offensive back. The linebacker gets into position.
2. On the coach's signal, the offensive back runs the pass route called by the coach.
3. The linebacker backpedals and calls out the pass route.

Coaching points: The linebacker should stay on the proper side of the running back during the drill but not react. No ball is used during the drill.

CALLING AND POINTING OUT PASS PATTERNS

Purpose: To train linebackers to concentrate on the running back, to learn pass routes, and to know where to go in coverage.

Procedure:

1. The linebacker gets into position on the line of scrimmage. A teammate lines up on the offensive side of the ball.

2. On the coach's signal, the linebacker starts to backpedal into coverage as his teammate begins to run a pass route at half speed.

3. The instant that he recognizes the pass route, the linebacker calls out the name of the pass pattern and points to his coverage area. He keeps backpedaling while calling out the name.

Coaching points: The linebacker should call the pattern and then point out where he should go to make his coverage. After he is successful at doing this, the linebacker can react to the pass route by rolling over and driving to the running back. He should stay between the back and his own goal line.

Variation: To practice getting in good position to cover, the linebacker drives at the receiver after he calls out the pattern.

MOVING TO ZONE COVERAGE

Purpose: To reinforce proper zone coverage technique.

Procedure:

1. The coach lines up as a quarterback with the ball.

2. Facing the linebacker, the coach calls out the zone for the linebacker to drop into.

3. To start the drill, the coach calls, "Hut."

4. The coach raises the ball as if to pass, and the linebacker stops his drop.

5. The coach then steps and goes through the pass motion, causing the linebacker to react.

6. When the linebacker is dropping, setting up, and reacting to the throwing motion, the coach can throw the ball to give the linebacker practice intercepting the pass.

Coaching points: The linebacker should sprint to his zone and then backpedal to get set. He must focus on the coach and the ball. No receiver is used in the drill.

REACTING TO DRAW AND SCREEN PLAYS

Purpose: To reinforce proper reaction to both plays from zone and man-to-man coverage.

Procedure:

1. The coach lines up as a quarterback with the ball, and players are at running back and offensive tackle.
2. Facing the linebacker, the coach calls out the type of coverage to be run.
3. The coach tells the offensive players the play—draw, screen, or drop-back pass.
4. To start the drill, the coach calls, "Hut."
5. The offense runs the play, and the coach observes the linebacker's reaction.

Coaching points: The coach checks to make certain that the linebacker is executing the correct movement for the pass coverage called. The linebacker must have the proper focus and must take the correct path to the ballcarrier. Tackling does not need to be part of the drill; the defensive player can react and be in position to make the tackle.

Variation: The drill can be run by adding an offensive guard and using both an inside linebacker and an outside linebacker.

DEFENSIVE BACKS

Defensive back may be the most exciting position on the football team. The position requires a positive but not cocky attitude. The defensive back should be ready to make a touchdown-saving tackle, deflect a long pass at the last moment, or best of all, make an interception.

Successful defensive backs can't wait for the next play to begin. Ready to compete, they are eager to match their skill against the skill of the offensive player. The defensive back's off-season conditioning program should prepare him physically to run for the entire course of the game. Besides physical stamina, mental toughness is required to succeed at this position.

The skills that a defensive back needs are the proper stance, the ability to start quickly on the snap and backpedal, knowledge and recognition of pass patterns, the ability to play zone and man-to-man coverage, the ability to execute the bump and run, and the ability to play the run.

STANCE AND START

The defensive backfield is the only defensive area on the football field in which the player's first movement is backward, not forward. The defensive back must be able to move backward at the speed of the receiver driving off the line. His beginning stance must allow him to explode into a backward run. If the defensive back does not have a specific man to cover, he may have the luxury of adjusting his stance.

Playing on the outside as a corner requires discipline. The corner gets into his stance by turning his front foot to the inside toward the center of his body, under his nose, until he can feel his weight on the outside edge of the foot. He should have enough weight on the front foot that he can easily lift the back foot. At this point, he is in a position to use the larger muscles in the front of the lower leg, not just his toes, to push back when he starts. He then leans forward with his shoulders and relaxes his arms. His shoulders should be slightly in front of his forward foot. He keeps his shoulders even, his back straight, and his head and eyes up (figure 9.1a).

An inside strong safety can stand more erect. This stance gives him a good view of the entire offensive backfield. Depending on the coverage, the inside strong safety usually can bring his outside foot straight forward instead of to the center of his body under his nose (figure 9.1b). A free safety has the freedom to line up with his feet even and spread comfortably apart (figure 9.1c). He can stand erect with only a slight forward lean of his shoulders. He needs to be able to see the entire field. Both the strong and free safety should learn the corner stance, especially if they might at times be asked to cover man-to-man on an inside wide receiver or play as a corner.

Every position on the team requires specific skills. For a defensive back, the ability to start properly is crucial. From the start, he must move with the same speed and quickness as the wide receiver does. Top defensive backs start every play in a game with speed and quickness. A successful defensive back perfects the important skills of the position and then molds them into one smooth movement. By developing this ability, he can cover even the fastest offensive wide receiver.

When starting to run backward, the defensive back must explode off his front foot. With his front foot under his nose and turned in, he is able to use the muscles in both the outside of his foot and his lower leg to provide this explosion. When pushing off the front foot, he must thrust his hips backward as he steps back with his back foot. As he takes his second step, his shoulders slowly begin to rise.

This start should be practiced repeatedly—pushing off the front foot, thrusting the hips back, stepping back with the back foot, and beginning to run backward in an easy, fluid motion.

Figure 9.1 Defensive back stances: *(a)* corner; *(b)* inside strong safety; *(c)* free safety.

Backpedaling

One of the most important skills for a defensive back to master is running backward. After the defensive back is comfortable getting into the stance and getting a good start, he is ready to continue his backward movement away from the line of scrimmage.

The speed and quickness of a good defensive back running backward or backpedaling into coverage is amazing. Many of the top cornerbacks can run backward for 10 or 15 yards almost as fast as a receiver can run forward.

After he has pushed back in his start and stepped with his back foot, the defensive back is in position to continue backpedaling. He accomplishes this by lifting his feet and stepping back with each stride. The defensive back must maintain good body position and movement as he runs backward. His hips remain over his feet, and he maintains a slight forward lean at the waist, keeping his shoulders in front of his hips. He reaches back with each step, hitting on the balls of his feet. His feet are no wider than his hips. He moves his arms in a normal running motion. He keeps his head up. The backpedal looks relaxed, smooth, and continuous. In man coverage, the defensive back focuses on the receiver. In zone coverage, he focuses on the quarterback.

The backward movement should be a true run. Some defensive backs lean so far back that their hips, shoulders, and head are behind their feet. A defensive back who makes this mistake will feel as if he is pushing himself backward rather than running backward, landing on his heels instead of the balls of his feet. When this happens, the defensive back should stop backpedaling, go back, and start again. To run backward correctly, he must keep his hips over his feet and his shoulders and head in front of his hips.

Angle Backpedaling

The defensive back must learn to adjust his backward run from a straight line to an angle. One of the goals of a good wide receiver is to adjust his pass route to force the defensive back to turn and leave his backward run. When the defensive back is running toward his own goal line, the receiver has a much better chance to separate from the defensive back on any short or medium pass route.

Learning to stay in the backward run requires practice, but mastering this skill enables the defensive back to provide better coverage. This technique requires the defensive back to change the direction of his backward run without crossing his feet or turning his shoulders. After backpedaling straight for 5 yards, the defensive back angles to his left by swinging his right leg around to change direction. As his right leg swings around, his hips and shoulders remain square and in the proper position for the backpedal. To return to a straight backpedal, he swings his left leg around to change direction. To angle backpedal to the right, he changes the direction of his backpedal by swinging his left leg back and around.

The distance between the defensive back's feet should be less than the width of his hips, and he should move back with each step, landing on the balls of his feet. His hips should stay over his feet, and he should have a slight forward bend at the waist so that his shoulders and head are in front of his hips and feet. The movement should be smooth. His arms should pump easily as he runs.

Rolling Over

Great wide receivers never lose their momentum when they go into their pattern and change direction. If anything, they get faster as they run their route. If the receiver maintains his speed, the defensive back needs to keep going at full speed. The key to keeping up momentum is to roll over the foot in the direction that the defensive back desires to go. Learning this skill and knowing exactly what path to take to get to the interception point makes a player a much better defensive back.

To get an idea of what it feels like to roll over, the player should stand on the sideline, facing the field. He keeps his feet even and hip-width apart. Without turning his body, he leans his head, shoulders, and upper body to the right. As his body moves over his right foot, he will feel his left leg automatically come across the front of his body, and he will take a step in the direction of his lean. He should repeat the drill leaning and rolling over his left foot.

The defensive back should try the same technique from the backward run. Starting at half speed, the defensive back runs backward for 10 yards. He leaves his backward run and quickly changes to a forward run at a 45-degree angle deep to his left by leaning his upper body back and to the left, rolling over his left foot. As he leans, he turns his shoulders to the left. He will feel his right foot automatically come across the front of his body as he continues his run.

Rolling over is one of the most basic and important techniques for defensive backs. If they can change from a backward run to a forward run without interrupting their momentum and losing their speed, they may have a chance to play in the NFL.

Players should remember that rolling over does not start with the feet. It starts with leaning the upper body in the direction that the defensive back desires to go and then allowing the feet to follow in natural, easy steps. If a player's feet slip out from under him or if the player has the receiver covered but in the next step sees him 2 yards away, the reason is often loss of momentum. This happens when the defensive back plants one foot, stops his momentum, and then starts chasing the receiver again.

MAN-TO-MAN COVERAGE

The defensive back must play the pass first. On every play, the defensive back should start by moving backward from the line of scrimmage. If the offense runs the ball, the defensive back can stop and come up to make the tackle. If he comes up first, thinking that the play is a run when it is a pass, the receiver may be so far down the field that the defensive back will not be able recover in time to make the tackle or cause an incompletion. The defensive back needs to remember that he is the last line of defense. He must think about the pass first. When he is sure that the offense will not be throwing a pass, he can get involved in stopping the run.

In man-to-man pass defense, the defensive back looks at the man he is covering; in zone pass defense, he looks at the quarterback. In zone pass defense, the defensive back should see the ball when it leaves the quarterback's hand, but in man-to-man he may not see the ball until the last instant.

Man-to-man pass defense is an exciting challenge for the defensive back. Usually the defensive back is on his own against his opponent. In some defenses, he may have help in the middle of the field, but he still knows that he is responsible for preventing the receiver from catching the ball.

Pass Route Zones

A defensive back playing man-to-man pass defense must understand the three sets of offensive pass patterns that are run at different distances down the field. The short zone starts at the line of scrimmage and covers the first 6 or 7 yards down the field. The medium zone begins at 7 or 8 yards and continues to about 12 yards past the line of scrimmage. The deep zone is from 13 yards to the goal line (see figure 4.16, page 89).

The defensive back must know and be able to recognize these three zones. During a play, he concentrates only on the pass patterns that can be run in that zone. If he worries about recognizing every pass route that a receiver might run at the start of every play, he will quickly become flustered and end up guessing rather than recognizing the pass pattern. When the defensive back knows the zones, he only has to think about and recognize the patterns that can be run in that area. Instead of thinking about 13 or 14 patterns, he can concentrate on recognizing the 3 or 4 runs in that zone.

When playing in pass coverage, the defensive back should always cover on one side of the wide receiver or the other. He should never be directly in front of the receiver.

Pattern Recognition

One of the most important skills for a defensive back to learn is to recognize offensive pass routes (pattern recognition). When learning to recognize offensive pass patterns, the defensive back should concentrate on recognition only and not reacting to the pattern. The first thing to do is learn the names of the pass routes that he will face.

The best way to start is with the short pass routes. For wide receivers, the slant, hitch, and quick out patterns are the short pass routes (figure 5.4, page 101). The tight end's short pass routes are the look-in, short, and flat pass routes (figure 6.7, page 124). Practicing with a teammate and alternating from offense to defense will help the player recognize a pattern and run the pattern correctly.

The point at which a defensive back recognizes the pass pattern is called the recognition point. The spot where the ball will be caught is called the interception point. To identify the interception point, the defensive back must know where the receiver can first catch the ball. On any short or medium pass pattern coming to the inside of the field, the receiver will run at least 6 yards from the recognition point before he can catch the pass (figure 9.2). For a short or medium pattern going toward the sideline, the receiver will cover at least 8 yards from the recognition point before he can make the reception (figure 9.2). To recognize the pattern early and find the interception point, the defensive back must concentrate on the receiver as he runs the route.

After learning to recognize short pass routes, the defensive back must learn the medium pass routes. For the wide receiver, the medium pass routes are the out, in, and hook routes (figure 5.6, page 102). The tight end's medium patterns are the in, out, cross, and hook (figures 6.8 and 6.9, pages 125-126). The medium pass zone covers from about 8 yards to 12 yards up the field.

After correctly identifying medium routes, the defensive back can learn the patterns used in the deep pass zone. After the receiver passes 12 yards, the defensive back should look for the deep pass routes. The wide receiver's deep routes are the post, corner, up, and comeback (figure 5.8, page 105). The tight end's deep routes are the post, up, and corner (figure 6.10, page 127). Even on these deep routes, the defensive back should try to keep 3 yards between himself and the receiver. Deep pass routes to the inside of the field have an interception point 10 yards beyond the recognition point (figure 9.3). The interception point for deep patterns to the outside of the field is 13 or more yards beyond the recognition point (figure 9.3).

Figure 9.2 Defensive back recognition and interception points for a medium pass pattern to the inside of the field and a short pattern to the sideline.

Figure 9.3 Defensive back recognition and interception points for deep pass routes to the inside and outside.

The defensive back should focus only on the patterns in the zone where the receiver is. When the receiver passes 7 yards, the defensive back can forget about the pass patterns run in the short zone and concentrate on recognizing the pass patterns run in the medium zone. After the receiver passes 12 yards, the defensive back should focus only on deep pass patterns. This thought process is important because it helps the defensive back relax during his backward run and look only for the patterns run in that zone. The patterns to look for change as the receiver comes off the line of scrimmage and runs up the field.

ZONE COVERAGE

For a defensive back, zone coverage is very different from man-to-man coverage. When playing man-to-man coverage, the defensive back covers one offensive receiver all over the field for the entire play. The focus is on that one receiver, and the receiver dictates where the defensive back should go. The only real chance to look for the ball is when the defensive back is in position to see both the receiver and the ball.

Playing zone pass coverage requires the defensive back to change his way of thinking. On the snap of the ball, the defensive back moves to a predetermined area of the field. His focus is on the quarterback, not on a particular receiver. The direction of the pass, not a receiver's pass pattern, tells him where to go (ball reaction).

The defensive back can and should use all the techniques of man-to-man coverage in zone pass defense. He can backpedal into his zone and angle backpedal if necessary to stay in the proper position on the field. After the ball leaves the quarterback's hand, he should roll over to leave his backpedal. Although the techniques are the same, the defensive back must change his focus to the quarterback. He must not allow himself to get distracted by receivers running across the zone.

Zone defenses can be broken down into three types of zone pass coverages: a two-deep zone, a three-deep zone, and a four-deep zone (sometimes used against wide-open passing teams). In all three zone defenses, the number one rule for the defensive back who is covering a deep zone is to backpedal deep enough to stay between his goal line and the deepest offensive receiver in his zone.

Before the play begins, the defensive back must know which type of pass coverage has been called, zone or man-to-man. If zone pass coverage is called, he needs to know where to go, which zone to cover, how he is going to get to his zone, and what his responsibilities are when he reaches his zone.

Two-Deep Zone

In a two-deep zone (figure 9.4, page 184), usually both safeties drop deep. Each safety covers half the field. The safeties need to backpedal quickly, get as deep as possible, stay deeper than any receiver in their half of the field, look at the quarterback, and react the instant that the quarterback steps and throws the ball (get a jump).

Both corners, who cover the outside underneath zones with the linebackers, should leave their original alignment before the play begins and move 5 yards from the line of scrimmage. After the snap, the corners take position just outside the offensive receivers as they move up the field. They bump the receivers to the inside, interrupting their runs up the field and forcing them in toward the safeties. The corners then drop back to 12 yards using their backpedal technique and focus on the quarterback. They react when the ball leaves the quarterback's hand.

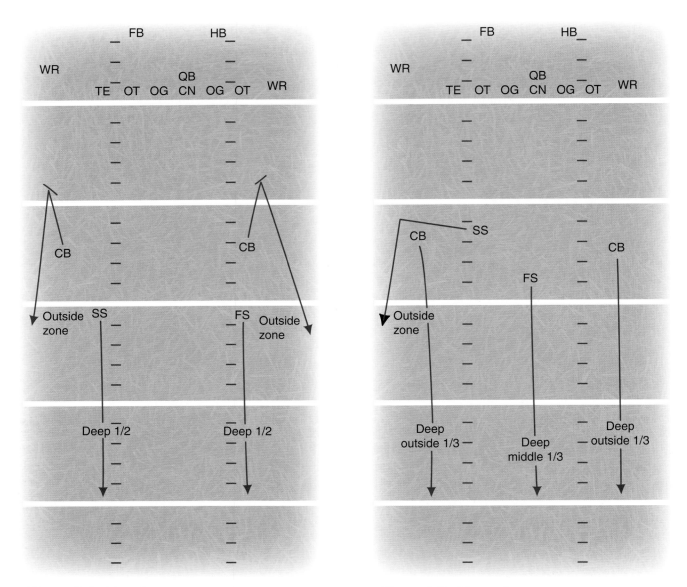

Figure 9.4 Two-deep zone coverage.   **Figure 9.5** Three-deep zone coverage.

Three-Deep Zone

In a three-deep zone (figure 9.5), three of the four defensive backs drop into a deep zone. One of the defensive backs, usually the strong safety, moves up and to the outside to cover the under zone on his side of the field.

Instead of only two defensive backs covering deep, there now are three. Each defensive back, usually the two corners and the free safety, is responsible for covering one-third of the field, or they may have one-quarter, one-quarter, and half coverage. The two corners have the outside third of the field on their side and the free safety moves to cover the center of the field. With three defensive backs going deep, the offense will be much less likely to complete a pass in the deep zone.

The defensive back must backpedal quickly, get as deep as he can, stay deeper than any receiver in his third of the field, look at the quarterback, and react the instant that the quarterback steps and throws the ball.

The safety who does not have deep coverage uses a different technique to drop into his zone. The technique that he uses depends on how wide from his original position he has to go to get into his zone. The wider he has to go, the more he will have to sprint to get there. When he sprints, he rolls over the foot in the direction that he needs to go and runs as fast as he can to his area. He constantly looks back over his shoulder to the quarterback. After he reaches his zone, he swings his inside leg around and gets into his backpedal. As he starts his backpedal, he focuses on the quarterback. He stops his backpedal when he sees that the quarterback is ready to throw. He runs in place, keeping his feet moving in short, choppy steps. He must be prepared to move to either his right or his left when he sees the quarterback start the throwing motion. He breaks to the ball by rolling over the foot in the direction that he needs to go.

Four-Deep Zone

A four-deep zone coverage probably will be used only when the coach knows that the offense has to throw deep to win the game or when the offense uses four or more wide receivers in a formation.

In a four-deep zone (figure 9.6), both corners and both safeties drop deep and cover one-quarter of the field. Any ball thrown deep should either be knocked down, causing an incompletion, or be intercepted. All the techniques for defensive backs covering in a deep zone apply in a four-deep zone defense.

The defensive backs should let the quarterback and the ball take them to the receiver. When playing zone defense, the main rules are to recognize the pass, go immediately to the appropriate zone, get as deep as possible before the quarterback sets to throw, focus on the quarterback and the ball, and react to the pass, letting the ball direct him to the receiver.

One challenge for a defensive back when playing zone defense is resisting the urge to take his eyes off the quarterback and look at a receiver running in his zone. Another is withstanding the temptation to come up before the ball is thrown to cover a receiver running in front of him. Both of these challenges can be overcome if the defensive back practices alone, goes to his zone, looks where the quarterback will set up, stops and settles into his backpedal, and then reacts to the right or left. Focusing on the quarterback and the ball gives the defensive back a great chance to make the interception.

BUMP AND RUN

At times a defensive back will want to line up on the line of scrimmage in front of a receiver. The technique that the defensive player uses will depend on the pass coverage called in the huddle.

Figure 9.6 Four-deep zone coverage.

Head-Up Technique

The head-up technique is usually used when the defensive back's assignment is to drop back into the outside zone on a zone pass defense. In this case, the goal of the defender is to disrupt the timing of the pass play by keeping the receiver on the line of scrimmage as long as possible. To accomplish his task, the defender must have a balanced stance with his feet spread shoulder-width apart, knees bent, and hips down so that he is in a semisquat position. His back should be straight and his head up. Both hands should be up in front of his chest, and his elbows should be close to his sides. He needs to be squarely in front of the receiver. The defensive back must not lunge at the receiver. Instead, he should wait for the receiver to attempt a release to either his right or his left. When the receiver commits to one side or the other, the defensive back needs to step back with his foot on the side of the release, drive his hand on that side into the sternum of the receiver, and impede the receiver's movement down the field, being careful not to push him away in the direction that he wants to go (figure 9.7). After making contact, the defender can move into his backpedal and drop into his zone.

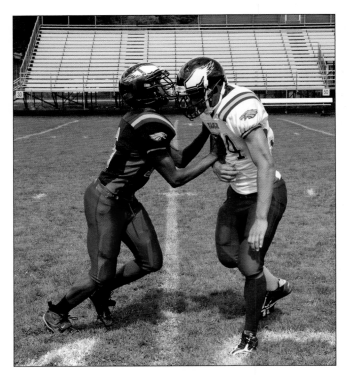

Figure 9.7 Defensive back using head-up bump and run technique.

Inside Technique

When using this technique, the defender lines up at a 45-degree angle to the sideline and places his outside foot directly in front of the nose of the receiver. The stance of the defensive back will be the same as when he is in a head-up position except that he is inside the receiver and facing him at an angle. Again, the defender should force the bump only if the receiver releases in a manner that allows the defensive back to make contact without lunging or stepping forward to make the hit. Should the receiver take a wide release to the outside, the defensive back leans his upper body in that direction, opens up with his foot on the side of the release, and runs with the receiver up the field, maintaining a position on the inside shoulder of the receiver. When the receiver tries to force an inside release, the defender opens up with his foot on that side, makes contact with his hand on that side, and drives the receiver straight down the line of scrimmage. This technique would be used in any type of man-to-man pass coverage, especially a blitz situation when the defensive back is as fast as the receiver and does not have any deep help on the inside of the field.

Outside Technique

For the outside bump and run, the defensive back lines up on the outside of the receiver at a 45-degree angle and places his inside foot directly in front of the receiver's nose. His stance, reaction, and movements are the same as what he used for the head-up and inside technique, but here the goal is to force the receiver into the center of the field where additional coverage can prevent the receiver from making the reception. This technique could be used for a man-to-man coverage with free safety help in the center of the field or with a two-deep zone when the goal is to funnel the receiver to the deep safety (figure 9.8).

Figure 9.8 Defensive back using outside bump and run technique.

PLAYING THE RUN

A defensive back's first concern is to play pass defense. His second is to know what to do when the offense runs the ball. His action and technique are determined by the defense that the coach calls for the play. The defensive back must understand his responsibility for the defense called, know what the offense must do before he leaves his pass coverage to attack the line of scrimmage (run force), know where and what his responsibilities are when he forces the run, understand which offensive players can block him, and know how to meet the blocker.

When the defense is called, the defensive back knows that he will play either zone or man-to-man pass defense. If the defensive back is responsible for covering a deep zone, he must go to that zone until the ballcarrier crosses the line of scrimmage. If he is to cover a receiver man-to-man, he needs to run with his receiver until the receiver blocks or the ballcarrier crosses the line of scrimmage. In either case, the defensive back pursues the ballcarrier after he is certain that the ball cannot be passed.

A defensive back playing zone defense but not assigned to a deep zone needs to leave his zone and come to the line of scrimmage if the end man on the defensive back's side blocks. If the player he is covering man-to-man blocks immediately, like a tight end on a linebacker, the defensive back may have to come up and help stop the run. The defensive back must not look at the running back or he will be fooled if the running back fakes the run on a pass play. Who is blocking and how they block will give the defensive back a better idea whether the offense is running or passing the ball.

When coming up to force the run, the defensive back usually is the outside man of the defense. His job is to force the ballcarrier back to the inside of the field. Forcing the ballcarrier back to the inside is important because all the other defensive players will be pursuing from that direction. The defensive back should not allow the ballcarrier to go around him and get to the outside. The defensive back should set a predetermined spot for the force 2 yards in the offensive backfield and 3 yards outside his next defensive teammate. If he can reach this spot, he can force the ballcarrier back to the inside and not give the ballcarrier a huge running lane up the field.

As he is crossing the line of scrimmage, the defensive back should look for the offensive player who has been assigned to block him. This blocker is often the fullback but can be the offensive tackle or guard. Before the defensive back even thinks about tackling the ballcarrier, he must pick out and defeat this offensive blocker.

The defensive back needs to keep his outside arm and leg free from the blocker. If the ballcarrier does try to go around him, the defensive back will be in position to turn to the sideline and make the tackle.

The defensive back should not sit and wait for the blocker to come to him, especially if the blocker is a big offensive lineman. He is far better off if he attacks the blocker, getting his shoulder pads under the offensive man's shoulder pads. He should hit the blocker as hard as he can with his inside forearm. He can bounce back if necessary, but he should stay on his feet.

Sometime during every game, the defensive back will be asked to force on a running play. Playing the run is 70 percent desire. The defensive back must be ready and understand how important it is for him to come up as soon as he sees that the play is a run, not a pass.

After the ballcarrier crosses the line of scrimmage and the pass is no longer an option for the offense, defensive backs are the last line of defense. They must take a proper angle of pursuit.

The basic rule for a defensive back is that the farther he is from the ballcarrier when he crosses the line of scrimmage, the deeper his angle must be to have an opportunity to make a touchdown-saving tackle.

The defensive backfield must work as a unit. Each player must go full out to reach the ballcarrier, making certain not to run in the footsteps of another defensive player. The defensive backs should react to the ballcarrier like the spokes on a wheel, fanning out, each on a separate path but all leading to one objective.

Each defensive back should adjust his pursuit path to put himself between the ballcarrier and the goal line.

DEFENSIVE BACK DRILLS

During every practice, defensive backs should go through drills designed to perfect their coverage techniques: start, backpedal, angle backpedal, and rolling over. Every practice should include a tackling drill, and at least two catching drills should be run each week (see chapter 1). The drills should be conducted at half speed and can increase in tempo as the players' skills improve. The time spent on these daily drills should diminish as the players begin to master the individual techniques.

EXPLODING AT THE START

Purpose: To teach defensive backs to explode at the start of the play.

Procedure:

1. **The coach lines up in front of the defensive back.**
2. **When the defensive back is in a proper stance, the coach calls, "Hut."**
3. **The defensive back explodes at the start, moving back.**

Coaching points: The player must step back with his back foot and propel his hips away from the line of scrimmage. His head and shoulders should come up gradually and never be behind the feet and hips.

Variation: To include backpedaling, use the same setup. The coach can stand at the side of the defensive back if he thinks that the defensive back is leaning back. To practice the angle backpedal, the coach points in the direction that the defensive back should go after backpedaling for 10 yards.

STAYING IN THE BACKPEDAL

Purpose: To reinforce proper backpedal and angle backpedal technique.

Procedure:

1. The defensive back lines up in position. The coach stands in front of the defensive back.
2. On the coach's signal, the defensive back explodes at the start and begins to backpedal.
3. After the defensive back runs 5 yards straight back, the coach signals him to angle to the left.
4. After the defensive back runs 5 yards on the angle, the coach signals him to return to the straight backpedal.
5. After the defensive back goes 5 yards straight back, the coach signals him to angle to the right. The defensive back runs the right angle for 5 yards.

Coaching points: The defensive back maintains the backward run throughout the drill. He must maintain proper body position during the entire 20 yards. He must never cross his feet during the angle drill. The player must change direction for a rollover by leaning his body in the direction indicated, rolling over the foot on that side, and turning into a forward run.

Variation: After the player can do the drill for 20 yards, he can roll over in the direction that the coach indicates rather than angle in that direction, going from a backpedal to a forward run.

PASS ZONES

Purpose: To teach defensive backs the passing zones.

Procedure:

1. The coach lines up to the side of the defensive back. Another defensive back, acting as a wide receiver, lines up.
2. The defensive back lines up 9 yards away from the wide receiver.
3. The coach calls the snap count to start the play.
4. The wide receiver jogs up the field. The defensive back backpedals for 20 yards.
5. When the wide receiver enters the short zone, the defensive back calls out, "Short, short, short." When the wide receiver passes 6 yards, the defensive back calls out, "Medium, medium, medium." Finally, after 12 yards, the defensive back calls out, "Deep, deep, deep."

(continued)

Pass Zones   *(continued)*

Coaching points: When practicing with a teammate, the defensive back can start 9 or 10 yards away from the receiver, allowing him to stay in his backward run the entire time the receiver runs up the field 20 yards. He is practicing recognizing the pass zones, not working on the backward run. The receiver should run at half speed at first, increasing his speed as the defensive back correctly calls out the distance for each zone.

During this drill, the defensive back lines up on one side of the receiver and stays on that side as the receiver runs up the field. The defensive back should always cover on one side or the other and never end up directly in front of the receiver.

RECOGNIZING PASS PATTERNS

Purpose: To give defensive backs experience recognizing pass patterns.

Procedure:

1. The coach lines up behind a defensive back who is acting as a wide receiver. The defensive back lines up in his normal position and stance.
2. The coach tells the wide receiver which route to run: short, medium, or deep.
3. The coach calls out the snap, and the receiver runs the route.
4. As the receiver starts off the line, the defensive back goes into his backward run.
5. The moment that he recognizes the pattern (recognition point), the defensive back calls out the name of the pattern and points to where the receiver will catch the ball (interception point). He keeps moving backward as he does so.

Coaching points: The player should work on one zone at a time. Only after the defensive back correctly calls and points out each pattern run in each zone without a mistake should the receiver and the defensive back run patterns in another zone. The drill does not require a ball. The defensive back needs to concentrate on the receiver and react to his pass route.

Variation: After the player can correctly call and point out all the pass routes in the three zones, the coach can run with the drill and have the defensive back break to the interception point for each pass route.

PLAYING A TWO-DEEP ZONE

Purpose: To give the defensive backs experience playing a two-deep zone.

Procedure:

1. The coach lines up in the quarterback position with a ball. Four defensive backs line up in their normal positions.
2. The coach calls out which defensive backs are to drop back and snaps the ball to start the drill.
3. Defensive backs drop back into their coverage. The coach should raise the ball to indicate that the pass is about to be thrown.

Coaching points: Players covering a deep zone should work hard to get deep as quickly as they can. Any defensive back in an under zone should move quickly to his zone and then backpedal to get his depth until the coach raises the ball to throw. As he steps toward a target area, all four defensive backs should move in that direction. The coach should teach zone coverage using a ball, not a receiver.

Variation: This drill is also good for practicing three-deep and four-deep zones. To give the defensive backs practice following the ball to the receiver, the coach can throw the ball. The defensive backs should move to the ball.

BUMP AND RUN

Purpose: To help the defensive back react properly to the receiver's release using all three bump and run techniques.

Procedure:

1. The defensive back lines up across from a receiver. The coach lines up behind the defensive back, facing the receiver.
2. The coach tells the defender how to line up—head up, inside, or outside— and tells the receiver where to release.
3. The coach gives the snap count and then observes and corrects the defensive player's reaction to the release of the receiver. Contact between players should be limited.

Coaching points: The defender's stance must be balanced. The coach should focus on the defender's first step and be sure that he is not stepping forward and lunging at the receiver. The defensive back's contact hand should stop the forward movement of the receiver and not push the receiver into his pass route. Each defensive back should have an opportunity to operate from all three positions with both an inside and an outside release.

Variation: From the same setup, the coach tells the receiver what pass route to run and tells the defensive back the coverage call made in the huddle. The defender must line up in the proper position for the coverage called and use the proper technique when the receiver releases off the line.

PASS OR RUN

Purpose: To help the defensive back understand his responsibility for the called defense.

Procedure:

1. The coach lines up facing the defensive back and even with the fullback. Another defensive back lines up as a tight end, and a third lines up as a linebacker in front of the tight end.
2. The coach calls out the coverage and the offensive play: sweep or pass.
3. If the play is a sweep, the tight end blocks, and the fullback becomes a blocker on the defensive back.
4. If the play is a pass, the tight end releases up the field, and the fullback sets up to pass protect.
5. The defensive back comes up or drops back based on the play.

(continued)

Pass or Run *(continued)*

Coaching points: Considering the coverage called by the coach, the designated defensive back who does not have deep zone coverage (corner or safety) must key the tight end and react accordingly. He should locate his force spot, 2 yards across the line of scrimmage and 3 yards outside the linebacker, and head there the moment that the tight end blocks. If the tight end releases upfield, the defensive back reacts according to the coverage called. He should take on any blocker with his inside shoulder and keep his outside leg and arm free when coming up on any running play.

ESTABLISHING PROPER PURSUIT PATHS

Purpose: To help the defensive backfield learn the proper pursuit paths to take when the ball crosses the line of scrimmage.

Procedure:

1. The coach lines up facing the defensive backfield, which is spread out across the field. A player is lined up wide on either side of the coach as a receiver.
2. The coach calls out the coverage and points to the receiver with the ball.
3. The receiver sprints straight up the field for 20 yards, and each of the defenders begins moving in the proper pursuit path.
4. The coach observes the path of each defensive back and makes corrections.
5. The coach repeats the drill to the other side of the field.

Coaching points: All four players must react to the ballcarrier the instant that he crosses the line of scrimmage. Each defensive back must run full out and must not follow in the footsteps of a fellow defender.

Variation: The same drill can be run with the addition of a running back. The coach tells the running back where to run and hands him the ball. The ballcarrier runs up the middle, to the right, or to the left, and each defensive back takes the proper pursuit angle to keep him from scoring.

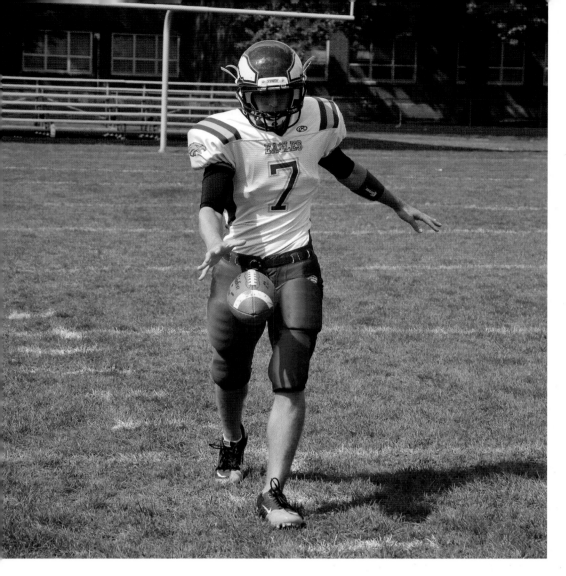

SPECIAL-TEAMS PLAYERS

S pecial-teams play involves a lot of players and many skills. This chapter covers punts, field goals, kickoffs, and kick returns. Special-teams players include the placekicker, short snapper, and holder, who must work as one unit; the punter and the long snapper, who also work as a unit; and kickoff and punt returners.

KICKERS

The punter and placekicker can have a strong impact on their team's success or failure. Other players have the luxury of knowing that if they mess up on a play, they will have many more opportunities during the game to make up for their mistake. A punter or placekicker typically has only a few opportunities during a game, and the pressure is on to get it right every time.

The most important attribute for a kicker is the ability to focus on the upcoming kick. He must be able to concentrate on making one kick at a time. Great kickers and punters work hard to be the best-conditioned athletes on the team and to have the mental toughness that allows them to focus completely on the job at hand. Whether punting out of his own end zone or lining up for a last-second, game-winning field goal, the kicker's attitude is, "Give me the chance. Let's get out on the field, and I will get the job done."

Every kicker experiences problems when he starts out. Beginning kickers must work hard, focus, stay positive, and try to improve with every kick. This chapter covers the techniques for punting and placekicking, the stance and steps for both, the drop when punting, the plant foot when placekicking, and the mental and physical skills that a kicker needs to be successful.

The kicker's beginning stance must be functional and help him perform the physical movements of punting or placekicking. A good stance can improve performance and is essential to becoming a great punter or placekicker.

A good start is crucial for both the punter and the placekicker. Their initial steps greatly influence the outcome of the kick. Each kicker must have a set, practiced start in his kicking motion. A true beginner should start learning the steps by walking through them and then slowly increasing his forward movement as he becomes comfortable with the action.

When the kicker is first learning technique, he shouldn't use the ball. It is human nature to want to kick the ball immediately, but after the ball is introduced, it becomes the center of attention. All the hard work on stance, steps, and kicking can be overlooked if kicking the ball becomes the only focus. The more techniques the kicker masters before using the ball, the greater his opportunity for success becomes. The kicker should focus first on getting the techniques down and making them automatic. This preparation makes kicking the ball much easier.

After a punter or placekicker has practiced getting into a comfortable stance and thinks that he has established the correct steps, the next technique to work on is his kicking. He must establish a fluid kicking motion. Both placekickers and punters should practice their kicking motions repeatedly without using a ball. Every phase is important. They must use a proper stance, use the correct steps, and develop a fluid kicking motion.

After kickers have mastered the basic techniques, the ball can be introduced into practice. If at any time the player has trouble punting or placekicking, he should practice without the ball to sharpen his technique.

THREE-PLAYER UNIT: PLACEKICKER, SHORT SNAPPER, AND HOLDER

Success is a team effort. To produce a successful kick, the kicker and his teammates must do their jobs. The blockers must keep the defensive players from blocking the kick. The center must make the snap. The holder must catch the snap and place the ball on the spot. The kicker must concentrate and kick the ball correctly.

For a placekicker to be successful, two other players must do their jobs correctly. The placekicker should understand the role of the short snapper and holder because any field goal or extra point is a joint effort. Improper technique by any of the three can result in the failure of the kick.

Placekicker

The placekicker is in a unique position. Every time that he goes out on the field, he has the opportunity to score points. No other player has this opportunity, but with this opportunity comes tremendous responsibility.

The placekicker's stance should be comfortable (figure 10.1a). The placekicker gets into his stance the same way every time. First, he stands straight up and steps forward with his nonkicking (plant) foot. The heel of the plant foot is just ahead of the toe of his kicking foot. His feet are no wider than his hips, and his weight is distributed evenly on both feet. He slightly bends both knees and bends forward at the waist, moving his shoulders forward so that they are in front of his hips. He relaxes his shoulders and allows his hands and arms to hang comfortably. He focuses on the kicking tee.

When the player is in a comfortable stance, he is ready to start moving to make the kick. The initial movement forward toward the placement spot starts with a slight forward lean of his shoulders. Then he takes a short momentum step forward with his plant foot (figure 10.1b), a normal forward step with his kicking foot, and a longer step with his plant foot. The step with his plant foot should bring the kicker's foot even with and 6 inches outside the placement spot (where the holder will place the ball for the kick). In this position, the kicker has room and is in position to make contact with the ball. Soon he will feel that his steps are the correct length and that he is ending in the proper position to make the kick, with his head down and his eyes on the placement spot.

Most placekickers prefer a soccer-style kick rather than the straight-ahead kick that was once popular. Many kickers have soccer experience, and this style generally produces greater accuracy and distance. The power for the soccer-style kick starts when the hips move forward and the kicking leg comes forward in a full arc. The knee of the kicking leg must precede the foot toward the placement spot (figure 10.1c). The knee of the kicking leg should be bent back slightly. The position of the kicking foot is important. The toes should point down, and the kicker's ankle should be locked and stable.

The toe of the kicking foot passes just outside the placement spot. The center of the inside of the kicking foot passes directly over the center of the placement spot. The top inside of the center of the kicking foot is the part of the foot that makes contact with the ball (figure 10.1d).

The follow-through (figure 10.1e) is an excellent indication of how the kick will go. When the kicking foot moves over the placement spot, the entire body must move straight at

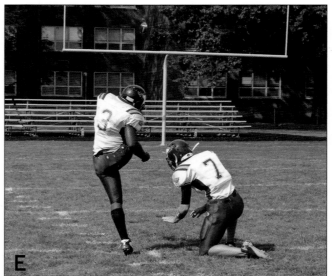

Figure 10.1 Placekicker's motion: He *(a)* takes the initial stance, *(b)* steps to the ball, *(c)* swings the kicking leg, *(d)* makes contact with the ball, and *(e)* follows through.

the target. As his kicking foot moves over the placement spot, the kicker's body is balanced, his head is down, and his eyes are focused on the placement spot. His hips lead the way to the target. Throughout the kicking motion, the kicker's shoulders precede his feet. A coach or teammate can line up 4 or 5 yards in front of the placement spot to watch the kicker's motion, making certain that the kicker follows through by moving straight toward him.

Before the kicker can get into his kicking motion with a ball, he must learn to align himself properly to the placement spot. When practicing by himself, the kicker can place a kicking tee, a cup, or a piece of tape on the ground to indicate the placement spot. After he establishes this spot, he needs to step correctly to get into proper position to start the kick. To line up to make the kick, the kicker places his plant foot so that the instep of the foot is next to the placement spot, and he places his kicking foot directly behind the placement spot. Beginning with his kicking foot, he takes three normal steps straight back from the placement spot and then two steps at a right angle with his plant foot. He turns and faces the placement spot and gets into his stance.

When first learning to kick, the kicker may find that he is not stepping straight back from the placement spot. One way to correct this error is to put the placement spot on a marked sideline on the field. Then he can see whether he has stepped straight down the line. When moving forward with his steps, the kicker's plant foot should come down even with and 6 inches outside the placement spot. Because there is no actual target, he points his toe in exactly the same direction as the kicking spot. This foot position is easy to monitor when working on the sideline.

Each time the kicker practices a kick, he should establish a placement spot. He needs to take the time to follow the exact steps to get lined up properly. After he is in position, he assumes a comfortable stance. When ready, he takes the correct steps to the placement spot and makes sure that his plant foot comes down in the right position. He executes his kicking motion in a smooth manner and makes certain that his body follows through directly at the target.

The kicker needs to be alert to whether his follow-through goes off to the left or the right instead of straight to the target. If he is going off to the left, he should make sure that his shoulders are not behind his hips. Going off to the right is caused by misplacing his plant foot or putting his shoulders too far in front of his feet.

After the entire kicking motion has become automatic and the kicker feels comfortable with every phase of the kick, the ball can be added. Eliminating the goalpost and focusing solely on kicking the ball in a straight line will help the kicker concentrate on technique. To kick without a goalpost, the kicker should practice on a sideline, making the placement spot a point where a yard line meets the sideline. The kicker takes his steps and sets up. A coach or a fellow kicker places the ball on the placement spot, making certain that the laces of the ball point straight down the sideline. The kicker finishes by kicking the ball in a straight line directly down the sideline. He should make sure to perform each technique correctly.

To stay smooth and accurate, the kicker needs to kick with a natural motion. Because the kicker is focusing on accuracy, no center is needed. The kicker should be careful to not overkick (kick too hard) when he is practicing with the ball.

Accuracy, not distance, is the goal. Range and the distance of the kick will increase with learning and perfecting proper technique, good core conditioning, and natural physical development. By kicking the ball down the sideline, the kicker will be able to tell quickly whether he is hooking or pushing the ball as he kicks. If he finds that he cannot get the ball to travel straight down the sideline, he needs to take the ball out of the drill and review each part of his kicking motion with the coach.

When the season rolls around, a kicker's participation in practice time may be limited, especially if he does not play another position. Still, he needs to keep busy during the season. He must work on his conditioning every day. He should develop a daily stretching program to improve flexibility, a daily running program that includes sprints and distance running, and a program to increase the strength of his abdominal muscles. The kicker needs to work as hard as his teammates do during practice and be in the best condition possible. This approach benefits the kicker physically and makes him feel more a part of the team.

The player and the coach should set the exact number of kicks that the kicker will make each day, and the kicker should perform that number. His concentration should be on using the proper technique for each kick.

Short Snapper

The ball originates with the center. The center needs to position his body to make the snap to the holder, who is 7 yards away. The center makes the snap primarily with one hand. The other hand is on the ball, but only as a guide.

The center must think of the snap to the holder as a pass thrown back between his legs. To execute this passing motion, he must make certain the ball is in front of him when he gets into his stance. The center should use a comfortable, balanced stance. His feet should be at least shoulder-width apart or more and about even with one another (figure 10.2a). If he feels more comfortable, the foot on the side of his snapping hand can be slightly behind his other foot. His shoulders should be square to the line of scrimmage, and his hips and shoulders should be even. The center's hips control the height of his snap—high hips, high snap; low hips, low snap.

After he is in this position, the center reaches out for the ball. He should rotate the laces of the ball to the outside and down so that they are just past the center point. The center should grip the ball just as if he were a quarterback throwing a forward pass. A proper grip ensures the desired accuracy and velocity.

The size of the player's hands determines the way that he is able to grasp the football. Regardless of the size of his snapping hand, he starts by gripping the ball near the center (figure 10.2b). He places three fingers of his snapping hand on or over the laces of the

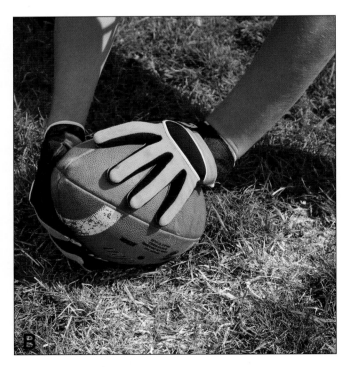

Figure 10.2 Short snapper's *(a)* stance and *(b)* grip.

ball. The index finger is near the tip of the ball off the laces and across the seam of the ball where the laces are. The middle and third finger are across the laces. The fingertips of these two fingers are on the surface of the ball, not on the laces. The little finger just reaches the laces of the ball. He feels most of the pressure between the ball and the passing hand just in front of the center point on the front of the ball.

At this point, the center places his other hand lightly on top of the ball and prepares to snap. He looks back through his legs to the holder. The holder's hands are always the center's target. When the holder has both hands extended and is ready to catch the ball, the center knows that he can snap the ball back to the holder.

As he snaps the ball back between his legs, the center makes certain to follow through with both hands. The fingers of both hands should point directly at the holder's hands. In a good follow-through, he will feel his entire body move slightly back toward the holder and kicker as he makes the snap.

Holder

The holder must position himself on the opposite side of the placement spot from the kicker. When he is even with the tee, the holder kneels down with his back knee on the ground 7 yards from the center (figure 10.3). The foot of his front leg is up, and his toe is pointed directly at the goalpost. From this position, he leans slightly forward toward the center.

The holder places his back hand on the center of the tee and extends his front hand and arm, palm down, toward the center. The holder's front arm and hand form the top part of the center's target. They should be even with the center of the holder's chest. The holder then asks the kicker whether he is ready. When the kicker says that he is ready, the holder brings his other hand off the ground and forms a target for the center's snap. His thumbs should be touching so that he can catch the ball correctly. The center will see that the holder has extended both hands toward him, and the center will feel free to snap the ball at any time. The holder must be alert!

Obviously, the center wants the ball to zip back into the holder's hands at the right spot on every kick. But that will not always be the case, and the holder must be prepared to catch the snap no matter where it is. The holder's first job is to make the catch and then get the ball down onto the kicking tee. After making the catch, the holder uses one smooth motion to place the ball on the tee. He turns the ball so that the laces face the goalposts as he brings the ball down. The holder rotates the ball to the correct position with his front hand as he places the tip of the ball on the tee. He places the index finger of his back hand lightly on the top point of the ball to balance it at the correct position for the kicker (figure 10.4).

Figure 10.3 Holder ready for the snap.

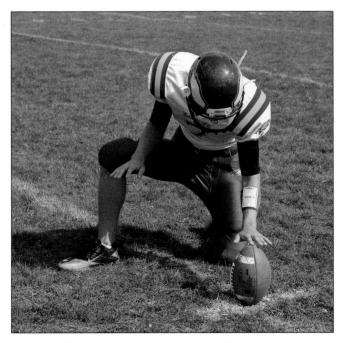

Figure 10.4 Holder ready for the kick.

To produce a successful kick, everyone must do his job. After the center completes the snap, after the holder makes the catch and places the ball on the placement spot, and after the blockers stop the rushers, it all comes down to executing the kick. The kicker must concentrate on the placement spot, stay smooth during his approach, maintain his technique, be fluid in his kicking motion, keep his head down, use a good follow-through, and listen for the crowd to tell him whether the kick was good. Players should make kicking a year-round priority. The most productive approach is for the kicker, short snapper, and holder to work together throughout the year. Spring and summer workouts are a great time for players to focus on their separate skills without the pressure of the game.

TWO-PLAYER UNIT: PUNTER AND LONG SNAPPER

Every punt can affect the outcome of the game. A successful punt requires the work of all 11 players on the field. The blockers must keep the defensive players from blocking the kick, the center must make the long snap back to the punter, and the punter must catch the ball and execute the punt. Everyone must cover the kick to tackle the return man before he can gain yardage. Everyone must do his job, but the center and the punter are responsible for executing the punt, and they must work in unison as a smooth two-man unit.

Punter

The team's punter is in a unique position. He has the opportunity to cause a significant change in field position with every punt. With a good punt and good coverage, he has the opportunity to pin the opposition deep in their end of the field.

In any game, a time will come when the offense has trouble moving the ball. The punter's kick moves the ball away from his team's goal line, giving the defense an opportunity to go in and stop the opponent and, at the same time, giving the offense a chance to regroup.

Conventional Punt

The punter's stance must allow him to move forward to punt the ball. His stance must also put him in position to move to the right or left, bend to the ground, or leap high into the air to catch a poorly snapped ball. To get into his stance, the punter stands straight up with his feet even. He spreads his feet about hip-width apart or slightly wider. He takes a slight step forward with his nonpunting foot so that the toe of his back foot is even with the middle of his front foot (figure 10.5). He feels his weight on the balls of both feet. He bends his knees a little and brings his shoulders forward so that they are slightly in front of his hips. His head is up, and his eyes are looking straight ahead.

From this position, the punter should practice moving in every direction without the ball. He must feel comfortable going after any snapped ball no matter where it is, including one sailing

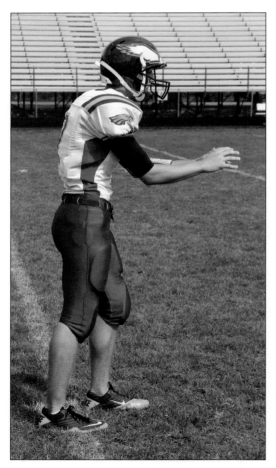
Figure 10.5 Punter's stance.

over his head. If the punter practices these movements without the ball and without a rush, he will be ready to perform when they occur in practice or a game.

A punter may use either a two-step or three-step punting motion. With either motion, the punter's steps should be smooth, and he should not overstride. He should picture himself walking toward the ball, never hurrying or leaning back as he steps. Because the risk of a blocked punt is lower with the two-step style, he should focus on it.

To begin the two-step punt, the punter should be in a comfortable stance with his kicking foot slightly in front of his other foot. He takes a short step with his front foot slightly to the outside instead of straight ahead, landing on the ball of his kicking foot. Next he takes a normal step with the other foot. The length of this step is the same as if he were walking. This step lands slightly across the center of his body. The punter wants to land on the ball of his foot so that he can transfer power to the kick.

Maintaining balance and control of the body while moving forward is essential to good punting. One way to develop good control is for the punter to practice the steps with his hands on his hips. In this position, the feet do the work and the player can easily see whether he is losing his balance. After he has learned to move with good balance and control, he is ready to practice positioning the hands and arms to receive the snap. Unlike a placekicker, the punter must learn to receive the snap by himself.

After assuming the proper stance, the punter extends the hand and arm on the same side as his kicking foot directly out in front of his shoulder. He moves the arm so that the hand is near the center of his body. He then turns the hand over so that the palm faces the ground. This position gives the center the top part of the target. Next, the punter reaches out with the other hand and arm to a level even with the middle of his belly. The palm of this hand faces up. This arm and hand form the bottom half of the center's target.

When the punter is ready and the center has seen the target, the punter moves his top hand down until it is even with his bottom hand. At this point, the palms of both hands face up and the little fingers almost touch (figure 10.6).

To see both his hands and the ball when the ball is snapped, the punter extends his arms away from his body. At first the punter should practice without the ball. He starts his normal steps. Both hands remain in position during his first step. When he begins his second step, the punter drops the hand away from his kicking foot. This hand swings back behind his hip. At the same time, he pushes forward the hand on the same side as the kicking foot. This hand should be slightly outside the thigh of the kicking leg. The punter allows the extended hand to drop naturally to his side as the kicking leg comes through in a practice kicking motion (figure 10.7, page 202).

The fun of kicking for the punter, of course, is seeing the ball go where he wants it to go. Even NFL kickers know that beginning kickers need to practice the motion of the kick repeatedly before bringing the ball out on the field. Eventually, though, the punter has to punt the ball. He has the additional task of catching the ball from the center, adjusting it in a proper grip, extending it correctly, and dropping it accurately to his punting foot. The punter should work on the handling of the ball and the drop before working with the center.

Figure 10.6 Punter ready for the snap.

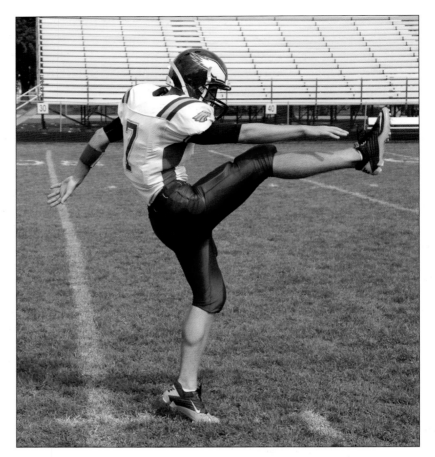

Figure 10.7 At first the punter should practice the kicking motion without the ball.

The first thing that the punter must do after receiving the ball is to grip it correctly. The laces must be facing straight up. The punter holds the ball with the hand on the side of the kicking leg. The back tip of the ball should touch the palm of the hand. The thumb should be on the inside top panel of the ball. The forefinger and second finger should be on the outside top panel of the ball. The remaining two fingers—the ring and little finger—should be on the outside bottom panel of the ball. The pressure from the thumb and fingers of the drop hand should allow the punter to hold the ball comfortably and securely (figure 10.8).

The other hand, the support hand, should be on the front inside of the ball. Four fingers should be on the inside bottom panel, and the thumb should be on the top inside panel just above the side seam. The punter should grasp the ball with as little pressure as necessary. Holding the ball with too much pressure adversely affects the way that the punter drops the ball onto his foot.

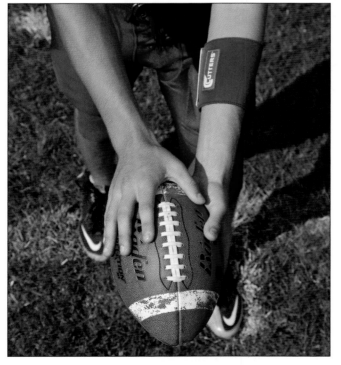

Figure 10.8 Punter's grip on the ball.

After the punter is holding the ball properly in both hands, he is ready to proceed with the hand, arm, and drop action of the kick. While learning these techniques, he should not actually kick the ball. This approach allows the punter to go through these movements many times in a short period. He also does not step while learning the kick.

The actual kicking movement starts when the punter moves his support hand away from his kicking foot. The punter allows this hand and arm to swing back to the outside at waist height, providing balance for the kick. As the hand swings back, the punter's hips turn slightly to the inside in the direction of his arm swing and his opposite shoulder rotates slightly forward. This action allows his ball hand and arm to extend easily in front of his body (figure 10.9a).

As he extends the ball, the hand on the side of the punter's kicking foot, his drop hand, rotates the point of the ball slightly to the inside until the ball is aimed in the same direction as the punter's hips. The punter is steady at the wrist and keeps the ball level, not pointing up or down, just above his waist. When the ball is slightly outside the thigh of the kicking leg, he pulls the drop hand away and allows the ball to drop to the ground (figure 10.9b).

During practice when the punter is not actually kicking the ball, a ball that has been dropped correctly should hit the ground and bounce straight back to the kicking leg. The punter will know exactly where the ball is going if he focuses on it as he should during an actual kick. The direction that the ball takes after it hits the ground tells the punter whether something was wrong with the drop so that he can correct the error. If the ball bounces back to the punter but not straight back to his kicking leg, the front point of the

Figure 10.9 Punter's drop action: He *(a)* extends his ball hand and arm and *(b)* releases his hand and drops the ball.

ball was the first part to strike the ground. If the ball bounces forward and away from his kicking leg, the back of the ball struck the ground first. The punter should repeat the drill until the ball bounces back to his kicking leg every time he drops it to the ground. He should follow each step in the process, from stance through drop action, noting the amount of pressure that he uses to grip the ball. He should keep the wrist of his drop hand locked as he extends the ball forward in preparation for release.

Figure 10.10   Punter's kicking action.

When the ball is first introduced in punting practice, the concern is not hang time or distance. The goal is to perform the correct steps—a smooth movement to the point of the kick, a good drop, and an easy leg motion in the kick. Power, distance, and hang time will come after the punter masters the fundamentals of the kick.

When first learning the kicking motion, the punter can start on the sideline. The punter positions himself and holds the ball waist high in both hands in front of the center of his body. He begins by stepping forward with his kicking foot. During this step, he keeps the ball secure in both hands. The punter makes certain that the length of this step allows him to land on the ball of his kicking foot. He then takes a step with his nonkicking foot. He moves his support hand away from the ball as he takes this step. His hand and arm swing back and outside his hip in a smooth motion. The drop hand extends forward and slightly outside the kicking leg as the nonkicking foot hits the ground. The punter is now in position to drop the ball to his kicking foot as his kicking leg comes through in a smooth, coordinated motion (figure 10.10).

For the drop to be successful, the punter must be sure to rotate the ball slightly to the inside until it points in the same direction as his hips. The ball must be level; the point should not aim up or down. The ball should be just above the waist. The punter needs to concentrate on the ball all the way from his drop hand to his kicking foot.

Up to this point, the punter has worked independently on the various segments of the punting action. Now he will attempt to put them all together. In the beginning, the punter may look jerky moving through the kick. This awkward action is expected and will improve quickly. The important thing for the punter is to stay positive.

A common mistake for the punter is to take a longer first or second step, landing on the heel rather than the ball of the foot. This action stops the punter's forward momentum and prevents him from moving smoothly through the entire kicking motion. To prevent or correct this problem, the punter needs to control the length of his stride.

Another mistake that beginning punters often make is forgetting to keep the shoulders and head in front of the hips. This stance causes the punter to lean back, putting him out of position to drop the ball properly to his kicking foot. Leaning back also can cause the punter to come down on the heel of his foot, even if his stride is the proper length. The punter must focus on keeping the upper body in front of the hips.

When something is wrong, the punter should go back to practicing the fundamentals without the ball. If one particular aspect is not working, the punter should work on that segment of the kick by itself without the ball until he is doing it properly. Practicing punting the ball when part of the punt is wrong only reinforces bad habits. The punter must understand what makes a punt successful, what causes a poor punt, and which part of the kicking motion he needs to review to ensure a successful punt.

Game situations may require a punt to the right or left rather than straight down the field. The punter may need to kick away from a good return man or try to keep his coverage area to one side of the field. The punter's goal when using a directional kick may be to kick the ball out of bounds to pin the opponent deep in his own end of the field.

Good directional punting starts before the punter ever gets the snap from the center. The key is adjusting the placement of the foot opposite the kicking foot. This foot needs to be turned slightly to point in the direction that the punter desires to kick before he receives the snap. A right-footed punter adjusts his left foot; a left-footed punter adjusts his right foot.

When a right-footed punter kicks to the left, he turns his left foot to the left so that the toe of his left foot points directly where he wants to kick the ball (figure 10.11). If the left foot is not turned, the punter will step across his body with his right foot, disrupting his natural punting motion. By turning the foot before the snap, his first step will be natural. His hips and shoulders will be square and pointed directly where he wants the ball to go.

Kicking to the right for a right-footed kicker requires a similar adjustment with the left foot. This time he turns his left foot to the right and points the toe where he wants to kick the ball. A right-footed punter tends to step to the right in his natural punting motion. Because of this tendency, he does not have to turn the left foot as much as he does when punting to the left. A slight turn of the left foot to the right keeps his hips and shoulders square and pointed right where he wants the punt to go.

Figure 10.11 Right-footed punter angles his left foot to direct the ball.

Rugby-Style Punt

Interest in the rugby-style punt is increasing. A major difference between a conventional punter and a rugby punter is the direction in which the punter is moving when he makes the kick. Instead of moving straight ahead toward the line of scrimmage to punt the ball, the rugby punter runs laterally toward the sideline while angling slightly forward toward the line of scrimmage.

Because the punter is running with the ball, he is always a threat to continue to run the ball and advance it enough to make a first down. This threat keeps the return-team players on the line of scrimmage and delays them from setting up for the return.

With the rugby-style punt, the ball is usually kicked low and does not have the same hang time as a conventionally punted ball. The flight of the ball may be end over end, not in a spiral. This kind of kick can be more difficult for the returner to catch and run back. Because the ball is going end over end, it often achieves greater total distance on the kick because after hitting the ground it rolls toward the opponent's goal line.

The rugby-style punter's stance must allow him to move laterally to punt the ball. His stance must also put him in position to move to the right or left, bend to the ground, or leap high into the air to catch a poorly snapped ball. To get into his stance, the punter stands straight up with his feet even. He spreads his feet about hip-width apart or slightly wider. He takes a slight step forward with his nonpunting foot so that the toe of his punting foot is even with the middle of his front foot. He feels his weight on the balls of both feet. He bends his knees a little and brings his shoulders forward so that they are slightly in front of his hips. His head is up, and his eyes are looking straight ahead.

After assuming the proper stance, the rugby-style punter extends the hand and arm on the side of his kicking foot directly out in front of his shoulder. He moves the arm so that the hand is near the center of his body. He then turns the hand over so that the palm faces the ground. This position gives the center the top part of the target. Next, the punter reaches out with the other hand and arm to a level even with the middle of his belly. The palm of this hand faces up. This arm and hand form the bottom half of the center's target.

When the punter is ready and the center has seen the target, the punter moves his top hand down until it is even with his bottom hand (figure 10.12a). At this point, he places the palms of both hands up and brings the little fingers of each hand together so that they almost touch. To see both his hands and the ball when the ball is snapped, he extends his arms forward away from his body.

Ideally, the ball will arrive from the center on the kicking-foot side of the punter's body. This position allows him the take a first lateral step toward the sideline with his punting foot, starting his running motion (figure 10.12b).

As the punter runs toward the sideline, he needs to angle forward toward the line of scrimmage to be in position to run the ball if the opportunity presents itself. As he makes his run, he needs to secure the ball in both hands with the fingers of both hands on the lower panels and the thumbs on the upper panel near the laces of the ball. The punter needs to continue his run until he sees a rush developing or sees that he cannot run successfully. This run can continue for four or more steps.

To kick the ball, the punter needs to control the ball in one hand by transferring the ball to the hand on the side of his kicking foot. The ball should be extended away from the body, below the waist, with the front point of the ball angled down (figure 10.12c).

Figure 10.12 Rugby-style punt: *(a)* Punter in position for the snap from center; *(b)* punter's first lateral step; *(c)* punter's drop action; *(d)* punter's contact and follow-through.

The punter needs to make contact with the ball at knee height or lower. His kicking foot is pointed down, and the laces of his kicking shoe make contact with the ball. During the punt, the kicker needs to focus on the ball and drive his kicking leg and foot through the ball (figure 10.12d). This action should cause his body to come up off the ground, allowing him to land on his kicking foot after the kick.

Because of the lateral movement, the speed generated by the punter, and the across-the-body kicking motion, this style of punt takes a great deal of practice and needs to be coached step by step before the punter uses it in a game.

Long Snapper

One of the most important positions in punting is the center. Teams usually punt 7 to 10 times a game, and every snap that the center makes must be close to perfect. The center and the punter must work as one unit.

For a punter to be successful, he must have faith that the center is going to deliver the ball into his hands so that he can concentrate on his movement and making the kick. If the punter has to worry about where the snap is going to go, he cannot fully concentrate on the catch, steps, drop, and kick.

The long snap is similar to the short snap in placekicking. Because the stance and grip of the ball are the same, the stance and grip information for placekicking (see pages 198-199) apply here. The snap for a placekick and the snap for a punt differ in two important ways. First, the distance of the snap for a placekick is 7 yards; for a punt, it's 15 yards. Second, the height of the snap differs. The short snap for a placekick goes to a holder, who is on his knees waiting for the ball. The target area for a long snap on a punt is the numbers of the punter's jersey as he stands and waits for the snap.

Because of the increased distance and higher target, the center needs to make two changes to his snap. First, he needs to lift the front point of the ball off the ground. Second, he must increase the velocity of the snap.

Before centering the ball, the center needs to establish the target area for the snap. The center looks through his legs at the punter's hands for the target (figure 10.13a). When he sees the punter adjust his hands by turning both palms up, the center knows that the punter is ready to receive the ball. When making the snap (figure 10.13b), the center needs to follow through with both hands, allowing the palms to rotate out and the hands to follow the path of the ball. If the center does this with the proper velocity, he may find that his entire body moves back toward the punter. This movement is normal.

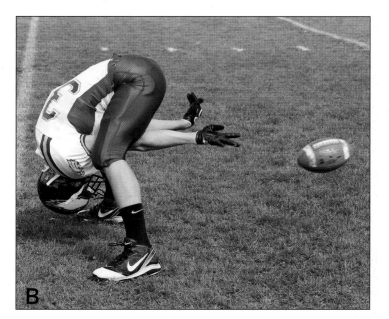

Figure 10.13   Long snap: Center (a) looks to the target area and (b) snaps the ball and follows through with both hands.

Snapping the ball to the punter is the center's first and most important job during a punt, but it is not his only job. After his release and follow-though, the center can help block any rushers in his immediate area. After the ball is punted, he can sprint downfield to cover the kick and make or help on the tackle of the return man. Often he will be one of the first players down the field to cover the kick. If he has the ability to tackle in the open field, he can become an extremely valuable player.

KICKING OFF

On kickoffs the kicker has the opportunity to force the opponent to start their offensive series deep in their end of the field. The kicker must always try to kick the ball high and far. This type of kick gives the cover men time to run down the field and tackle the return man before he can gain many yards. Kickoff consistency is important.

One of the easiest ways for the kicker to get into a good, comfortable stance is to stand with both feet together and take a normal step forward with the nonkicking foot. Then the kicker brings that foot back about half the distance to his body. He flexes his knees slightly. He positions his shoulders slightly in front of his hips and allows his arms and hands to hang down in a relaxed manner. After the kicker has assumed his stance a number of times, he will automatically know the distance to take with the half step.

When beginning to work on his setup, stance, steps, and kicking motion, the kicker should use a kicking tee without a ball as a point of reference. Later the ball can be added to practice. The kicking tee should be placed on a yard line facing the field. This location provides a good reference for setting up and a point for positioning the kicker's plant foot. After the kicking tee is in place, the kicker lines up with his kicking foot directly behind the tee and his nonkicking foot to the side of the tee. From this position, he takes one step away from the tee with his kicking foot and then turns around so that he faces away from the tee. He takes eight normal steps away from the ball straight down the yard line, ending with his kicking foot on the yard line. He turns to face the tee, making sure that he is not to the right or left of the yard line. He turns in the direction of his nonkicking foot and takes five normal steps. Then he turns back to face the tee and prepares to get into his stance. He should end up at a 45-degree angle to the kicking tee as he gets into his stance.

After the kicker is in position and in the proper stance, he is ready to move to the ball. He starts his forward movement by leaning his shoulders forward. As he leans, he takes a short half step forward with his nonkicking foot to start his approach to the ball. He stays relaxed during his steps for the first 5 yards of his approach. His pace quickens with each step in the final 5 yards as he approaches the tee. The kicker attacks the tee and prepares for the actual kicking motion.

Figure 10.14 Placement of the plant foot before the kick.

One of the keys to a good kickoff is to place the plant foot correctly at the start of the kicking motion. The plant foot should strike the ground 2 to 4 inches behind the tee and 6 inches to the left of the tee. His foot should point straight down the field in the direction of the kick (figure 10.14). When the plant foot makes contact with the ground, the kicker must keep his head down and focus his eyes on the tee. His shoulders should be in front of his hips.

For a kicker who uses a soccer-style motion, the most common style used today, the kicking motion (figure 10.15a) begins with a forward motion of the hips. The kicking leg moves forward in a high arc. The toe points down, and the knee is in front of the foot. The kicker's foot comes through so that the inside of the instep strikes an inch below the center of the ball. The foot should come through with such power that the kicker lifts off the ground and lands 2 to 3 feet in front of the tee (figure 10.15b).

After the kicker is able to move in the correct way, he can start practicing with the ball. When the ball is on the tee, it should be nearly vertical. The laces should be in front, lined up facing where the kicker wants the kick to go.

At first the kicker should not overkick or see how far he can kick the ball. Instead, he needs to concentrate on kicking with a smooth motion, striking the ball properly, and seeing that the ball goes straight down the yard line. The kicker can work up to attacking the ball and adding distance to the kickoff in practice sessions.

If the kicker experiences problems with any part of the kick, taking the ball out of practice and reviewing each segment is helpful. Kickoffs will be smooth and effective after the kicker has corrected any faulty part of his kick.

RETURNING KICKS

A kick returner must be dedicated and fearless in his approach to his job. Every return must be important to him. When returning punts or kickoffs, the kick returner must understand that his return can greatly influence the team's field position. He must focus only on the ball and not be concerned with the opposing players who are racing at him. His concentration must be on making the catch. He must completely secure the ball until the whistle blows, ending the return. He must accept that he will likely be hit by multiple tacklers every time he returns a kick.

Although the kick returner needs the same attributes and has the same responsibilities for both punts and kickoffs, there are some differences. First, the flight of the ball differs. A punt typically comes in a spiral, whereas a kickoff travels end over end. Also, a

A

B

Figure 10.15 Kicking motion for kickoffs: *(a)* backswing of the kicking leg; *(b)* kicker lifts off the ground and eventually lands in front of the tee on the follow-through.

punt usually is much higher than a kickoff. On a punt, the return man may not be able to see the ball the instant that it is punted, but he will have a clear view on a kickoff. Opposing coverage men may be right in front of him when he fields a punt, whereas on a kickoff he usually has time to make the catch and start up the field before the coverage men reach him. When blocking for the return of a punt, blockers try to keep the coverage men from getting down the field. Then they block any opposing player in a specific area. For kickoff returns, blockers are assigned specific players for the entire play. The return man does not have to catch every punt. He can allow the punt to be recovered by the opponent because it will still be his team's ball, but on a kickoff he must catch or fall on the ball because a kickoff is a free ball. Finally, smaller players often return punts, whereas bigger, stronger players return kickoffs.

Kickoff Returns

Where the return man positions himself to catch a kickoff depends on the ability of the player kicking the ball. The return man normally lines up 10 yards closer to his own goal line than the distance that he thinks the kicker can kick the ball. If the kicker normally sends the kickoff to the 15-yard line, the return man would position himself on his own

Figure 10.16 Returning a kickoff: Return man *(a)* gets in position and *(b)* prepares his hands for the catch.

5-yard line. One incontrovertible rule is that the return man should not line up in his own end zone. He should never line up deeper than his own 1-yard line, just to be safe.

The return man's focus is on the kicking tee and the ball. He wants to see immediately where the kickoff is going. After he sees the direction of the end-over-end flight of the ball, he changes his position to get directly in the path of the ball (figure 10.16a). He adjusts his forward movement to make the catch as he is going forward. To prepare for the catch, the return man places his little fingers together and brings the outside of his hands together with his palms, forming a catching basket for the ball (figure 10.16b). Both elbows are in close to his body. At the moment of the catch, the return man reaches out with his arms and hands so that he can see his hands and the ball at the same time (figure 10.16c).

The instant that he makes the catch, the return man secures the ball. If he is moving forward when he makes the catch, he will have momentum for the return. The return man must know where to run. Good kickoff return men know not only where they are supposed to run but also the blocking that will be used on the return. Most long returns occur when the return man catches the ball and runs straight to a designated area of the field (figure 10.16d).

Figure 10.16 *(continued)*   Returning a kickoff: Return man *(c)* makes the catch and *(d)* starts up the field.

As he heads upfield with the ball, the return man looks for any small space to sprint through. This seam usually appears only for an instant, so he has to get through it as fast as he can. He should not hesitate, stop, or change direction when returning a kickoff. This tentative approach can only get him in trouble and makes it hard for his teammates to execute good blocks.

Kickoff return men need to remember that the kickoff is a free ball. Players from either team can fall on the ball and gain possession, including kicks that go into the end zone. The return man's primary focus must be on making the catch. He must get to the ball and secure it before an opposing player can reach it. He should be prepared to fall on the ball, although he usually has time to pick it up and return it up the field. The return man should try to return every kickoff with abandon. He should head for the seam and have faith that his teammates will keep it open. He should never let the kicker make the tackle.

The return man must be alert for the short kick. On a short kickoff, the ball will hit the ground before the return man can catch it. As he moves forward to retrieve the short kick, the return man moves in front of the ball regardless of where it bounces. He concentrates on the ball, not on the opposing players.

Punt Returns

The punter's ability determines where the punt return man lines up. If the punter can kick the ball 35 yards, the return man should line up 40 yards behind the line of scrimmage.

Figure 10.17   **Returning a punt: Return man *(a)* gets in position and *(b)* prepares his hands for the catch.**

He wants to give himself room to move up and get under the ball to make the catch. This alignment also gives him protection if the punter makes an exceptional kick. The deepest position that he should line up or catch a punt is his own 10-yard line. He should never break this rule. Most punts that come down inside the 10-yard line will bounce into the end zone, creating a touchback that will result in the ball being brought out to the 20-yard line for the next play.

Because of the mass of players that are usually in front of the punter, the return man may not see the ball when it is kicked. The key is to locate the ball as soon as possible. After he sees the ball, he should adjust his position to be in a direct line with the flight of the ball (figure 10.17a).

After he is in position to make the catch, the punt return man comes under control with both palms up and the tips of his little fingers together (figure 10.17b). He cocks his wrist to form the catching area and reaches up with his arms and hands. He should see both hands and the ball at the moment of the catch (figure 10.17c). After catching the ball, the return man secures it and starts up the field (figure 10.17d).

When watching the ball in flight, the punt return man should try to see whether the front or back of the ball is coming down first. On longer punts, the front point of the ball comes down first. This type of punt usually moves to the return man's right. If the back point of the ball comes down first, the punt is shorter. The return man has to come up farther, and the ball will sail to his left.

Figure 10.17 (continued) Returning a punt: Return man (c) makes the catch and (d) starts up the field.

Figure 10.18   Signaling a fair catch.

Not every punt has to be caught. After the ball leaves the punter's foot, it is the receiving team's ball even if the return man does not catch it or the kicking team downs it. The return man needs to think through the situation. If he does not think that he can get in position to catch the punt securely, he should let it hit the ground and move away from it, yelling to his teammates to move away from the ball as well. If a player from the punting team falls on a bouncing punt after it has touched one of the return team's players, the punting team regains possession.

If the punt return man thinks that he can make the catch but not execute a return, he should signal a fair catch while the punt is still in the air by waving one hand back and forth over his head (figure 10.18). A fair-catch signal allows him to make the catch without being tackled. He cannot advance the ball after the catch, but his team does get the ball at the spot of the catch. He should consider making a fair-catch signal if the punt is extremely high, if the punt is a short kick that he can safely catch, or if he senses that the cover men are right on top of him.

If he thinks that he can gain yardage, the return man must be ready to run immediately after he catches the punt and secures the ball. Before the ball is kicked, he must know where to return the punt if he gets a chance to run with the ball.

Legal blocking on any kick return is difficult, and it is almost impossible if the return man does not return the punt where his teammates think he will. He should always try to return in the direction called by the coach. The one exception to this rule occurs when the call is for a right return and the punt is kicked near the left sideline. In this case, if the return man can safely make the catch, the best choice might be to return up the left sideline. He may not have blocking and may not make many yards, but he will not have to run all the way across the field before turning and starting up toward the opponent's goal line.

Stopping, starting, and changing direction create trouble for the blockers and hurt the return. After he has secured the ball, the return man needs to turn on the speed, hit the return area as fast as he can, get as many yards as possible, and never let the punter make the tackle.

SPECIAL-TEAMS DRILLS

The drills for special-teams players usually involve only a few players, but because of their importance, practice time must be allowed for them. Beginning punters and place-kickers should initially practice the skills without the ball. After the ball comes into the drill, it becomes the focus of the workout.

PLACEKICKING

Purpose: To reinforce placekicking techniques.

Procedure:

1. **The placekicker kicks the ball. The coach faces the kicker to observe his stance, steps, and kicking motion.**

2. **For the stance, the coach faces the kicker as the kicker lines up in his stance.**

3. **For the steps, the coach lines up in front and to the side of the placement spot to observe the kicker's motion. A tee or the ball is not used; a piece of tape can be used as the placement spot.**

4. **To check the kicker's steps, the coach lines up in front and to the side of the placement spot. The kicker needs to take the proper steps away from the placement spot and then to the side before assuming his presnap stance. On the coach's command, the kicker takes the correct steps, places his plant foot, and goes through his normal kicking motion.**

5. **The coach lines up 5 yards in front of the placement spot and observes the kicking motion, including the follow-through.**

Coaching points: The kicker needs to have his head and shoulders in front of his hips and his plant foot in the correct position. His kicking motion should be in a straight line. He should keep his eyes focused on the placement spot throughout his kick.

SHORT SNAPPING

Purpose: To reinforce proper technique when executing the short snap.

Procedure:

1. **The coach lines up in front of the ball and observes the center's stance and grip.**

2. **After the center is comfortable with the proper stance and grip, the coach lines up as the holder or in front of the center to observe the center's snap.**

Coaching points: The center should have his hips even with his shoulders before the snap. The center must check that the holder is ready before the snap, have a good follow-through with both hands on the snap, and expect to block after he releases the ball.

HOLDING FOR THE KICK

Purpose: To reinforce proper technique for catching, placing, and holding the ball for the placekicker.

Procedure:

1. The coach lines up directly in front of the center.
2. The holder assumes his proper stance, checks that the kicker is ready, and prepares to receive the snap.
3. When the center snaps the ball, the holder catches it and places it for the kick.

Coaching points: The holder must be comfortable in his stance. The holder should catch the ball, move it to the placement spot, adjust the laces to the front, and lean the ball in one smooth motion. Some practice time should be spent fielding poorly snapped balls.

KICKING FOR ACCURACY

Purpose: To help kickers develop accuracy in their kicks.

Procedure:

1. The kicker lines up at the intersection of the sideline and end line in one end zone.
2. The tee is placed at the kicking spot facing in toward the goal post.
3. The kicker makes the proper steps and sets up. When the ball is placed on the tee, he moves forward to make the kick.
4. The goal of the kicker is to hit the upright on the near side of the goal post with the ball.
5. If a coach is available, he can position himself behind the holder and observe the entire procedure, offering corrections as needed.
6. Kickers can do this drill on their own when all the coaches are occupied with other areas in practice.

Coaching points: The kicker must take the proper steps to set up correctly to make the kick. He needs to have his head and shoulders in front of his hips and his plant foot in the correct position. His kicking motion should be in a straight line. He should keep his eyes focused on the placement spot throughout his kick.

GETTING ON THE FIELD QUICKLY

Purpose: To practice getting the point-after-touchdown and field goal (PAT and FG) team on the field quickly for kicks before the end of the half or game or when no timeouts are available.

Procedure:

1. The entire offense is on the field and runs a play.
2. The coach blows a whistle, and another coach moves to spot the ball.

3. When the whistle blows, any members of the PAT and FG team not on the field for the offensive play sprint to the ball to get lined up.

4. At the same time, any members of the offensive team not on the PAT and FG team must sprint off the field.

5. The ball is snapped, and the kick is made. The coaches record the time required to execute the play.

Coaching points: The holder must immediately establish the placement spot. The kicker needs to take his steps quickly and get into his stance to make the kick. The holder must make certain that all players are set in their stances. He then signals the center when the kicker is ready. The center makes the snap, the holder places the ball on the spot, and the kicker makes the kick. The kicker needs to have his head and shoulders in front of his hips and his plant foot in the correct position. His kicking motion should be in a straight line. He should keep his eyes focused on the placement spot throughout his kick. All players must be told and understand that speed is vitally important if the kick is to occur before the end of the half or game.

PUNTING—CONVENTIONAL

Purpose: To reinforce punting technique by focusing on each segment of the punt.

Procedure:

1. The coach lines up 15 yards in front of the punter and observes his stance, making corrections if necessary.

2. After the stance is correct, the coach observes the punter's steps as he uses the two-step punting technique.

3. After the stance and steps are correct, the coach observes how the punter sets up and places his hands to receive the snap. The punter should make sure that he can see both the ball and his hands at the same time.

4. For the grip and drop, the coach stands to the side of the punter's kicking leg and hands him the ball. The coach observes the punter's grip and drop, making corrections if necessary.

5. The punter punts the ball, going through the entire motion.

6. To practice adjusting the nonkicking foot for directional punts, the coach sets up behind the punter, indicates the direction for the punt, and observes the punter's movement.

7. The center joins in the drill after the punter establishes the kicking motion.

Coaching points: The punter must have a balanced stance, step on the balls of his feet, keep his shoulders in front of his hips, drop the ball onto his kicking foot correctly, and follow through with every kick. The techniques can be perfected individually and then combined without a ball. Next, the ball can be used without a center, and finally, the center joins in the drill. Punters should not kick with poor technique. The ball should be eliminated if they are having trouble.

PUNTING—RUGBY STYLE

Purpose: To reinforce punting technique by focusing on each segment of the punt.

Procedure:

1. The coach lines up 15 yards in front of the punter and observes his stance, making corrections if necessary.
2. After the stance is correct, the coach observes the punter's steps as he starts laterally to begin his lateral run. The punter can assume his initial stance on one hash mark and move laterally to the other.
3. The coach should observe the punter's lateral movement and kicking motion.
4. After the stance and steps are correct, the coach observes how the punter sets up and places his hands to receive the snap. The punter should make sure that he can see both the ball and his hands at the same time.
5. For the grip and drop, the coach hands the punter the ball and stands between the punter and the sideline. The coach observes the punter's grip and drop as the punter runs to the sideline, making corrections if necessary.
6. The punter punts the ball, going through the entire motion.
7. The center joins in the drill after the punter establishes the kicking motion.

Coaching points: The punter must have a proper stance and take the first step toward the sideline on the side of his kicking foot with his kicking foot. As he runs laterally and forward, he needs to keep his shoulders in front of his hips, drop the ball onto his kicking foot correctly, and follow through with every kick. The techniques can be perfected individually and then combined without a ball. Punters should not practice kicking with poor technique. The ball should be eliminated if they are having trouble with the steps or kicking motion.

This drill can be divided into three separate drills:

- Drill 1: Use only the coach, the punter, and no ball to practice only the steps, body position, and kicking motion.
- Drill 2: Use the coach, the punter, and a ball to practice the lateral run and an actual kick.
- Drill 3: Use the coach, the punter, the center, and a ball to practice the snap, run, and kick as described earlier.

LONG SNAPPING

Purpose: To reinforce proper technique when executing the long snap.

Procedure:

1. The coach lines up directly in front of the center and observes his stance and grip.
2. After the center is comfortable with the stance and grip, the coach observes the center's snapping motion.

Coaching points: The coach should check that the front point of the ball is up before the snap. The center must see that the punter is ready and then fire the ball back to the punter. The center needs good follow-through with both hands on the snap. After the snap, he must be prepared to block and then cover down the field.

KICKOFFS

Purpose: To reinforce proper kickoff technique by focusing on each segment of the kickoff.

Procedure:

1. The coach sets up to the side of the tee opposite the kicker's foot.
2. The kicker takes his stance and goes through his steps, making adjustments as necessary.
3. After mastering the stance and steps, the kicker goes through the approach and kicking motion without the ball as the coach observes.
4. After the kicker is comfortable performing the motions without the ball, the kicker can kick the ball to the returner.

Coaching points: The kicker must set up in the proper location, attack the ball while keeping his head and shoulder in front of his hips, and ensure that his plant foot is in the proper location to allow his leg to move through the kick. The kicking motion should propel the kicker's body forward. The kicker must concentrate on the tee and the ball all through the kick.

RETURNING KICKOFFS

Purpose: To reinforce proper technique for returning kickoffs.

Procedure:

1. The coach lines up in the end zone behind the kick return man.
2. The return man uses the proper positioning, catch technique, and start.
3. The actual kick is added after the return man is set on the techniques for making the catch.

Coaching points: The return man should position himself directly in front of the flight of the ball on every kick and be moving forward as he makes the catch. He must look the ball into his hands on every catch and cover all kicks.

RETURNING PUNTS

Purpose: To reinforce proper technique for returning punts.

Procedure:

1. The coach lines up behind the punt return man.
2. The punt return man uses the proper positioning, catch technique, and start.
3. After the return man is set on the techniques for making the catch, the punter can punt the ball to the returner.

Coaching points: The return man should move quickly to get in front of every punt. He needs to determine whether to make the catch, call for the fair catch, or let the ball bounce. The returner must look the ball into his hands on every catch. The coach can throw the ball to the return man if the punter is not available or is inconsistent in his punts.

Drill	Ball Handling	Blocking	Defeating Blocks	Kicking	Movement & Agility	Reading the Opposition	Receiving	Running	Rushing	Snapping	Stance & Body Position	Tackling	Page #
Chapter 1: All Players													
Angle tackling					X							X	5
Straight-ahead tackling					X							X	6
Sideline tackling					X							X	7
Palms-up catching							X				X		10
Thumbs-together catching							X				X		10
Simulated receiving							X				X		10
Running and protecting the ball	X				X			X					12
Gaining possession on the ground	X				X						X		14
Retrieving a fumble in the open field	X				X			X			X		14
Rolling the hips for forward motion					X								15
Chapter 2: Quarterbacks													
Stance											X		22
Snap with movement	X									X	X		22
Shotgun snap with movement	X									X	X		23

Drill	Ball Handling	Blocking	Defeating Blocks	Kicking	Movement & Agility	Reading the Opposition	Receiving	Running	Rushing	Snapping	Stance & Body Position	Tackling	Page #
Chapter 2: Quarterbacks													
Adjusting the ball	X				X					X			23
Coming down the line	X				X			X		X	X		28
Reading for the option play	X					X	X	X		X	X		28
Angle footwork	X				X			X		X	X		29
Making the handoff on a sweep	X				X			X		X	X		29
Turning on a reverse pivot	X				X						X		29
Making a pitch from a reverse pivot	X				X			X			X		30
One-hand fake	X				X			X			X		30
Two-hand fake	X				X			X			X		31
Center and quarterback pass play					X					X	X		39
Three-step drop					X					X	X		40
Throwing the bubble screen	X				X		X			X	X		40
Five- and seven-step drops	X				X					X	X		41
Slow screen action	X				X		X	X		X			41

(continued)

Drill	Ball Handling	Blocking	Defeating Blocks	Kicking	Movement & Agility	Reading the Opposition	Receiving	Running	Rushing	Snapping	Stance & Body Position	Tackling	Page #
Chapter 2: Quarterbacks *(continued)*													
Arm strength	X				X		X						42
Multiple quarterbacks, multiple receivers	X				X			X					43
Turning and stepping to the target	X				X		X			X			44
Faking the pitch and running a bootleg	X				X			X		X			44
Rollout passing	X				X			X		X			45
Sprint-out passing	X				X			X		X			46
Chapter 3: Offensive Linemen													
Getting off on the snap		X			X						X		50
Drive block		X			X						X		60
Blocking a linebacker		X			X						X		60
Hook block		X			X						X		60
Angle block		X			X						X		61
Double-team block		X			X						X		61
Combination block		X			X						X		61

Drill	Ball Handling	Blocking	Defeating Blocks	Kicking	Movement & Agility	Reading the Opposition	Receiving	Running	Rushing	Snapping	Stance & Body Position	Tackling	Page #
Chapter 3: Offensive Linemen													
Pull and drive block		X			X						X		62
Center snap	X									X	X		65
Shotgun center snap	X									X	X		65
Pass protection		X								X	X		69
Screen pass blocking		X			X								70
Chapter 4: Running Backs													
Running back's stance											X		75
Running back's directional step					X			X					75
Running back's crossover first step					X			X					75
Taking the handoff	X							X					77
Catching the option toss							X	X			X		78
Catching the pitch	X				X		X				X		78
Executing the run pass	X				X			X			X		80
The cut	X				X			X					84

(continued)

Drill	Ball Handling	Blocking	Defeating Blocks	Kicking	Movement & Agility	Reading the Opposition	Receiving	Running	Rushing	Snapping	Stance & Body Position	Tackling	Page #
Chapter 4: Running Backs *(continued)*													
Evasive crossover step	X				X			X					84
Run to the sideline	X				X			X					85
Inside cut	X				X			X					85
Spin to get free					X			X					85
Running pass routes					X		X	X					90
Blocking the outside linebacker		X						X					95
Screen pass	X	X					X	X					96
Chapter 5: Wide Receivers													
Short pass routes					X		X	X			X		107
Out and in patterns					X		X	X			X		107
Special medium routes					X		X	X			X		107
Corner and comeback					X		X	X					108
Fade route					X		X	X					109
Pivot in and pivot out routes					X		X	X					110

Drill	Ball Handling	Blocking	Defeating Blocks	Kicking	Movement & Agility	Reading the Opposition	Receiving	Running	Rushing	Snapping	Stance & Body Position	Tackling	Page #
Chapter 5: Wide Receivers													
Perfecting the bubble screen							X	X					111
Reading the defense						X		X					113
Reacting to the defender		X			X								115
Chapter 6: Tight Ends													
Pass protection		X									X		122
Solo pattern practice	X						X	X			X		129
Running short routes					X			X					129
Running short routes after pass blocking		X			X			X					130
Running deep routes					X			X					130
Chapter 7: Defensive Linemen													
Instant movement on the ball					X						X		147
Facing the drive block			X		X						X		147
Playing the angle block			X		X								148
Blocker in the hole			X			X							148

(continued)

Drill	Ball Handling	Blocking	Defeating Blocks	Kicking	Movement & Agility	Reading the Opposition	Receiving	Running	Rushing	Snapping	Stance & Body Position	Tackling	Page #
Chapter 7: Defensive Linemen *(continued)*													
Attacking the target area			X		X			X			X		149
Straight-ahead bull rush			X					X	X				149
Reacting off a pass rush			X		X	X							150
Chapter 8: Linebackers													
Starting forward to the blocker					X								170
Beating the drive block			X		X								170
Defeating the hook block			X		X								170
Defeating the angle block			X		X								171
Defeating the trap block			X		X	X							171
Finding the target area					X			X					171
Arm-over rush			X					X	X		X		172
Backpedaling					X			X					172
Rolling over					X			X			X		173
Backward to forward run					X			X			X		173

Drill	Ball Handling	Blocking	Defeating Blocks	Kicking	Movement & Agility	Reading the Opposition	Receiving	Running	Rushing	Snapping	Stance & Body Position	Tackling	Page #
Chapter 8: Linebackers													
Learning pass routes					X	X		X					173
Calling and pointing out pass patterns					X	X		X					174
Moving to zone coverage					X			X					174
Reacting to draw and screen plays			X		X			X					175
Chapter 9: Defensive Backs													
Exploding at the start					X						X		188
Staying in the backpedal					X			X					189
Pass zones						X		X					189
Recognizing pass patterns						X		X					190
Playing a two-deep zone					X								190
Bump and run					X						X		191
Pass or run	X					X		X					191
Establishing proper pursuit paths					X			X					192

Drill	Ball Handling	Blocking	Defeating Blocks	Kicking	Movement & Agility	Reading the Opposition	Receiving	Running	Rushing	Snapping	Stance & Body Position	Tackling	Page #
Chapter 10: Special-Teams Players													
Placekicking				X	X						X		215
Short snapping										X	X		215
Holding for the kick	X				X		X				X		216
Kicking for accuracy				X							X		216
Getting on the field quickly					X			X			X		216
Punting—conventional	X			X							X		217
Punting—rugby style	X			X				X			X		218
Long snapping	X									X	X		218
Kickoffs				X	X						X		219
Returning kickoffs	X				X		X	X			X		219
Returning punts	X				X		X	X			X		219

ABOUT THE AUTHOR

Tom Bass coached with three NFL teams—the Cincinnati Bengals, the Tampa Bay Buccaneers, and the San Diego Chargers—as well as at the collegiate level at San Jose State University and San Diego State University.

For the past ten years coach Bass has served as the technical writer and advisor for USA Football and was a major contributor to the content of USA Football's new multi-level youth football age specific coaching certification program. He serves as the chairman of the technical committee for USA Football and hosts the "Let's Talk Football" Q&A column on their website www.USAFootball.com. Coach Bass also interacts with and advises football coaches, players, parents, and fans.

Bass is the creator of Coach Bass Sport Maps, the author of NFL Nintendo Game for NFL Properties, and the author of several books. He is a longtime editor of the official Super Bowl Program. He has been a featured guest on numerous sports talk and interview shows on radio and television, including HBO, ABC Nightly News, and ESPN. Bass resides in Carlsbad, California.

You'll find other outstanding football resources at

www.HumanKinetics.com/football

In the U.S. call 1-800-747-4457

Australia 08 8372 0999 • Canada 1-800-465-7301
Europe +44 (0) 113 255 5665 • New Zealand 0800 222 062

HUMAN KINETICS
The Premier Publisher for Sports & Fitness
P.O. Box 5076 • Champaign, IL 61825-5076 USA

eBook
available at
HumanKinetics.com